Mastering Keyboarding Skills 1

SECOND EDITION

Sandra D. Ubelacker, B.A., M.A., Ph.D.
Professor
Department of Secondary Education
University of Alberta

Rita M. Guest, B.A.A.
Business Education Department
Thistletown Collegiate Institute

Gerald W. McConaghy, B.Ed., M.Ed.
Graduate Student
University of Alberta

Copp Clark Pitman Ltd.
A Longman Company
Toronto

ISBN 0-7730-4933-9

Editing Jennie Bedford
Design Patti Brown
Typesetting and Assembly Compeer Typographic
  Services Ltd.
Cover design and illustrations Allan Moon
Printing and Binding DW Friesen

Canadian Cataloguing in Publication Data
Ubelacker, Sandra D.
  Mastering keyboarding skills 1

Includes index.
ISBN 0-7730-4933-9

1. Typewriting.   2. Typewriting — Problems, exercises,
etc.   I. Guest, Rita M.   II. McConaghy, Gerald W.
III. Title.

Z49.U25   652.3'024   C83-094159-2

Disclaimer
An honest attempt has been made to secure permission
for and acknowledge contributions of all material used.
If there are errors or omissions, these are wholly
unintentional and the publisher will be grateful to learn
of them.

Copp Clark Pitman Ltd.
2775 Matheson Blvd. East
Mississauga, Ontario   L4W 4P7

Printed and bound in Canada

7 8 9 10   4933-9   99 98 97 96

Mastering Keyboarding Skills 1

SECOND EDITION

Contents

Acknowledgements

To the many people who have reviewed the developmental stages of both editions of *Mastering Keyboarding Skills 1*, the authors and publisher would like to extend our sincere appreciation. Without your constructive criticism there would not have been the regional input that is necessary to produce a truly Canadian program.

The following business educators were asked for detailed reviews of draft material and deserve a special note of thanks:

- Cathy Abbrossimoff, McNair High School, Richmond, British Columbia
- Stan Baker, Centennial Secondary School, Coquitlam, British Columbia
- John Bennett, Vernon Secondary School, Vernon, British Columbia
- Mhora Hepburn, Communications Consultant
- Lily Kretchman, Co-ordinator of Business Education, Peel Board of Education, Mississauga, Ontario
- Eileen Laker, Clarkson Secondary School, Mississauga, Ontario
- Betty MacDonald, Fredericton High School, Fredericton, New Brunswick
- Arnold MacPherson, Business Education Consultant, Department of Education, Fredericton, New Brunswick
- F. Willard McShane, Sussex Regional High School, Sussex, New Brunswick
- Sandra C. Richard, Simonds High School, Saint John, New Brunswick
- Terry Taylor, KLO Secondary School, Kelowna, British Columbia

We also sincerely thank M. Bernice Casey of Lakeshore Collegiate Institute, Etobicoke, Ontario and Elaine Sands of Harry Ainlay Composite High School, Edmonton, Alberta who field tested the text for us.

For permission to reproduce forms and letterheads as well as the use of other material, we acknowledge the following organizations:

- The Bank of Nova Scotia
- Beaver Lumber Company Limited
- Bell Canada
- Canada Employment and Immigration
- Canada Post
- Canadian Tire Corporation, Limited
- CHUM Limited
- Cooper Canada Limited
- Finning Tractor & Equipment Company Limited
- Frederick Harris Music Co. Limited
- Laura Secord
- MacMillan Bloedel Limited
- Mimico High School
- Ministry of Government Services, Province of Ontario
- North American Air Defence Command
- Olympia Sports Camp
- Royal York Minor Hockey League
- Spruce Grove Composite High School
- 3M Canada Inc.
- Tembo Music Canada, from whom every effort has been made to obtain permission to reproduce the words to "Canada Is"
- West Edmonton Mall
- Westcoast Energy Inc.

Introduction

You are ready to begin *Mastering Keyboarding Skills 1, Second Edition.* After completing the program, you will be able to input by touch and apply your skill to personal and business applications, such as letters, tables, forms, reports, and résumés.

Organization of the Text

Mastering Keyboarding Skills 1, Second Edition, organized into four units of twenty-five lessons each. Each lesson is designed for *one* 70- to 80-minute class period, or for *two* 35- to 40-minute class periods. Each unit deals with specific topics: Unit I introduces the keyboard and centring; Unit II, tabulations; Unit III, letters; and Unit IV, reports, résumés, and application letters/forms. Numbers are introduced as a logical extension of the second-row keys. Beginning with lesson two, you will practise numbers daily through drill material and apply number skill in the production exercises. Numeric keypad drills are available in the Additional Production Practice Section following Unit IV. Special symbols are introduced as they are needed.

In each unit, lessons are planned with directed drill material, production practice, and applications in spelling, English usage, editing practice, composition, and number practice. Hyphenation, capitalization, and metric rules are introduced and practised in the first three units and reviewed in the last unit. The last lesson of each unit is a test to evaluate your progress. A pre-test and post-test are provided in the *Teacher's Resource Book* and will be supplied by your teacher.

Additional production practice and timed writings are available at the end of the text, following Unit IV.

Drill Material

The marginal instructions should be used as guidelines. Teachers should time as many drills as possible.

Each unit has analytical practice and graduated speed practice drills. Analytical practice provides additional reinforcement for the alphabetic and numeric keys that may be causing errors. Graduated speed practice provides timed, short drill material for either speed or accuracy development. Specific practice goals should be set each day for all types of drills (for a complete listing see the index under Drills). Drills should be timed, and you should continually measure and evaluate your progress. You should set your own individual goals with the assistance of your teacher or according to the marginal instructions.

Timed Writings

Each lesson has a timed writing with the difficulty specified in terms of syllabic intensity (SI). The difficulty increases as the SI increases. A record of gross words per minute (GWPM) and the number of errors for your best timing should be kept on your Personal Progress Chart. The best timing is the one with the highest GWPM and with the number of errors below the maximum set by your teacher. If you are working without a teacher, refer to the timed writing objectives given on each unit objectives page.

Additional timed writings with a high syllabic intensity are available at the end of the text, following Unit IV.

Production Material

Editors' symbols are introduced as they are needed for production exercises. Material is presented in arranged, handwritten, and unarranged format. Handwritten and edited copy is introduced early in each unit. Formatting Guides summarize the new theory presented in each unit.

The number of words in each production exercise is given in the *Teacher's Resource Book*. This word count is the number of words in the production exercise. Allowance has not been made for the use of service mechanisms (setting tabs, return/enter key, etc.). Production exercises should be timed and the word count should be used as a guide in assessing production skill. A production word count, which makes allowance for the use of service mechanisms, is given for each unit test and will be supplied by your teacher.

Refer to the end of the text for additional production practice.

Teacher's Resource Book

The *Teacher's Resource Book* includes teaching and evaluation suggestions, complete answer keys, pre- and post-tests, as well as black-line and transparency masters. These masters include the forms, letterhead paper, and envelopes which can be duplicated for the production exercises. The letterheads are from actual Canadian companies.

Pica or Elite

To determine if your typewriter or printer has elite (12 pitch) or pica (10 pitch) type, input 12 i's and compare with the following:

Elite type (12 pitch)   iiiiiiiiiiii

Pica type (10 pitch)   iiiiiiiiii

Alternatively, take a full sheet of paper, and place the left edge at zero on the front scale of your typewriter or printer. Measure the width of the paper. Pica measures 85 spaces and elite measures 102 spaces.

Setting Margins on a Typewriter

Locate the print indicator, the alignment scale, and paper guide. Then, locate the margin stops on your typewriter.

Steps for Setting Margins

1. If the paper guide is at zero, the centre point of the paper is 50 (elite) or 42 (pica).

   The basic principle for setting margins is: Half of the line should be to the right of the centre point and half to the left of the centre point.

2. Calculate the margin settings.

   40-character line

Left Margin	Centre Point	Right Margin
30	50 (elite)	75
50		50
−20		+20
30		70 + 5* = 75

*Add 5 characters to the right margin for signal allowance.

3. Set the margins for the line length desired.
   * Set your new left margin first.
   * Set your new right margin.

Note: The word processing program loaded in your computer will have a set line length which is called the line length default. It also has a type pitch default which is usually 10 pitch (pica). The margin and type pitch defaults can be changed at any time. Ask your teacher or read the software manual for the steps to reset the margins and the pitch.

You are now ready to start lesson one. Follow the instructions and read the explanations carefully as you progress through *Mastering Keyboarding Skills, Second Edition*.

Operative Parts of an Electronic Typewriter

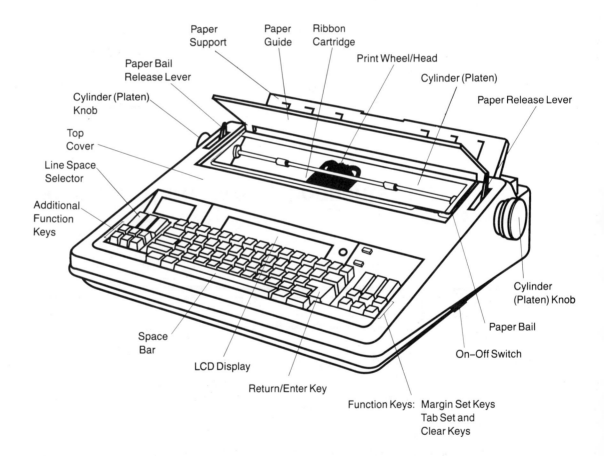

TYPEWRITER KEYBOARD

Computer Hardware Components

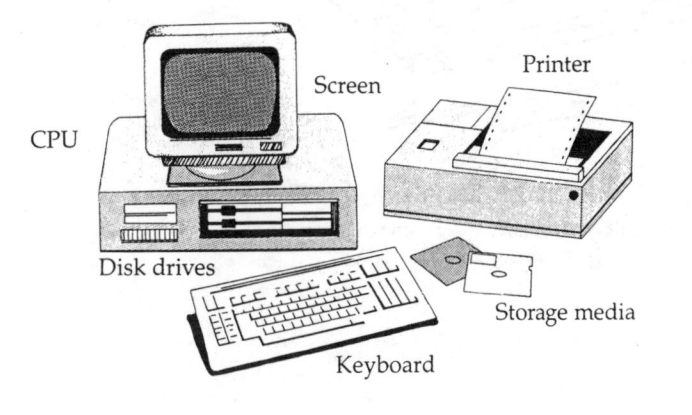

CPU
Screen
Printer
Disk drives
Keyboard
Storage media

COMPUTER KEYBOARD

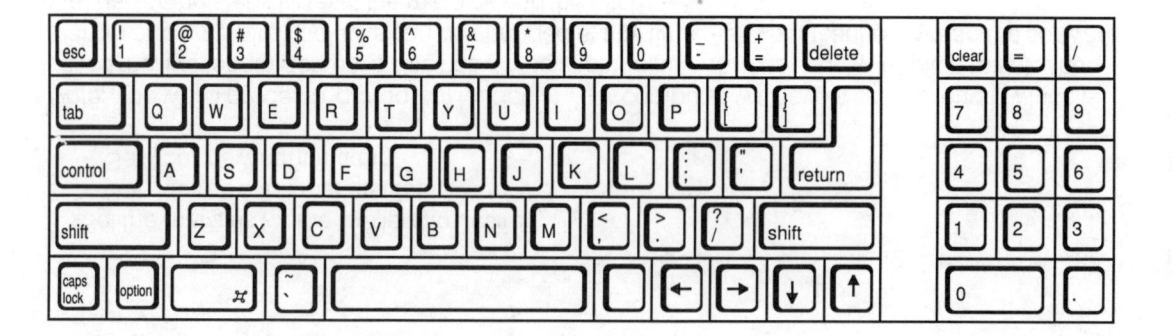

EXPANDED COMPUTER KEYBOARD

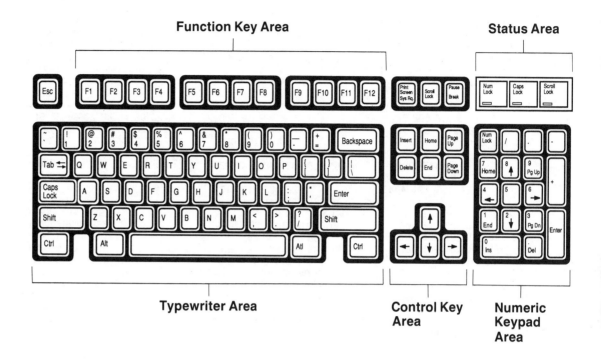

Maintaining Computer Hardware and Software

To ensure that your computer hardware and software function reliably, you should:
1. Avoid exposing your hardware and software to contaminants such as dust, dirt, smoke, powder, or erasure particles.
2. Avoid exposing your software to direct sunlight, excessive heat, or magnetic fields (including paper clips).
3. Do not bend or put pressure on floppy disks. Store your disks in an upright position, preferably in a box or a cabinet. Use a felt-tipped pen to label your disks.
4. Check your hardware wiring and cabling regularly to ensure that it is in good condition. Any faulty wiring or cabling should be repaired immediately.
5. Use an anti-static spray in your work area to prevent static build-up.

Copyright

It is against the law to copy any computer software without the permission of the manufacturer unless you have a Licensing Agreement. *Never* accept illegal copies of computer software from *anyone*.

Index

Unit I

Objectives

By completing this unit *you* will:

1 Develop correct keyboarding technique.

2 Learn the alphabetic and numeric keyboard by touch.

3 Learn the correct use of a standard keyboard and service mechanisms or options.

4 Input paragraphs and format material on a page using vertical centring.

5 Work toward developing a minimum speed of 20 words per minute with four or fewer errors on a two-minute timing.

Note: Additional production practice for this unit may be found on page 329.

This includes four production exercises for inputting paragraphs.

Three- or Five-Minute Timing

In many countries of the world, motion pictures are one
of the most important ways of having fun and spreading ideas
to the general public. When we see movies, we sense that we
are part of what we hear and observe. We may cheer the hero
and hiss the villain in a western. We often become involved
in the problems and conflicts presented in a serious drama.

Besides providing entertainment, movies are also useful
in science, education, industry, and various other areas. A
scientist can observe a research experiment and a doctor can
view an operation. A sales staff could learn better selling
techniques from films. Millions of people enjoy making home
movies, which are usually very entertaining.

Screen writers delve into all periods of history to get
material for their stories. They also present some thoughts
about the future. Stories from the Bible and from the lives
of famous people are retold. Recollections of serious world
conflicts point out the dangers and bravery involved in war.
Gangster movies show the various evils and effects of crime.

1	CW	3
12	12	4
24	24	8
36	36	12
48	48	16
60	60	20
72	72	24
12	84	28
24	96	32
36	108	36
48	120	40
60	132	44
69	141	47
12	153	51
24	165	55
36	177	59
48	189	63
60	201	67
72	213	71

1 min
3 min

SI 1.59

• • • • 1 • • • • 2 • • • • 3 • • • • 4 • • • • 5 • • • • 6 • • • • 7 • • • • 8 • • • • 9 • • • •10• • • •11• • • •12
        1   2   3   4

1

■ Are you ready?

A / S / D / F J / K / L / ;

Your Work Station

1. Is your keyboard even with the front of your desk?
2. Is your desk clear except for your text book which is to the right of your keyboard?
3. Is your text book standing upright?

Your Posture

1. Are you sitting erect?
2. Are you sitting approximately a hand span from the edge of your keyboard?
3. Is your body centred opposite the **J** key?
4. Are your feet flat on the floor?
5. Are your hands relaxed at your sides?

Your Typewriter

■ Did you set the line space regulator for single spacing?

1. Is the paper guide set so that the left edge of the paper is at 0 on the margin scale?
2. Is the line space regulator set for single spacing?
3. Are your margins set for a 40-character line?
4. Can you locate and use the paper bail and paper release?
5. Can you insert a piece of paper in your typewriter?
6. Is your typewriter plugged in?

for trees to survive. This thinly populated region has many

deposits of copper, gold, nickel, and zinc. Several forests

stretch across the southern half of the region. Balsam fir,

spruce, and other trees provide wood for furniture factories

and paper mills.

SI 1.61

	36	117	39
	48	129	43
	60	141	47
	72	153	51
	75	156	52

• • • •1• • • •2• • • •3• • • •4• • • •5• • • •6• • • •7• • • •8• • • •9• • • •10• • • •11• • • •12   1 min

       1   2   3   4   3 min

Three- or Five-Minute Timing

1	CW	3

Radio broadcasting has been a leading source of general

information and knowledge for many years. It is very useful

in keeping large numbers of people informed about major news

events soon after they occur or while they are happening. A

top news story can be an on-the-spot report. Announcers and

crews travel great distances to provide major news coverage.

Despite the popularity of television, millions continue

to listen to the radio. Important changes have been made in

radio programming to maintain listeners. Transistors enable

music, sports, news, etc., to be heard in various locations.

Years ago most people listened to their crystal receiver for

the thrill of picking up some distant and exciting stations.

Most commercial radio stations are organized into three

departments: programming, engineering, and sales. Programs

on the air are determined by the programming staff. Keeping

the station on the air is the job of the engineers. A sales

staff sells time on the air to advertisers. Larger stations

SI 1.68

might be operated with a television or affiliated network.

1	CW	3
12	12	4
24	24	8
36	36	12
48	48	16
60	60	20
72	72	24
12	84	28
24	96	32
36	108	36
48	120	40
60	132	44
72	144	48
12	156	52
24	168	56
36	180	60
48	192	64
60	204	68
72	216	72

• • • •1• • • •2• • • •3• • • •4• • • •5• • • •6• • • •7• • • •8• • • •9• • • •10• • • •11• • • •12   1 min

       1   2   3   4   3 min

Your Computer

1. Is your computer plugged in OR Is the network ready?
2. Is your computer turned *on*?
3. Is your monitor turned *on*?
4. Is the program loaded for word processing?
5. Is your formatted data disk loaded?
6. Is your monitor displaying a screen ready for word processing?
7. Is the paper in the printer aligned so the left edge of each sheet of paper is at zero on the margin scale?

Your Hands

1. Place the fingers of your left hand on **A S D F**.
2. Place the fingers of your right hand on **J K L ;**.
3. Curve your fingers slightly in order to strike the keys with the ends of your fingers.
4. Place your fingers gently *on* the keys.
5. Keep your elbows relaxed at your sides and your hands parallel with the slant of the keyboard.
6. Keep the palms of your hands above the keyboard.

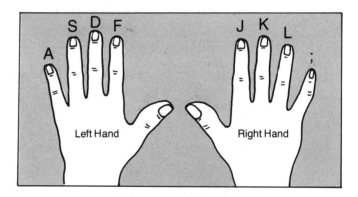

Three-Minute Timing

		1	CW	3
Vancouver has the leading seaport on the Pacific Coast.		12	12	4
It is situated on Burrard Inlet, which is one of the world's		24	24	8
greatest harbours. Vancouver is the fourth largest Canadian		36	36	12
city. The city is well served by railways and highways too.		48	48	16
The airport is one of the largest and busiest we have. Many		60	60	20
overseas flights leave from here. Many forest, fishing, and		72	72	24
manufacturing industries have their headquarters here.		83	83	28
Gardens have always been a feature of the city. Almost		12	95	32
every home endeavours to provide a display of some kind. If		24	107	36
you visit this beautiful city, be sure you see Stanley Park.		36	119	40
It is one of the finest parks on our continent. In addition		48	131	44
to gardens, its attractions include large semiwild areas, an		60	143	48
aquarium and a zoo. Queen Elizabeth Gardens offers a superb		72	155	52
tropical display. You can spend many enjoyable hours there.		84	167	56

• • • 1 • • • • 2 • • • 3 • • • • 4 • • • • 5 • • • 6 • • • 7 • • • • 8 • • • 9 • • • •10 • • • •11 • • • •12   1 min

1   2   3   4   3 min

SI 1.57

Three-Minute Timing

		1	CW	3
Manitoba is the sixth largest province in this country.		12	12	4
It was the fifth province to become part of our nation. Now		24	24	8
it ranks among the leaders in the western world in producing		36	36	12
nickel and zinc. Manufacturing is always a source of income		48	48	16
for the province. Food processing, stockyards, clothing and		60	60	20
railway equipment factories, and petroleum refineries assure		72	72	24
a stable and reliable labour force and economy.		81	81	27
A vast rocky region lies across the northern two thirds		12	93	31
of the province. Much of this northern region is too chilly		24	105	35

■ Is the power switch *on*?

The Space Bar

1. Strike the space bar with your right thumb or with the thumb of your writing hand.
   - Do not rest your thumb on the space bar.
   - Do not hold the space bar down.

2. Keep your right hand, wrists, and other fingers as motionless as possible when striking the space bar.

Practice

Space Bar Drill

(*space*) once once once twice twice once twice once

The Return OR Enter Key

1. Anchor your index finger over the **J** key.
2. Reach with your little or semicolon finger of your right hand to the return or enter key.
3. Strike the return or enter key. Then return your finger to home row.
4. The return or enter key should be one continuous motion.

■ Some electric typewriters and word processing software have automatic word wrap as a default. This can be used in Unit III.

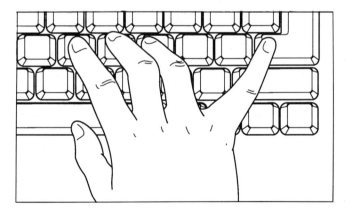

Practice

Return/Enter Key Drill

(*space*)   once once twice once (*return or enter*)
             twice twice once twice (*return or enter*)

Two-Minute Timing

Despite the difficulties of geography and history, most of the fine people of Prince Edward Island have lived a life of rugged independence on the farm and by the sea. They are close to nature and its wonderful gifts--to the countryside, to fishing, swimming, golfing, to country fairs, and to many other benefits of small-town living. These gifts are easily accessible to all and provide the people with a good deal of enjoyment.

1	2
12	6
24	12
36	18
48	24
60	30
72	36
84	42
86	43

• • • • 1 • • • • 2 • • • • 3 • • • • 4 • • • • 5 • • • • 6 • • • • 7 • • • • 8 • • • • 9 • • • • 10 • • • • 11 • • • • 12   1 min

1   2   3   4   5   6   2 min

SI 1.52

Three-Minute Timing

Prince Edward Island is the smallest province in Canada in both area and population. The Island received its proper name in 1799. This Island is crescent-shaped. It is 190 km long and around 5 to 65 km wide. The coastline is irregular with large bays and long inlets. It has white sandy beaches and majestic shores. All the inland waters are tidal inlets except for one river and one lake.

The soil is rich and a distinctive red color. The rock is mostly sandstone and quite sparse. The landscape is flat and rolling. Minerals have not been found in any great mass but there has been exploration for oil and gas off shore and on land. Major finds in these areas could greatly alter the lives of the people.

1	CW	3
12	12	4
24	24	8
36	36	12
48	48	16
60	60	20
72	72	24
79	79	26
12	91	30
24	103	34
36	115	38
48	127	42
60	139	46
64	143	48

• • • • 1 • • • • 2 • • • • 3 • • • • 4 • • • • 5 • • • 6 • • • • 7 • • • • 8 • • • • 9 • • • • 10 • • • • 11 • • • • 12   1 min

1   2   3   4   3 min

SI 1.60

Format
40-character line
Single spacing

Double space before each
new drill line.
This leaves one blank line
between lines of text.
To double space press the
return or enter key twice.

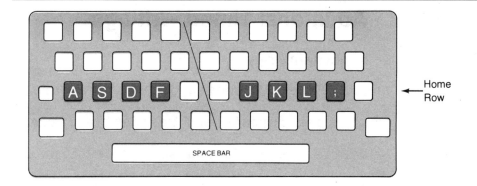

Home
Row

Place your fingers gently on **Home Row**. Place the fingers of your
left hand on **A S D F**. Place the fingers of your right hand on **J K L ;**
Curve your fingers slightly.

The J and F Keys

Use index finger of right hand
for **j**.
Use index finger of left hand
for **f**.
Use your thumb to strike the
space bar.
Practise each line once.

1 jjj fff jjj fff jf jf jjj fff jjj fff fj

2 jjj fff jjj fff jf jf jjj fff jjj fff fj

3 fjf fjf fff jf jf jfj jfj fj fj fjf fjfj

4 fjf fjf fff jf jf jfj jfj fj fj fjf fjfj

The L and D Keys

Use ring finger of right hand
for **l**.
Use middle finger of left hand
for **d**.
Practise each line once.

5 lll ddd lll ddd ld ld lll ddd lll ddd ld

6 lll ddd lll ddd ld ld lll ddd lll ddd ld

7 dld dld ddd ld ld ldl ldl dl dl dld dl l

8 dld dld ddd ld ld ldl ldl dl dl dld dl l

The K and S Keys

Use middle finger of right hand
for **k**.
Use ring finger of left hand
for **s**.
Practise each line once.

9 kkk sss kkk sss ks ks kkk sss kkk sss ks

10 kkk sss kkk sss ks ks kkk sss kkk sss ks

11 sks sks sss ksk sks ks ks sks sk sk ss k

12 sks sks sss ksk sks ks ks sks sk sk ss k

Additional Timed Writings

Two-Minute Timing

	1	2

Several species of oak trees are found in our Canadian forests and residential areas. The white oak is one of Canada's largest hardwood trees. It is very valuable because it provides strong, high-quality lumber which is used for doors, furniture, and flooring. The oak's large, spreading branches make it a favourite shade tree. Its acorns are an important source of food for animals.

SI 1.59

1	2
10	5
20	10
30	15
40	20
50	25
60	30
70	35
77	38

· · · 1 · · · · 2 · · · · 3 · · · · 4 · · · · 5 · · · 6 · · · · 7 · · · · 8 · · · · 9 · · · · 10   1 min
    1   2   3   4   5   2 min

Two-Minute Timing

	1	CW	2

Amateur athletes are indeed committed to their training programs. They work year after year to attain a great level of excellence. Few of them receive the praise and adoration that professionals enjoy. In many cases their hours of work get little notice. The rewards come from within the person.

The best of these athletes represent our country in the Olympic games. These athletes have worked hard to raise our standings in several events, and they have been particularly successful in sailing. We now have winning teams and should give them our support. Our Olympic representatives are very dedicated and deserve every encouragement.

SI 1.65

1	CW	2
12	12	6
24	24	12
36	36	18
48	48	24
60	60	30
12	72	36
24	84	42
36	96	48
48	108	54
60	120	60
68	128	64

· · · 1 · · · · 2 · · · · 3 · · · · 4 · · · · 5 · · · 6 · · · · 7 · · · · 8 · · · · 9 · · · · 10 · · · · 11 · · · · 12   1 min
    1   2   3   4   5   6   2 min

The ; and A Keys

Use little finger of right hand for ;.
Use little finger of left hand for **a**.
Practise each line once.

13 ;;; aaa ;;; aaa ;a ;a ;;; aaa ;;; aaa ;a

14 ;;; aaa ;;; aaa ;a ;a ;;; aaa ;;; aaa ;a

15 a;a a;a aaa ;a; ;a; a; a; a;a a; a; aa ;

16 a;a a;a aaa ;a; ;a; a; a; a;a a; a; aa ;

Drill on New Keys

Practise each line twice.

17 a al all all al as alas alas all as alas

18 a as ask ask as ask ask as as asks ask a

19 ad dad ad fad fad ad lad lad add fad lad

20 all as alas as ask ad lad fad alas lad a

■ Leave one space after a semicolon.

21 dad asks; a lad asks; a lass asks; alas;

22 a fad falls; a sad lass falls; all fall;

23 add ask; add flask; alas; lad adds flask

24 dad adds alfalfa salad as a fad; sad dad

Drill on Letter Combinations

Practise each line twice.
Do the underscored letters as quickly as you can.

25 as ask lass flask asks alas ad fad salad

26 ad add dad fad lad sad al all alas falls

■ Did you open the paper release and pull the paper bail forward before removing the paper from your typewriter? OR Did you save this lesson as a file on your data disk?

Spacing Reminder: Semicolon ;
• One space follows a semicolon.
• No space before a semicolon.

two league winners compete in a playoff--the Japan Series--
at the end of the season.

Each team plays 130 games per season, which runs from
April through October.

There are over 10 000 baseball and softball fields
in Japan, including 4 203 owned by companies, 3 181 that
are public, and 1 759 that belong to elementary, junior
and high schools.

The leading home run hitter of all time is a Japanese--
Sadaharu Oh, who had 868 homeruns to his credit when he
retired in 1980.

2

Format

40-character line
Single spacing

■ Is your work station neat and organized?

Practise each line twice.
Practise as quickly as you can.

Use **K** finger.
Practise each line twice.

Use **K** finger.
Keep **J** finger in home position.
Practise each line twice.

Practise each line twice.

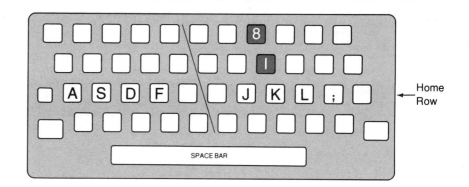

Home
Row

When each new key is introduced, look at your keyboard and watch your finger trace the reach. Then, keep your eyes on the copy. If you are uncertain about the location of any key, refer to the keyboard chart.
Beware—keyboard watching can be habit forming!

Review Home Row

1 jjj fff jf jf fjf fj lll ddd ld ld dld l

2 kkk sss sk sk sks ks ;;; aaa ;a ;a ;a; a

3 ad lad fad as ask lass alas flask all ad

4 as fads fall; alas; all sad lads ask; ad

Reach to the **I** Key

5 kkk kik kk ki ki ki kk ii kik kik kk iik

6 kik kik ki ki ik ik kiik kkk kik iii kki

Reach to the **8** Key

7 kkk kik ki8 ki8 ki8k k8k k8k k8 k8 k8k 8

8 kik ki8 8k 8k i8 i8 ki8k 88i k8i k8i i8k

Drill on the **I** Key

9 if is kid did aid ill ski skill fail lid

10 ill dill ail sail fail kiss lid silk aid

11 silk sails slid; disks skid; dials fail;

12 if all is said; if kids did kiss; if ill

· · · · 1 · · · · 2 · · · · 3 · · · · 4 · · · · 5 · · · · 6 · · · · 7 · · · · 8

The player, therefore, stays cooler and is able to conserve his or her energy.

To complete the Cooperall outfit, a matching sweater or hockey jersey is worn. The sweater is shorter and more tapered than the traditional one.

By actual weight, the total Cooperall system (gloves, shoulder pads, shinguards, pants and sweater) is about 40% lighter than the conventional uniform and protective equipment.   *spell out in words*

All components of the XL line are non-allergenic and completely washable.

Report

Production 4

Input the following short report.

BASEBALL (YAKYU)

Baseball (Yakyu) is one of Japan's most popular sports. It has been said that baseball is more popular in Japan than in the United states, where it was invented.

Baseball was introduced into Japan in 1873. It quickly became popular among university students and non-professional company teams. Professional baseball was started in Japan in 1934, but it did not really flourish until after World War II.

There are two baseball leagues in Japan: the Central League and the Pacific League, each with six teams. The

Drill on the 8 Key

Practise each line twice.

13 8 kids; 8 disks; 88 silk dials; 88 lids;

14 88 sails; 888 skills; aid 8 kids; 88 ifs

Line Indicator

One word is five characters (letters, numbers, and spaces). Therefore, there are eight words in a 40-character line. A line indicator, marked in five-character intervals, is given at the bottom of drill lines and timed writings. After the last character is input, read down vertically to the line indicator to calculate the number of words completed in the line. In the first example, six words have been input. In the second example, eight words have been input.

Example 1

a sad lass falls; all fall; as

· · · · 1 · · · · 2 · · · · 3 · · · · 4 · · · · 5 · · · · 6 · · · · 7 · · · · 8

Example 2

add ask; add flask; alas; lad adds flask

· · · · 1 · · · · 2 · · · · 3 · · · · 4 · · · · 5 · · · · 6 · · · · 7 · · · · 8

Drill and Practice

Practise each line once. Repeat or take two 15-s timings on each line.

15 a as did dial fail kiss sail jails alias

16 if dill fail fall sail disk silk slid is

17 all did ask kid lads flail dais ski kill

18 if sails skid; if aid fails; dill salad;

· · · · 1 · · · · 2 · · · · 3 · · · · 4 · · · · 5 · · · · 6 · · · · 7 · · · · 8

Number Drill and Practice

Practise each line once. Practise each line again.

19 88 silk sails; if 88 ail; 888 disks; 888

20 if 88; add 8 disks; dial 88 kids; 88 ads

21 if 8; if 88; if 888; is 8; is 88; is 888

· · · · 1 · · · · 2 · · · · 3 · · · · 4 · · · · 5 · · · · 6 · · · · 7 · · · · 8

Drill on Letter Combinations

Practise each line twice. Do the underscored letters as quickly as you can.

22 id did aid kids lids slid skid laid said

23 di dill did disk dial il kill flail silk

24 ai aid laid said ail sail fail jail dais

25 ki kids kiss kill skills skis skid skiff

· · · · 1 · · · · 2 · · · · 3 · · · · 4 · · · · 5 · · · · 6 · · · · 7 · · · · 8

■ Are you using a sharp, quick stroke?

the XL3 shoulder pad. All are moulded of a revolutionary new material, Plastafoam. The new gloves and pads are lighter, more flexible, longer lasting, and completely washable. Above all, they protect the player better than ever, particularly in the more vulnerable areas.

The total working model for Cooperall (the uniform of the future) was unveiled at the Winnipeg Jets rookie camp in Ste. Agathe, Quebec in 1979.

At first glance, it looks as if the player is wearing a streamlined pair of warm-up pants. What one sees is the outer shell of lightweight nylon that covers from waist to ankle and eliminates the need for stockings.

Under this shell is the inner girdle which covers from the top of the knees to the middle of the rib cage. The girdle, resembling somewhat a pair of football pants, is made of lightweight lycra with Plastafoam pads in strategically placed pockets. This system holds the pads close to the body, preventing injuries due to sticks or skates coming up under the pants. The girdle offers all the protection of conventional pants, plus extra slash pads at the back of the leg and on the inside of the thigh. Because the girdle is sewn with an inner lining, it is simple to add, alter, or remove pads.

All of the individual pads have a nubby texture on the inside, and have a series of small holes to allow maximum air circulation.

3

Format
40-character line
Single spacing

■ Are both your hands in home position?
■ Are your fingers slightly curved?

Practise each line twice.
Practise as quickly as you can.

Use **F** finger.
Practise each line twice.

Use **J** finger.
Practise each line twice.

Practise each line twice.

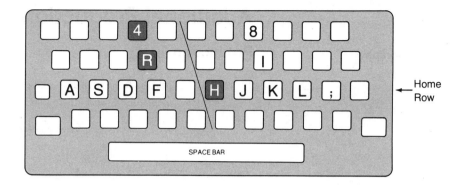

When each new key is introduced, look at your keyboard and watch your finger trace the reach. Then, keep your eyes on the copy. If you are uncertain about the location of any key, refer to the keyboard chart.
Beware—keyboard watching can be habit forming!

Review New Keys

1 jj ff kk dd ll ss ;; aa j f k d l s ; aa

2 kkk kik ki ki iik ki ki8k k8k k8 i8 8k 8

3 kid lid dill skill dial dais ski disk if

4 alas; add; flask; sail; sad; alias; lass

Reach to the R Key

5 fff frf fff frf frf rrr fr fr rf rf frfr

6 frf fr fr frr rfr rfr rrf rrf rf rf rrff

Reach to the H Key

7 jjj jhj jhj jjj hhh jh jh jjj hjh hj jhj

8 jhj jh jh jhh hjh hjh hhj hhj hj hj hj h

Drill on the R and H Keys

9 air fir sir iris fair dark jars risk far

10 his has hid half fish dish hark rash had

11 far hills; frail jars; rash drills; hark

12 his dark hair hid a radial rash; add all

· · · · 1 · · · · 2 · · · · 3 · · · · 4 · · · · 5 · · · · 6 · · · · 7 · · · · 8

Additional Production Practice (Unit IV)

Production 2

Input the following as a bibliography. Use correct format.

Bibliography

Lowry, Mary Ann et al. <u>People to People</u>. Toronto : Copp Clark Pitman Ltd., 1987.

Kretchman, M. Lily et al. <u>The Language of Business Communication</u>. Toronto : John Wiley & Sons, 1988.

Bryson, Bill. "A Little English is a Dangerous Thing." <u>Language at Work</u>. Toronto : Holt, Rinehard & Winston of Canada, Ltd., 1987, 26-28.

Misener, Judi and Sandra Steele. <u>The Business of English</u>. Toronto : Oxford University Press Canada, 1986.

Production 3

Input the following two-page report. Use a backing sheet to determine the bottom margin for page 1.

COOPERALL

Several years ago Cooper Canada's research and design team began an intensive program to improve protective hockey equipment. The aim was to make the equipment tougher, yet lighter--to make it as cool and comfortable as possible and still offer maximum protection.

The first result of this research and testing was the Cooper XL1 glove, introduced in 1978. It was followed by the XL2 shinguard and

Use **F** finger.
Keep other fingers in home
position.
Practise each line twice.

Practise each line twice.

Practise each line once.
Repeat *or* take two
15-s timings on each line.

Practise each line once.
Practise each line again.

Practise each line twice.
Do the underscored letters as
quickly as you can.

■ Do you think **space** for
each space bar stroke?

Reach to the 4 Key

13 fff frf fr4 fr4 fr4f f4f f4f f4 f4 f4f 4

14 frf f4f 4f 4f r4 r4 fr4f 44r f4r f4r r4f

Drill on the 4 Key

15 4 jars; 4 affairs; 4 fish; 4 halls; 4 44

16 hark 44 hairs; 44 raids; 444 drills; 444

Drill and Practice

17 if has far fall drill frail radar affair

18 sir his half risk dark frail radar drill

19 has had hid fair drill rails hard fir if

20 raid radish hill; a fair fish; dark hair

Number Drill and Practice

21 44 half firs; 44 radar drills; 444 risks

22 if 4; if 48; if 84; if 484; if 848; 4884

23 flash 48 fish; drill 84 lads; 484 hills;
· · · · 1 · · · · 2 · · · · 3 · · · · 4 · · · · 5 · · · · 6 · · · · 7 · · · · 8

Drill on Letter Combinations

24 ir air fir sir fair iris affair irk lair

25 ri rid risk riff drills arid frills iris

26 ar far jar dark jars arid radar hard ark

27 ra raid rail radar radial frail rash rad
· · · · 1 · · · · 2 · · · · 3 · · · · 4 · · · · 5 · · · · 6 · · · · 7 · · · · 8

Additional Production Practice (Unit IV)

Production 1

Input the following in report form.

Cold Water Safety

<u>Cold Water Can Kill</u>

What happens when a person plunges suddenly into cold water? Panic and shock are usually the first reactions. The initial shock of the cold water may place severe strain on the body and make the heart stop beating.

The hands and feet may become numb. Within minutes, severe pain makes clear thought difficult. Finally, deep hypothermia (exposure) sets in, which can lead to unconsciousness, then death. In the past 10 years, about half of the fatal drowning accidents in Canada took place in late spring or early fall, when the water was cold.

<u>What Can You Do?</u>

If you capsize or fall overboard, try to get out of the water as fast as possible. Either right your boat and get in it, or climb on top of it.

If you have to stay in the water, try to keep your body as warm as possible. Huddle with others who were in the boat. If you are alone, roll into a HELP (Heat Escape Lessening Position) ball. This is similar to the fetal position. You lose more body heat from swimming than you do if you remain still in the water.

4 Review

Format
40-character line
Single spacing

■ Is your paper guide set correctly on your typewriter or your printer?
■ Is your line space regulator set for single spacing on your typewriter?

Practise each line according to your teacher's directions *or* practise each line twice.

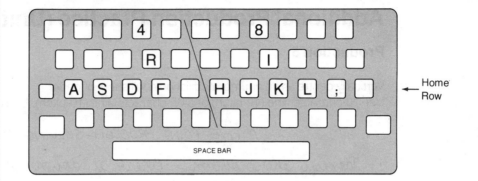

If you are uncertain about the location of any key, refer to the keyboard chart. *Beware* – keyboard watching can be habit forming!

Keyboarding Review

A 1 a;a a;a a;a aaa ;a; ;a; a; a; a;a a; a; aa ;

   2 as sad aid sail liar dial asks radar far

D 3 dld dld ddd ld ld ldl ldl dl dl dld dl d

   4 dad add salad kid did arid dais disk hid

F 5 fjf fjf fff jf jf jfj jfj fj fj fjf fjfj

   6 fad fall if fail fair riff flash affairs

H 7 jhj jh jh jhh hjh hjh hhj hhj hj hj hj h

   8 half fish hark dish hills has hair flash

I 9 kik kik ki ki ik ik kiik kkk kik iii kki

  10 if his kid dill aid iris fish fir radish

J 11 jjj fff jfj jfj jf jf jfj jfj fj fj fjfj

  12 jars ajar rajah jiff jail jails jai alai

K 13 kkk sks kkk ksk sks ks ks sks sk sk ss k

  14 ask kid skills disks kiss dark risk jars

L 15 lll dld lll ld ld ldl ldl dl dl dld dl l

  16 alas fall ill silk flair hall ail radial

· · · · 1 · · · · 2 · · · · 3 · · · · 4 · · · · 5 · · · · 6 · · · · 7 · · · · 8

Additional Production Practice (Unit III)

Production 5

Vertically centre as an enumerated list on a full sheet of paper.
Use 70-character line (12-pitch) or a 60-character line (10-pitch). Use correct format.

A FIVE-POINT PROBLEM-SOLVING PLAN

1. Identify the problem. Break it down to the bare essentials.

2. List the possible solutions to the problem. State alternatives.

3. Evaluate the alternatives. What are the positive and negative aspects of each one?

4. If possible, test the alternatives; then choose the one that seems to give the best results.

5. Re-evaluate regularly. After some time has gone by, decide if the choice was a good one. Use this knowledge for future decisions.

Production 6

Vertically centre as an enumerated list on a full sheet of paper. Use 70-character line (elite — 12-pitch) or a 60-character line (pica — 10-pitch). Use correct format.

Title: Cold Water Safety Tips

List: 1. Make sure your boat and equipment are in top condition. 2. Check the weather forecast before setting out on a trip. 3. Always tell someone where you are going and when you expect to return. 4. Have someone else with you in the boat, or go out with another boat. 5. Dress properly for the cold. Wool clothing offers the best protection. 6. Always wear an approved lifejacket or personal flotation device (PFD) when boating on cold water. 7. Know what actions to take in an emergency. 8. If you end up in the water, don't panic.

R 17 frf fr fr frr rfr rfr rrf rrf rf rf rrff
18 sir rid far hair radar rash frail affair

S 19 sss sks sss ksk sks ks ks sks sk sk ss k
20 as lass dais risk fish his has silk jars

; 21 ;;; a;a ;;; ;a; ;a; a; a; a;a a; a; ;; a
22 hall; liar; liars; dial; flair; dash; if

8 23 kik k8k 8k 8k i8 i8 ki8k 88k k8i k8i i8k
24 8 88 8 88 48 484 88 84 848 848 888 8 888

4 25 frf f4f 4f 4f r4 r4 r4 fr4f 44f f4f f4r4
26 4 44 4 44 84 848 444 48 484 44 8 444 844
· · · · 1 · · · · 2 · · · · 3 · · · · 4 · · · · 5 · · · · 6 · · · · 7 · · · · 8

Letter Review Practice

Take two 30-s timings on each line *or* practise each line twice.

27 his lad has half a fish as his salad fad

28 his dad hid; jar lids fall as sails fail

29 drill his frail kids as hard as all fads

Number Review Practice

Take two 30-s timings on each line *or* practise each line twice.

30 4 dark firs slid far as all 484 lads did

31 48 flair disks drill 88 radials as rails

32 44 jars rid all 48 lads as 8 raid flasks

33 8 liars kill 84 dills as 4 dark fish aid

34 all 8 ski as 44 sail far; 4 dial all ads

35 half his 84 lads dash as 48 hid his dish
· · · · 1 · · · · 2 · · · · 3 · · · · 4 · · · · 5 · · · · 6 · · · · 7 · · · · 8

Additional Production Practice (Unit III)

Production 4

Vertically centre as an enumerated list on a full sheet of paper. Use 70-character line (12-pitch) or a 60-character line (10-pitch). Use correct format.

WHAT COMPUTERS DO

1. Computers compute. They can process long and elaborate calculations very quickly.

2. Computers store information in data banks.

3. Computers process information. They can make multiple copies of information such as business letters, mailing lists, and bills.

4. Computers are used in research and medicine.

5. Computers can predict--they can forecast future trends in weather, the economy, etc.

6. Computers are used in education as a teaching tool.

7. Computers help design complex projects such as buildings, planes, and rockets.

8. Computers are used in simulations to show what can happen in a given situation.

9. Computers can monitor and control machines.

10. Computers are used in graphic arts, photography, and music.

11. Computers are explorers--they help find minerals, study the ocean floor, and explore space.

12. Computers play games.

Timed Writings

Timed writings are calculated on the *gross words* completed *per minute* (GWPM). One word is equivalent to five characters (letters, numbers, and spaces).

If eight words are completed in 60 s (1 min), it is equivalent to 8 GWPM. If eight words are completed in 30 s, it is equivalent to 16 GWPM. Each timed writing has a line indicator at the bottom as a guide for calculating the gross words per minute (GWPM) on each timed writing (timing).

Thirty-Second Timings

30 s

```
36 silk skis fail as air radar skill flairs     16

37 his dish hid a dark radish if a lad asks      16

38 fair hair alias dark flash all his jails      16
   · · · · 2 · · · · 4 · · · · 6 · · · · 8 · · · · 10 · · · · 12 · · · · 14 · · · · 16   30 s
        1         2         3         4         5         6         7         8          60 s
```

Additional Production Practice (Unit III)

Production 3

Input the following letter on MacMillan Bloedel letterhead. Use full block letter style with mixed punctuation. Input an appropriate envelope or an envelope label. Remember to include the missing letter parts.

MacMillan Bloedel Limited

1075 West Georgia Street
Vancouver, B.C. Canada V6E 3R9
Cable Address: "Harmac"   Telex No. 0451471
Telephone: (604) 661-8000

Mr. Egon P. Frisch
Co-ordinator, B.C. Project
Hausenerstrasse 15
7210 Rottweil
Wuerttemberg
FEDERAL REPUBLIC OF GERMANY

Thank you for your interest in MacMillan Bloedel.
Enclosed are brochures about our company and our
various regions within B.C., along with a few maps
of our logging roads on Vancouver Island.

If you are looking for material on the B.C. forest
industry in general, you might want to write to:

    Council of Forest Industries of B.C.
    1055 West Hastings Street
    Vancouver, British Columbia
    V6E 4A6

*If you would like additional copies of
anything I have sent to you, please let
me know and I will forward them to you.*

Yours very truly

*Jacqui Wills
Editorial Assistant*

5

T / 5 / ,

Format
40-character line
Single spacing

■ Are the palms of your hands and your wrists above the front of your keyboard?

Practise each line twice.
Practise as quickly as you can.

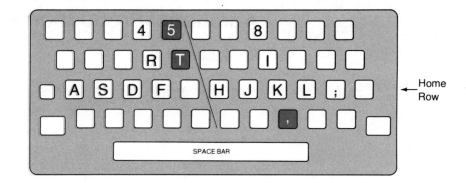

Review New Keys

1 a;sldkfj a;sldkfj kik ki ki ii ki8 k8 k8

2 frf fr frr rr fr4 f4 f4 44 jhj jhh jh jh

3 sir did raid half hills has flash radish

4 hall; 44 hills; 88 silk sails; 48 salads

Use **F** finger.
Practise each line twice.

Reach to the T Key

5 fff ftf ftf ftt ftf ttt ft ft tf tf ftft

6 ftf ft ft ftt tft tft ttf ttf tf tf ttff

Use **K** finger.
Practise each line twice.

Reach to the , Key

7 kkk k,k k,k k,, k,k ,,, k, k, ,k ,k k,k,

8 k,k k, k, k,, ,k, ,k, ,,k ,,k ,k ,k ,,kk

Practise each line twice.

Drill on the T and , Keys

9 it at fat fatal raft sat trail halt tilt

10 art rat kit hit tar stir that data trait

11 fat rat, tall hat, fast darts, trash art

12 this is, at last, his first thrift start

■ Leave one space after a comma.

Use **F** finger.
Keep other fingers in home position.
Practise each line twice.

Reach to the 5 Key

13 fff frf ftf frf f4f f5f ft5f f5f f5f f55

14 ftf f5f 5f 5f t5 t5 ft5f 55f f5t f5t t5f

• • • • 1 • • • 2 • • • 3 • • • 4 • • • 5 • • • 6 • • • 7 • • • 8

Additional Production Practice (Unit III)

Production 2

Input the following letter on Finning letterhead. Use full block letter style with mixed punctuation. Input an appropriate envelope or an envelope label. Remember to include the missing letter parts.

FINNING TRACTOR & EQUIPMENT COMPANY LIMITED　　

HEAD OFFICE: 555 GREAT NORTHERN WAY, VANCOUVER, B.C. V5T 1E2 • PHONE (604) 872-4444 • TELEX 04-508717 • CABLE ADDRESS "FINTRAC"

Mr. Ah-Suk Sug
Senior Director
Hyundai Construction
One Bridge Plaza, Suite 600
Fort Lee, NJ 07024-6001
U.S.A.

As the world's largest Caterpillar dealer, Finning has the size and resources to offer you quality construction equipment and unmatched product support services. Founded in British Columbia in 1933, Finning and its subsidiaries now sell, lease, and service a broad range of products from some 35 major centres in Western Canada, Northwestern United States, and the United Kingdom.

To further acquaint you with our commitment to the construction and resources industries, I have enclosed an information package, including our latest annual report.

As Finning has been the major equipment supplier on all large dams, tunnels, pipelines, highways, and rail projects in British Columbia, I am sure you will want to consider our expertise in any of your construction contracts.

B. Wright, Manager
Construction Sales

Drill on the 5 Key

Practise each line twice.

15 5 kits 5 tails 5 rats 5 tars 5 rafts 5 5

16 that is 55 art kits, 55 darts, 555 tails

Drill and Practice

Practise each line once.
Repeat or take two
15-s timings on each line.

17 that fast halt at third hit this fat rat

18 hit this task first, stir that tart last

19 hit it as far as that tall dark tar hill

20 5 raft thrills, 54 fatal trails, 5 darts

Number Drill and Practice

Practise each line once.
Practise each line again.

21 55 salads; 4 jars; 8 darts; 58 half fish

22 88 fat rats; his 45 skis; 85 fatal hills

23 5 hard flasks hit 4 fish as 85 lads talk

· · · · 1 · · · · 2 · · · · 3 · · · · 4 · · · · 5 · · · · 6 · · · · 7 · · · · 8

Drill on Letter Combinations

Practise each line twice.
Do the underscored letters as
quickly as you can.

■ Are you striking the return
or enter key by touch while
keeping your eyes on the
copy?

24 th that thrift third thirst filth faiths

25 at rat data that hat fat fatal atlas tat

26 ta task stall tail talk tart data tariff

· · · · 1 · · · · 2 · · · · 3 · · · · 4 · · · · 5 · · · · 6 · · · · 7 · · · · 8

Spacing Reminder: Comma ,

• One space follows a comma.
• No space before a comma.

Additional Production Practice (Unit III)

Production 1

Input the following letter on Westcoast letterhead. Use full block letter style mixed punctuation. Input an appropriate envelope or an envelope label. Remember to include the missing letter parts.

Westcoast Energy Inc.

1333 West Georgia Street
Vancouver, British Columbia
V6E 3K9
Telephone (604) 664-5500
Telex 04-51340
FAX (604) 664-5702

Ms. Connie Coniglio
1157 First Avenue
Chetwynd, British Columbia
V0C 2J0

Dear Connie

The Employee Suggestion Plan Committee has now completed its review of your proposal concerning improved access to the Utility Building at the Pine River Plant. I am pleased to tell you this has been accepted for implementation and an award has been approved.

Please choose a gift from Group A of the enclosed Suggestion Award Brochure, complete the order form and return it to Valerie Ward, who will arrange for the appropriate item to be sent to you.

We appreciate your interest in the Suggestion Plan and shall welcome any other ideas you may wish to submit.

Douglas G. MacKenzie
Chairman
Employee Suggestion Committee

6

E / 3 / .

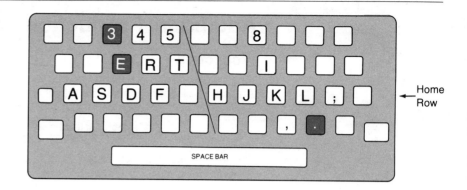

Format
40-character line
Single spacing

■ Do you keep your eyes on the copy except when tracing the new reaches?

Practise each line twice.
Practise as quickly as you can.

Use **D** finger.
Practise each line twice.

Use **L** finger.
Practise each line twice.

Practise each line twice.

The symbol ∧ means leave a space.

■ Leave two spaces after a period to indicate the end of a sentence.

Review New Keys

1 asdfjkl; ki ii k8 88 fr rr f4 f4 jh jh h

2 ftf ft ftt tt ft5 f5 f5 55 k,k k,, k, k,

3 at last, that is, stir fast fists thrift

4 55 rats, 45 rafts, 545 tasks, 555 54 445

Reach to the E Key

5 ddd ded ded dee ded eee de de ed ed dede

6 ded de de dee ede ede eed eed ed ed eedd

Reach to the . Key

7 lll l.l l.l l.. l.l ... l. l. .l .l l.l.

8 l.l l. l. l. l.. .l. .l. ..l ..l .l .l ..ll

Drill on the E and . Keys

9 the she are her date left heir deer kite

10 seas ate era diet shed these alter teeth

11 these are here.∧∧fear rides.∧∧idle life.

12 three tarts, fresh dates are their diet.

13 the deer at the tree at the lake is free

· · · · 1 · · · · 2 · · · · 3 · · · · 4 · · · · 5 · · · · 6 · · · · 7 · · · · 8

Additional Production Practice (Unit II)

Production 7

Arrange the following menu attractively on a full sheet of paper. Supply a suitable title.

North American Indian

Pakweijigan .... Quick Corn Bread
Sagamite .... Corn Soup with Beans and Meats

Chinese

Ling Moong Gai .... Lemon Chicken
Wonton .... Tiny Savoury Dumplings

French Canadian

Tourtière .... Minced Pork Pie
Tarte au Sirop D'Érable .... Maple Syrup Pie

Japanese

Harusame Tempura .... Deep-fried Seafood
Sukiyaki .... Quick-cooked Beef and Vegetables

Ukrainian

Borsch .... Beet Soup
Holubtse .... Stuffed Cabbage Rolls

Filipino

Rellenong Talong .... Stuffed Eggplant
Ensaimada .... Sweet Bread Rolls

Caribbean

Sancocho .... Beef and Vegetable Stew
Corn Pone .... Cornmeal Cake with Fruit

Korean

Galbi Jim .... Spareribs with Sesame Sauce
Oyi Namul .... Cucumber Salad

Reach to the 3 Key

14 ddd ded de3 de3 de3d d3d d3d d3 d3 d3d 3

15 ded d3d 3d 3d e3 e3 de3d 33d d3e d3e e3d

Drill on the 3 Key

16 3 sides. 3 herds. 33 tires. 33 series

17 3 fires. 33 aisles. 333 elk. 333 sets

Drill and Practice

18 after that, the kites tear like threads.

19 the tired deer are alerted at the trail.

20 read that tale after the three lads ski.

21 she left her red silk dress at the lake.

Number Drill and Practice

22 83 litres; 383 teeth; read at least 344;

23 585 after this; 435 free sleds; 843 deer

24 35 fake rides; 844 late lads; 343 fears;

· · · · 1 · · · · 2 · · · · 3 · · · · 4 · · · · 5 · · · · 6 · · · · 7 · · · · 8

Drill on Letter Combinations

25 ea deal heater sea area hear ease teases

26 te date rate test tell after steal alter

27 er era erase her here refer alert herded

28 re rest dress flare are area thread fret

29 ee feet feel free three sheet teeth deer

· · · · 1 · · · · 2 · · · · 3 · · · · 4 · · · · 5 · · · · 6 · · · · 7 · · · · 8

Sidebar:

Use **D** finger.
Keep other fingers in home position.
Practise each line twice.

Practise each line twice.

Practise each line once.
Repeat *or* take two
15-s timings on each line.

Practise each line once.
Practise each line again.

Practise each line twice.
Do the underscored letters as quickly as you can.

■ Are your wrists relaxed?

Additional Production Practice (Unit II)

Tables

Production 5

Centre the following table attractively on a half sheet of paper.

CAYUGA II
Daytime Schedule
Toronto—Niagara

Departure		Arrival	
Toronto	08:30	Niagara	11:00
Niagara	11:15	Toronto	13:45
Toronto	14:00	Niagara	16:15
Niagara	16:30	Toronto	19:15

[4] Align colons   [8]   [4] Align colons

Tables

Production 6

Centre the following table on a half sheet of paper. Arrange it attractively.

MUSICAL INSTRUMENTS AND EQUIPMENT

(Electronic)

Manufacturer	Item	Model
Guild	Guitar	Detonator
Norman Guitars	Bass	BAC-800
Hohner	Amp	Panther
Casio	Synthesizer	DG-10
Kaman	Microphone	Sony Musician
Sunrise	PA System	Rocky
Peavey	Effects Pedals	AOD-2

Format
40-character line
Single spacing

■ Did you check your posture?
feet? back? hands? eyes?

Practise each line twice.
Practise as quickly as you can.

Use **L** finger.
Practise each line twice.

Use **F** finger.
Practise each line twice.

Practise each line twice.

■ *rigor* or *rigour*

Know the preference in your
area of Canada.

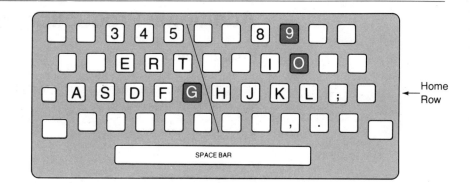

Review New Keys

1 asdfjkl; jj rr 88 44 hh ft tt f5 f55 k,k

2 ded de dee ee de3 d3 d3 33 l.l l.. l. l.

3 take three tales sheet least here delete

4 at least 33 fires. 435 sides. 33 53 34

Reach to the O Key

5 lll lol lol loo lol ooo lo lo ol ol lolo

6 lol lo lo loo olo olo ool ool ol ol ooll

Reach to the G Key

7 fff fgf fgf fgg fgf ggg fg fg gf gf fgfg

8 fgf fg fg fgg gfg gfg ggf ggf gf gf ggff

Drill on the O and G Keys

9 to do oat old foil silo riot load oriole

10 go fog ego logo igloo forge rigor giggle

11 he tried to get legal aid for his folks.

12 the old gate at the gorge is solid jade.

13 the jogger lags at the fork of the road.
· · · · 1 · · · · 2 · · · · 3 · · · · 4 · · · · 5 · · · · 6 · · · · 7 · · · · 8

Additional Production Practice (Unit II)

Production 3

Using the Backspace Method, centre the following display attractively on a full sheet of paper. Use block centring.

```
FAMOUS SAYINGS


Better late than never.
JOHN HEYWOOD

History is bunk.
HENRY FORD

Penny saved is a penny got.
HENRY FIELDING

We are not amused.
QUEEN VICTORIA

If a tree dies, plant another in its place.
CARL LINNAEUS

Fate makes our relatives, choice makes our friends.
JACQUES DELILLE

Every dog has his day.
MIGUEL DE CERVANTES

Come up and see me sometime.
MAE WEST

Every day is a fresh beginning.
SARAH CHAUNCEY WOOLSEY
```

Production 4

Centre the following table on a half sheet of paper. Use block centring for the column headings.

```
              CRIME AND MYSTERY STORIES


Title of Story                  Author

The Shadow of a Doubt           Fulton Oursler
The Manufactured Clue           Alan Hynd
Death in the Arctic             Arthur Train, Jr.
The Thirty-Nine Steps           John Buchan
The Pit and the Pendulum        Edgar Allan Poe
Death on the Nile               Agatha Christie
The Sound of Murder             Donald E. Westlake
```

Reach to the 9 Key

14 lll lol lo9 lo9 lo9l 191 191 19 19 191 9

15 191 191 9l 9l ol ol lo9l 991 19o 19o o9l

Drill on the 9 Key

16 9 tigers.   99 eagles.   99 otters.   9 oak

17 999 dolls, 99 sold.   999 ghosts, 9 soar.

Drill and Practice

18 hold their last order for the oak doors.

19 she agreed to sell her dogs to the lads.

20 do eat the fresh fish or the fried eggs.

21 the folks agreed to go to the gift sale.

22 lead the goat herd to the far east gate.

Number Drill and Practice

23 494 idle lads; taste 98 sodas; 498 goods

24 89 diet dates; 935 as 953; 955 soft sets

25 98 sore feet; 499 joggers; 39 fried eggs

· · · · 1 · · · · 2 · · · · 3 · · · · 4 · · · · 5 · · · · 6 · · · · 7 · · · · 8

Drill on Letter Combinations

26 oi oil foil soil hoist toil joist soiled

27 oa oak oat oaf loaf road soar goat oasis

28 gg egg jogger giggle trigger jagged eggs

29 gre great agree ogre greed regret grease

· · · · 1 · · · · 2 · · · · 3 · · · · 4 · · · · 5 · · · · 6 · · · · 7 · · · · 8

Use **L** finger.
Keep **J** finger in home position.
Practise each line twice.

Practise each line twice.

Practise each line once.
Repeat *or* take two
15-s timings on each line.

Practise each line once.
Practise each line again.

Practise each line twice.
Do the underscored letters as
quickly as you can.

■ Are your elbows and arms
motionless?

Additional Production Practice (Unit II)

Production 1

Centring

Centre the following display horizontally and vertically on a half sheet of paper.

```
                   COMPUTER FIRMS


                        IBM
                   SPERRY UNIVAC
                    HONEYWELL
                  HEWLETT-PACKARD
                      TANDY
                     DIGITAL
                    COMMODORE
                 OHIO SCIENTIFIC
                      WANG
                       AES
                      MICOM
                     OSBORNE
                      APPLE
```

Production 2

Centring

Centre the following display horizontally and vertically on a half sheet of paper.

```
               THE BANKS OF CANADA

            Domestic Chartered Banks


             The Royal Bank of Canada
                 Bank of Montreal
                Bank of Nova Scotia
               Toronto Dominion Bank
         Canadian Imperial Bank of Commerce
              National Bank of Canada
                 Bank of Alberta
         Western and Pacific Bank of Canada
```

Review

SPACE BAR

← Home Row

Format
40-character line
Single spacing

■ Is your textbook arranged at an angle for ease of reading?

Practise each line according to your teacher's directions *or* practise each line twice.

■ *odor* or *odour*

Know the preference in your area of Canada.

Keyboarding Review

E 1 ded de de dee ede ede eed eed ed ed eedd
2 aide herd idle tests the feel stereo ego

G 3 fgf fg fg fgg gfg gfg ggf ggf gf gf ggff
4 go egg high great garage digit eager gag

O 5 lol lo lo loo olo olo ool ool ol ol ooll
6 off old oil torso odor idols igloo forge

T 7 ftf ft ft ftt tft tft ttf ttf tf tf ttff
8 the data tart thirst state tooth theatre

, 9 k,k k k, k, k, k,, ,k, ,k, ,,k ,,k ,k ,k ,,kk
10 of the, to the, if she has, their, there

. 11 l.l l. l. l. ..l .l. .l. ..l ..l .l .l ..ll
12 alas, it is. go for it. so, to do. so

3 13 ded d3d 3d 3d e3 e3 de3e 33d d3e e3d d3e
14 3 33 3 33 43 343 33 83 383 33 3 333 5343

5 15 ftf f5f 5f 5f t5 t5 ft5f 55f f5t f5t t5f
16 5 55 5 55 45 535 55 85 585 555 5 555 435

9 17 l9l l9l 9l 9l ol ol lo9l 99l l9o l9o o9l
18 9 99 9 99 89 989 99 59 939 999 9 999 985

· · · · · 1 · · · · 2 · · · · 3 · · · · 4 · · · · 5 · · · · 6 · · · · 7 · · · · 8

Additional Production Practice (Unit II)

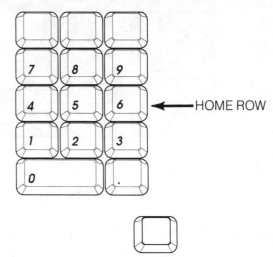

HOME ROW

Reach to the 7, 8 and 9 Keys

Use your index finger for **7**.

Use your middle finger for **8**.

Use your ring finger for **9**.

Practise each line twice.

5   789 898 987 788 877 999 787 988 798 97 887 788 977

6   877 989 779 879 977 789 899 979 78 889 987 798 897

7   700 809 970 780 880 909 707 890 970 80 709 808 990

8   8.09 7.98 9.08 7.07 8.97 9.98 7.89 8.70 9.087 7.88

Reach to the 1, 2, and 3 Keys

Use your index finger for **1**.

Use your middle finger for **2**.

Use your ring finger for **3**.

Practise each line twice.

9   123 232 322 133 212 331 233 123 321 211 112 33 231

10   323 131 231 322 122 331 223 311 132 233 312 13 223

11   101 230 302 110 201 310 203 101 300 120 220 10 301

12   2.13 1.30 3.21 1.22 2.02 3.01 1.23 2.013 3.31 1.32

Drill and Practice

Practise each line twice.

13   305 750 501 270 403 806 530 904 708 20 603 405 100

14   8.09 7.26 3.50 6.41 2.75 5.93 6.09 4.72 8.109 3.53

15   419 527 639 295 834 503 926 410 729 36 628 502 861

16   361 752 490 139 276 835 517 294 384 716 529 451 24

Letter Review Practice

Take two 30-s timings on each line *or* practise each line twice.

19 he forgot the address of the old estate.

20 the old sailor had tattoos of red roses.

21 he regrets that the eggs are still soft.

22 take the iris seeds off the third shelf.

23 stars fell to the left of the oat field.

24 go to the lake. get the red fire flare.

Number Review Practice

Take two 30-s timings on each line *or* practise each line twice.

25 let 53 go after 89 are fed so 44 sold it

26 845 tigers eat 93 eggs as 498 gals feast

27 oil 593 oak doors like 84 soft odd kites

28 94 told her 55 forts look old as the ark

· · · · 1 · · · · 2 · · · · 3 · · · · 4 · · · · 5 · · · · 6 · · · · 7 · · · · 8

One-Minute Timing

Timing

Take two 1-min timings on the set of three lines.

■ Are your hands parallel with the slant of the keyboard?

1 min

29 the lad rode the horse to the east hill.   8

30 list all the goods he takes to the lake.   16

31 she agreed to sell the old hotel stereo.   24

· · · · 1 · · · · 2 · · · · 3 · · · · 4 · · · · 5 · · · · 6 · · · · 7 · · · · 8

Additional Production Practice (Unit II)

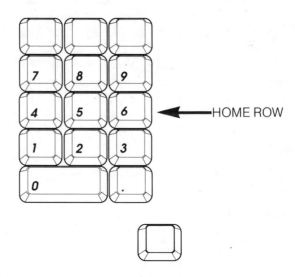

HOME ROW

Place the finger of your right hand on HOME ROW.
Use the index finger on **4**.
Use the middle finger on **5**.
Use the ring finger on **6**.

The 4, 5, and 6 Keys

Practise each line twice.

1 456 445 446 544 564 644 645 444 565 646 555 64 465

2 564 445 646 544 456 666 554 65 445 654 464 565 645

Reach to the 0 and • Keys

Use your index finger for 0.
Use your ring finger for .
Practise each line twice.

3 400 506 650 405 604 505 460 606 500 404 650 505 40

4 4.06 6060 5.45 6.04 4.45 5.05 6.55 4.54 5.00 6.065

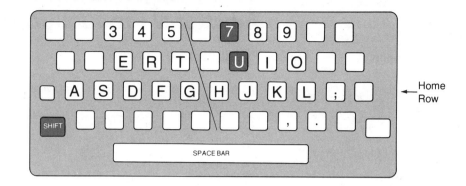

Format
40-character line
Single spacing

■ Is your chair or table adjusted to a comfortable height?

Practise each line twice.
Practise as quickly as you can.

Review New Keys

1 fjdksla; de ee d3 33 l. ft tt f5 55 ., .

2 lol lo loo oo lo9 l9 l9 99 fgf fgg fg fg

3 sold forth road hotel high glad gift ego

4 at least 99 orders. 99 rods; 98 459 398

Use **J** finger.
Practise each line twice.

Reach to the U Key

5 jjj juj juj juu juj uuu ju ju uj uj juju

6 juj ju ju juu uju uju uuj uuj uj uj uujj

Reach to the Left Shift Key

To capitalize the letters on the right side of the keyboard:
1. Keep **F** finger on the **F** key.
2. Depress left shift key with **A** finger.
3. Strike the letter to be capitalized with the correct finger of the right hand.
4. Release left shift key and quickly return **A** finger to home position.

Use **A** finger.
Keep **F** finger on **F** key.
Practise each line twice.

The symbol ∧ means leave a space.

7 Ida Kit Les Joe Ollie Jude Luke Jeff Ula

8 It is our rug.∧∧It did.∧∧Our auto skids.

Drill on the U and the Left Shift Key

Practise each line twice.

9 us use used rug four thus sure auto just

10 Lisa Hilda Lou Helga Jesse Ursula Louise

11 Our guests fuss. Juries judge. It did.

12 Our dog, Luke, guards the house outside.

13 I guessed the disguise of the huge Hulk.

· · · · · 1 · · · · 2 · · · · 3 · · · · 4 · · · · 5 · · · · 6 · · · · 7 · · · · 8

Additional Production Practice (Unit 1)

Production 4

Set a 40-character line. Input the following paragraphs using single spacing. Listen for the right margin signal.

        Rice is the most important item in the daily diet throughout Asia. There are thousands of varieties of rice. It has several different qualities: colour, fragrance, flavour, and texture.

        The desirable features of rice are not the same in every Asian country. In India and Pakistan, Sri Lanka and Burma, fluffy, dry rice is preferred. Long, thin grains are thought to be best, and rice is cooked with salt.

5⟩ In Malaysia, Indonesia, Thailand, and Vietnam, rice is preferred dry and separate, but it is cooked without salt. ¶In China, Korea, and Japan, glossy, pearly grains are desired. The rice should tend to cling together so that it can easily be picked up with chopsticks. No salt is used.

5⟩ In some Asian countries, rice is used in religious ceremonies. It is considered a symbol of prosperity and fertility. The Western world too has adopted some of the symbolism, for example, in the throwing of rice at weddings.

Reach to the 7 Key

14 jjj juj ju7 ju7 ju7j j7j j7j j7 j7 j7j 7

15 juj j7j 7j 7j u7 u7 ju7j 77j j7u j7u u7j

Drill on the 7 Key

16 7 rugs.   77 guests.   77 gulls.   77 duels

17 77 suits.   777 adults.   777 laughs.   777

Drill and Practice

18 I urged Ula to audit the figures for us.

19 Louis uses the usual route to get there.

20 Loud laughter outraged the adult guests.

21 Our guide shrugs as I hug four tourists.

22 Lulu likes to use the ukulele for hours.

Number Drill and Practice

23 87 fat sailors, 7 sad jailers, 7 old elk

24 97 full jugs; 797 guards; 794 used rugs;

25 78 rigid rules; 47 old guitars; 773 uses

· · · · 1 · · · · 2 · · · · 3 · · · · 4 · · · · 5 · · · · 6 · · · · 7 · · · · 8

Drill on Letter Combinations

26 ou out tough four route loud oust outlet

27 au auto aura audit fault gauge laugh auk

28 ur sure turf hurt urge hour figure lurks

29 ru trust rug fruit drug strut rule shrug

· · · · 1 · · · · 2 · · · · 3 · · · · 4 · · · · 5 · · · · 6 · · · · 7 · · · · 8

Use **J** finger.
Keep other fingers in home position.
Practise each line twice.

Practise each line twice.

Practise each line once.
Repeat *or* take two
15-s timings on each line.

Practise each line once.
Practise each line again.

Practise each line twice.
Do the underscored letters as quickly as you can.

■ Did you quickly return your little finger from the shift key?

Additional Production Practice (Unit I)

Production 3

Set a 40-character line. Vertically centre an exact copy of the following paragraphs.

One of the most popular computer applications is word processing. A word processing software program is used to input the words of a letter, report, or other document into the memory of the computer. Word processing makes it easy to change, delete, add, move, or print when needed.

The term database can refer to anything that is stored electronically in a computer. A database is also a special program that allows a user to enter, store, and call up information in an organized manner. New information is easily added or deleted as required.

A third type of computer application is the spreadsheet. A spreadsheet program is a type of electronic grid on which a series of calculations can be carried out. Spreadsheets are often used for financial planning in the preparation of budgets, analyses, and reports. Changes can be made easily and are automatically effected within all columns.

10

W / M / 2

Format
40-character line
Single spacing

■ Do you say each letter to yourself?

Practise each line twice.
Practise as quickly as you can.

Use **S** finger.
Keep **F** finger in home position.
Practise each line twice.

Use **J** finger.
Keep other fingers in home position.
Practise each line twice.

Practise each line twice.

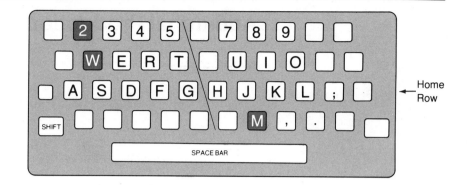

Review New Keys

1 de ee ft tt 33 55 k, lo lo 19 19 fg fggf

2 juj ju juu uu ju7 j7 j7 j7 77 jU kI 10 H

3 suit turf Use Hour Urge fluid rural glue

4 77 outlets. 77 tugs. 878 75 487 374 77

Reach to the W Key

5 sss sws sws sww sws www sw sw ws ws swsw

6 sws sw sw sww wsw wsw wws wws ws ws wwss

Reach to the M Key

7 jjj jmj jmj jmm jmj mmm jm jm mj mj jmjm

8 jmj jm jm jmm mjm mjm mmj mmj mj mj mmjj

Drill on the W and M Keys

9 owe who two was owl walk allow twig hawk

10 me am him them same more must item terms

11 Our weather was humid from time to time.

12 Loud hawks woke the owls at the willows.

13 Major wigwam walls were made from reeds.

· · · · 1 · · · · 2 · · · · 3 · · · · 4 · · · · 5 · · · · 6 · · · · 7 · · · · 8

Additional Production Practice (Unit I)

Production 1

Input the following paragraphs using a 40-character line.

If you had a chance to copy
someone else's work, would you do it?

Sometimes you may feel that
someone else can complete an
assignment better than you
can. However, you were given the
assignment to show what you could do
and to learn from what you couldn't
do. Copying someone else's work and
presenting it as your own is
unacceptable both at school and in
the workplace.

Production 2

Set a 40-character line. Vertically centre an exact copy of the following paragraphs.

It is said that Marco Polo brought
noodles to Italy from China more than 700
years ago. However, noodles were also
found in the ruins of Pompeii, the Italian
city buried by a volcano more than a
thousand years ago.

Pasta, noodles of all kinds, became
a national food of Italy. Noodles are
also popular in many Asian dishes, as well
as in the United States, Canada, Germany,
and France.

Pasta is made from flour mixed with
warm water. It is then kneaded into a
stiff dough. Spinach or eggs can also be
added to the dough. The dough is then
dried. Pasta dough can be cut or machine
shaped in over sixty ways.

Some of the more popular kinds of
pasta are spaghetti, macaroni, fettucini,
lasagna, linguini, pastini, and rotelli.

Use **S** finger.
Keep **F** finger in home position.
Practise each line twice.

Practise each line twice.

Practise each line once.
Repeat *or* take two
15-s timings on each line.

Practise each line once.
Practise each line again.

Practise each line twice.
Do the underscored letters as quickly as you can.

■ Is your body a hand span from the edge of your keyboard?

Reach to the 2 Key

14 sss sws sw2 sw2 sw2s s2s s2s s2 s2 s2s 2

15 s2s s2s 2s 2s w2 w2 sw2s 22s s2w s2w w2s

Drill on the 2 Key

16 2 wars. 22 widows. 22 forms. 22 sums.

17 22 terms. 222 maids, 22 work. 2 wishes

Drill and Practice

18 Mae must gather more twigs for the fire.

19 Jim, mow the grass. Jo, water the mums.

20 I will show them two major works of art.

21 I will mail two forms with a work order.

22 Kim likes the hot, humid summer weather.

Number Drill and Practice

23 2 straw wigs; 24 weak twigs; 2 fir items

24 22 dark rooms; '72 rest times; 2 old owls

25 allow 2 more; 234 weak motors; 292 forms

· · · · 1 · · · · 2 · · · · 3 · · · · 4 · · · · 5 · · · · 6 · · · · 7 · · · · 8

Drill on Letter Combinations

26 wh who what where wheel whale wheat whet

27 me time meet same method summer home met

28 we awe ewe well weir welt west week ewes

· · · · 1 · · · · 2 · · · · 3 · · · · 4 · · · · 5 · · · · 6 · · · · 7 · · · · 8

Production 3

Input the following in report form. Use correct format.

Title: Planning Ahead

    Beginning a new job is an exciting challenge. Your step-by-step planning strategy has earned you the position you wanted! What now? How do you keep that position and show your employer that you are worth promoting?

Side Heading: A Valued Employee

    Everyone wants to be thought of as a valued employee. Demonstrate to your employer that hiring you was a good decision by doing the best job you can. Complete work as quickly and as accurately as possible. Check to see that your work is error-free before submitting it.
¶ Follow instructions. Make notes when you are given directions, so that there can be no misunderstanding later. ¶ Be dependable. Arrive on time. Follow up on promises.

Side Heading: A Team Player

    When you were hired, you became a team player. Work at getting along with others. Treat customers and fellow employees as you would want to be treated--with courtesy and respect.

Side Heading: Attitude Counts

    Have a positive attitude. It is difficult to work with a "negative" person. ¶ Show initiative. Where possible, work without direction. When given the opportunity, do more than you are asked to. Show interest by learning as much as you can about the company.

Side Heading: Keep Up the Image

    Dress and act the part. You represent your company in all dealings with the public. Be business-like. Take pride in the good work you do--and your employer will too.

11

Y / 6 / Right Shift

Format
40-character line
Single spacing

■ Are your feet flat on the floor with one foot slightly ahead of the other?

Practise each line twice.
Practise as quickly as you can.

Use **J** finger.
Practise each line twice.

Use **;** finger.
Keep **J** finger on **J** key.
Practise each line twice.

Practise each line twice.

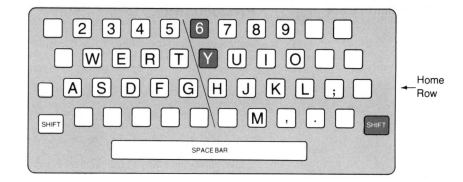

Review New Keys

1 lo oo fg gg l9 99 ee tt 33 55 ,, . lo9 g

2 sws sw sww ww sw2 s2 s2 22 jmj jmm jm jm

3 mail watt straw who am me from major awe

4 wild west 22; east 23; 222 73 432 527 24

Reach to the Y Key

5 jjj jyj jyj jyy jyj yyy jy jy yj yj jyjy

6 jyj jy jy jyy yyy yjy yyj yyj yj yj yyjj

Reach to the Right Shift Key

To capitalize the letters on the left side of the keyboard:
1. Keep **J** finger on the **J** key.
2. Depress right shift key with **;** finger.
3. Strike the letter to be capitalized with the correct finger of the left hand.
4. Release right shift key and quickly return **;** finger to home position.

7 Roy Sara Dad Willy Fred Doug Amy Gord Al

8 The day is short. She is away. Fay is.

Drill on the Y Key and the Right Shift Key

9 my you day yet your they gym sorry study

10 Wally Sally Roger Gary Wesley Terry Rory

11 Sally, your eyes always tell your story.

12 The gym is the key to your daily health.

13 Terry made a yellow Easter hat for Rita.
· · · · · 1 · · · · 2 · · · · 3 · · · · 4 · · · · 5 · · · · 6 · · · · 7 · · · · 8

Production 1

Vertically centre the following as an enumerated list on a full sheet of paper. Use a 60-character line. Use correct format.

Title: Questions Frequently Asked During an Interview
1. Tell me about yourself. 2. What are your special talents and abilities? ^3^ What is your major weakness? 4. Which subjects do you like the most? the least? 5. How do you spend your spare time? 6. Why should I hire you? 7. Why do you want to work for this company? 8. What jobs have you held? Why did you leave them? 9. What do you know about this company? 10. What salary do you expect? 11. Do you prefer working alone or with others? 12. What are your career plans?

Production 2

Input the following as a bibliography. Use correct format.

Bibliography

Employment and Immigration Canada. <u>Creative Job Search Techniques</u>. Minister of Supply and Services Canada, 1985.

Bolles, Richard N. <u>The 1989 What Colour is Your Parachute</u>. Berkeley, California : Ten Speed Press, 1989.

UPCA. <u>Career Planning Annual</u>. Toronto : University and College Placement Association, 1986.

Gates, Anita. <u>21 Steps to a Better Job</u>. New York : Monarch Press 1983.

Kent, George. <u>You're Hired. Job Search Strategies for the 90s</u>. Toronto : Copp Clark Pitman Ltd., 1989.

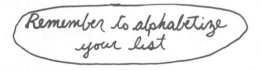

Remember to alphabetize your list

Use **J** finger.
Keep other fingers in home position.
Practise each line twice.

Practise each line twice.

Practise each line once.
Repeat *or* take two
15-s timings on each line.

Practise each line twice.
■ Leave one space after a period at the end of an abbreviation as it is part of the word.

Practise each line once.
Practise each line again.

Practise each line twice.
Do the underscored letters as quickly as you can.

Reach to the 6 Key

14 jjj jyj jy6 jy6 jy6j j6j j6j j6 j6 j6j 6

15 j6j j6j 6j 6j y6 y6 jy6j 66j j6y j6y y6j

Drill on the 6 Key

16 6 days. 66 gyms. 66 yams. 66 trays 66

17 66 yards. 666 yells. 666 ways. 6 toys

Drill and Practice

18 As you walk away, tell her what Al said.

19 Mary should get ready for the day shift.

20 Gary or Ray will dry the yellow flowers.

21 Dad wishes Roy would try to study daily.

22 Yes, you must study for all major tests.

Drill on Abbreviations

23 Mr. Wm. Elder; Mrs. R. York; Ms. Amy Roy

24 Mr. Jos. Dory will meet the mayor today.
· · · · 1 · · · · 2 · · · · 3 · · · · 4 · · · · 5 · · · · 6 · · · · 7 · · · · 8

Number Drill and Practice

25 6 days; 62 dry eyes; 26 dyes; 6 old jugs

26 66 yellow toys; 76 grey days; 6 key guys

27 try 6 ways; key 726 styles; your 65 ways

Drill on Letter Combinations

28 ay lay ray day tray way stay gayly stray

29 ye yet eye yellow year ey they grey eyes
· · · · 1 · · · · 2 · · · · 3 · · · · 4 · · · · 5 · · · · 6 · · · · 7 · · · · 8

Spacing Reminder: Period .

- Two spaces follow a period at the end of a sentence.
- One space follows a period at the end of an abbreviation as the period is part of the word.
- No space before a period.

Evaluate Your Progress

Format

60-character line
Single spacing

Practise each line twice.
Practise as quickly as you can.

Practise each line twice.

Common Phrases

1 it is/it must/it can/it may/it won't/it will/it can't/it did/

2 at any time/at any cost/at the same time/at last/at any rate/

Common-Word Sentences

3 Vic revised the bibliography without making any more errors.

4 Record profits were announced at the annual meeting in June.

5 All examinations are scheduled to begin this coming Tuesday.

· · · · 1 · · · · 2 · · · · 3 · · · · 4 · · · · 5 · · · · 6 · · · · 7 · · · · 8 · · · · 9 · · · 10 · · · 11 · · · 12

Assess Your Progress

Set for double spacing. Take
two 3-min or two 5-min timings.
Circle all errors. Calculate
Gross Words Per Minute
(GWPM).
Record your best timing on
your personal progress chart.

Three- or Five-Minute Timing

		1	CW	3
Before the northern winters begin, many birds fly south		12	12	4
to warmer climates. Some four-legged animals also travel to		24	24	8
places that remain unfrozen during the winter months. Hardy		36	36	12
creatures, such as rabbits, wolves, and coyotes, live in the		48	48	16
same location all year. They are as active in winter months		60	60	20
as they are in summer months.		66	66	22
However, many animals neither move to a new home in the		12	78	26
balmy south nor remain active. They locate sheltered places		24	90	30
and become so quiet that they often appear to be dead. Some		36	102	34
people think this motionless state of being is a deep sleep.		48	114	38
It is actually hibernation. Animals inherit the tendency to		60	126	42
hibernate, the same as they inherit shape, size, and colour.		72	138	46
Many insects survive their times of inactivity as grubs		12	150	50
or larvae. They hide under dead leaves, tunnel into rotting		24	162	54
logs, or burrow into the ground. In the ocean, certain fish		36	174	58
wriggle into the mud or sand in shallow inlets or quiet bays		48	186	62
and hibernate. Most freshwater fish stay active all winter,		60	198	66
although some species become sluggish and likely do not eat.		72	210	70

· · · · 1 · · · · 2 · · · · 3 · · · · 4 · · · · 5 · · · · 6 · · · · 7 · · · · 8 · · · · 9 · · · 10 · · · 11 · · · 12   1 min

     1   2   3   4   3 min

12

Review / Editing

Format
40-character line
Single spacing

■ Is your work station neat and organized?

Practise each line according to your teacher's directions *or* practise each line twice.

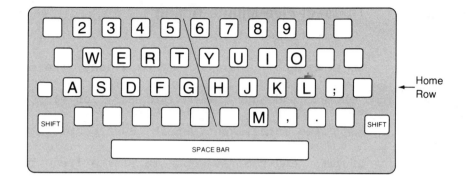

Home
Row

Keyboarding Review

M 1 jmj jm jm jmm mjm mjm mmj mmj mj mj mmjj
  2 me am them from time yam gym summer milk

U 3 juj ju ju juu uju uju uuj uuj uj uj uujj
  4 sue rule your usual must study tutor jug

W 5 sws sw sw sww wsw wsw wws wws ws ws wwss
  6 why owl twig wheel willow would widow we

Y 7 jyj jy jy jyy yjy yjy yyj yyj yj yj yyjj
  8 my day style year sorry they eye lye way

Shift 9 Harry Ross Mother Kim Duke Ella Dale May

2 10 s2s s2s 2s 2s w2 w2 sw2s 22w s2w s2w w2s
  11 2 22 2 22 32 232 22 24 253 222 2 222 932

6 12 j6j j6j 6j y6 jy6j 66j j6y j6y y6j y6 y6
  13 6 66 6 66 56 656 66 62 643 666 6 666 675

7 14 juj j7j 7j 7j u7 ju7j 77j j7u j7u u7j u7
  15 7 777 7 67 767 77 78 387 777 7 777 297 7
  · · · · 1 · · · · 2 · · · · 3 · · · · 4 · · · · 5 · · · · 6 · · · · 7 · · · · 8

Assess Your Progress

Set for double spacing. Take two 3-min *or* two 5-min timings. Circle all errors. Calculate Gross Words Per Minute (GWPM).
Record your best timing on your personal progress chart.

SI 1.53

Three- or Five-Minute Timing

		1	CW	3

Sometimes it is difficult to know if one is telling the | 12 | 12 | 4

truth or not. The eyes may be steady, the manner confident, | 24 | 24 | 8

relaxed, and sure. With the exception of young children and | 36 | 36 | 12

some less intelligent people, most people have some feelings | 48 | 48 | 16

of guilt and remorse about telling a lie. They cannot avoid | 60 | 60 | 20

inward reactions, such as changes in blood pressure. | 70 | 70 | 23

A sensitive machine, however, can detect and record any | 12 | 82 | 27

hidden reactions. This instrument is popularly called a lie | 24 | 94 | 31

detector. It usually consists of an arm cuff to measure the | 36 | 106 | 35

blood pressure and pulse, a chest tube to record the rate of | 48 | 118 | 39

breathing, and a galvanograph to record the flow of sweat in | 60 | 130 | 43

the hands. Thus, all body reactions are documented. | 70 | 140 | 47

Lie detectors are widely used in crime detection. They | 12 | 152 | 51

are also used in business to verify the honesty of employees | 24 | 164 | 55

who have responsible positions. The indicators are attached | 36 | 176 | 59

to the subject, and an examiner reads aloud the questions to | 48 | 188 | 63

be answered in the test. This avoids startling the subject. | 60 | 200 | 67

Then the machine is started and the same questions are asked | 72 | 212 | 71

again. The path of the graph lines indicate if the truth is | 84 | 224 | 74

being told. | 86 | 226 | 75

```
• • • • 1 • • • • 2 • • • 3 • • • • 4 • • • • 5 • • • 6 • • • • 7 • • • • 8 • • • • 9 • • • •10• • • •11• • • •12        1 min
          1                    2                    3                  4          3 min
```

Editing for Changes (Proofreading)

The paper bail method of editing is most accurate and efficient on the typewriter. After you have finished your copy, do not remove the paper from the typewriter. Use the cylinder knob or the reverse index to return to the first line (position the first line just above the paper bail).

Read each line twice: First, read each word for correctness and then reread for meaning. On the paper copy in your typewriter, circle the entire word if an error has been made. If you are using a computer, read your monitor before printing the file. Circle the entire word on the printed copy if an error has been made. Only one error is charged to any one word, no matter how many errors it contains.

The following are examples of various types of errors.

Edit (you r) work while the (psper) is

   Extra Spacing   Keying Error

still in the machine. Position the first

   Omitted Spacing   Incorrect Spacing

line above the paper bail Circle (circle)

                   Omitted Punctuation   Repeated Word

any error in that line Use the

                  Punctuation

cylinder knob to (con tineu) down (the)

               Spacing / Keying Error   Strikeover

page. Read each carefully.

         Omitted Word

■ Did you ask your teacher or read the software manual for the scrolling option?

Career Bulletin 7

```
CAREER PLANNING

Employment Tests


     Be prepared to take a number of tests if you are
applying for a job.  Depending on the position, you may
be asked to take aptitude, personality, or intelligence
tests.  In addition, an employer may wish to test
specific skills--keyboarding, math, spelling, or English
usage.
```

Career Bulletin 8

```
CAREER PLANNING

Following Up on the Interview


     It is important to follow up each interview with a
brief, business-like, thank-you letter.

     Express your interest again in working for the
company, and mention that you are available if a second
interview is required.
```

Production Practice

Production 4

Prepare a thank-you letter for a job interview with a company in your area.

Editing Practice

Edit each line by correcting two errors.
Practise each line once with the corrections.

16 We were sorry that Harry had togo away.

17 laurie says that she will meet us their.

18 We met th e 73 delegates at the show art.

19 Millie sells red,yellow or white kites

20 Mrs Wm. Dwight will talk to the ladies.

21 My father or mother wil go tothe game.
· · · 1 · · · · 2 · · · · 3 · · · · 4 · · · · 5 · · · · 6 · · · · 7 · · · · 8

■ Did you read Editing for Changes?

Letter Review Practice

Take two 30-s timings on each line or practise each line twice.

22 Look for the old home with the red roof.

23 We must use some well water for my wash.

24 Gerald hit the drum with his small fist.

Number Review Practice

Take two 30-s timings on each line or practise each line twice.

25 We made 27 more hats for the 63 dresses.

26 Mr. Roma made 64 sets of lot 297 of red.

27 Ira must sell 46 or 47 rugs for 29 days.

28 Use 72 of our 459 jugs for the 36 loads.

29 Start with all 376 models or 254 styles.

30 They must make 79 items for the 58 toys.
· · · · 1 · · · · 2 · · · · 3 · · · · 4 · · · · 5 · · · · 6 · · · · 7 · · · · 8

One-Minute Timing

Timing

Take two 1-min timings on the set of three lines.

1 min

31 Write to them while I make you some tea. | 8

32 Dagmar was away from work for four days. | 16

33 We will take Lisa with us if we go away. | 24
· · · · 1 · · · · 2 · · · · 3 · · · · 4 · · · · 5 · · · · 6 · · · · 7 · · · · 8

Production 3

Input the following in report form. Use correct format.

CAREER PLANNING

During the Interview

It is natural to be nervous during an interview. It helps to smile when you greet your interviewer--it will make both of you feel more comfortable.

Introduce yourself and be prepared to shake the employer's hand. Mention which job you are applying for: "How do you do, ...; I am ...; I am here about the stock clerk position." Do not sit down until you are invited to do so. Do not chew gum or smoke.

Be pleasant. An interviewer is looking to see how well you get along with others and how you take direction.

Look at the interviewer. Concentrate on each question being asked. It will help you to develop your answers. Try not to give one-word answers.

Be enthusiastic about the company. If you have done your research, you will have questions to ask which will indicate your interest. Be aware of why you want this job. Stress your good points.

Don't give up part of the way through an interview because you think you are doing poorly; you do not know how other candidates have done.

Thank the employer (and the receptionist) at the end of the interview. Be courteous, even if you know you have not obtained the position. Every interview is a worthwhile experience which will help you towards the next one!

P / O / C

Format
40-character line
Single spacing

■ Do you practise evenly without hesitating or stopping?

Practise each line twice.
Practise as quickly as you can.

Use **;** finger.
Keep other fingers in home position.
Practise each line twice.

Use **D** finger.
Keep other fingers in home position.
Practise each line twice.

Practise each line twice.

Use **;** finger.
Keep **J** finger on **J** key.
Practise each line twice.

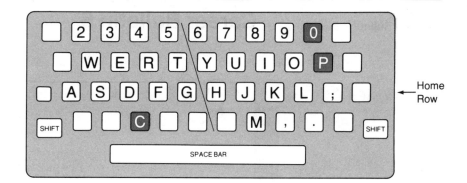

Review New Keys

1 sw ww s2 s2 juj jm ju j7 jm ju7jmj jum m

2 jyj jy jyy yy ju6 j6 j6 66 66 fR dE sW 6

3 66 Yams, 67 Days, 876 Rays, 9364 68 5762

4 my you day way yet why your they eye guy

Reach to the P Key

5 ;;; ;p; ;p; ;pp ;p; ppp ;p ;p p; p; ;p;p

6 ;p; ;p ;p ;pp p;p p;p pp; pp; p; p; pp;;

Reach to the C Key

7 ddd dcd dcd dcc dcd ccc dc dc cd cd dcdc

8 dcd dc dc dcc cdc cdc ccd ccd cd cd ccdd

Drill on the P and C Keys

9 par up apt tap wipe stamp spill page pay

10 call ice acid cast cafe close decor ache

11 Cal samples each plate of chili peppers.

12 Cut up pork or peapods for steamed rice.

13 Carrie must cram for all the chem tests.

Reach to the 0 Key

14 ;;; ;p; ;p0 ;p0 ;p0 ;0; ;0; ;0; ;0 ;0;0

15 ;0; ;0; 0; 0; ;0 ;0 ;p0 00; ;0p ;0p p0;

· · · · 1 · · · · 2 · · · · 3 · · · · 4 · · · · 5 · · · · 6 · · · · 7 · · · · 8

Career Bulletin 6

CAREER PLANNING

Preparing for the Interview

Ideally, the interview is a discussion between two interested parties. It is not a quiz; rather, it is an exchange of information.

Here are some suggestions which will help you to prepare for an interview:

1. Take a dry run at getting to the interview. On the day of the interview, provide extra time for transit or traffic delays. Plan to arrive 10 to 15 minutes early.

2. Obtain literature on the company and its products. Be prepared to ask a few questions.

3. Rehearse the interview with a friend. Ask for feedback and advice.

4. Bring an extra copy of your résumé, a list of your references, a pen, and a notepad to the interview.

5. Dress appropriately. Be neat and clean.

6. Go alone to the interview--leave friends and family at home.

7. Finally, just before you go in the door, take a <u>deep</u> breath. It does help!

Drill on the 0 Key

Practise each line twice.

16 200 plus 20 is 220.   300 less 50 is 250.

17 00 90 80 70 60 50 40 30 20 98765432 0987

Drill and Practice

Practise each line once.
Repeat or take two
15-s timings on each line.

18 Her eyes glow as she writes her memoirs.

19 Chill ripe apples to make proper ciders.

20 Please throw away the empty cups of ice.

21 The comics taped each puppet show twice.

22 Call some cycle shops for the road trip.

Number Drill and Practice

Practise each line once.
Practise each line again.

23 50 thick pipes; 80 stamps; 600 or 700 or

24 60 cold peas; 800 copper pots; 700 packs

25 Place 30 or 40 paper cups at 200 depots.

· · · · 1 · · · · 2 · · · · 3 · · · · 4 · · · · 5 · · · · 6 · · · · 7 · · · · 8

Drill on Abbreviations

Practise each line twice.

26 The date of the party is Tues., Mar. 20.

27 Dr. Palma resides at 80 St. Clair Rd. E.

Drill on Letter Combinations

Practise each line twice.
Do the underscored letters as
quickly as you can.

28 ip pipe hippo grip trip wipe triple whip

29 op prop people slope drop stop poppy top

30 ch each echo ache yacht chew etch church

31 cr cracks crimes cruel credit cry crowds

32 ck deck shocks track chicks socket stuck

· · · · 1 · · · · 2 · · · · 3 · · · · 4 · · · · 5 · · · · 6 · · · · 7 · · · · 8

■ Are your elbows
motionless?
■ Are your wrists relaxed?

Production 2

Complete the Application Form for Part-Time Employment.

CANADIAN TIRE

APPLICATION FOR EMPLOYMENT

FOR OFFICE USE ONLY	
Work Location _____	Rate _____
Position _____	Date _____

FOR OFFICE USE ONLY	
Possible Work Locations	Possible Positions

Name _____
first name   initial   last name

Social Insurance Number ☐☐☐ ☐☐☐ ☐☐☐

Address _____
number and street city postal code

How long there _____

Phone number _____

What type of work do you prefer: _____ Full time ☐

Languages spoken: English ☐ French ☐ Part time ☐

Typing speed _____ Temporary ☐

Languages written: English ☐ French ☐

Rate of pay expected _____ /week/annually

Circle last grade completed successfully:

	GRADE	COURSE
Elementary and High School	1 2 3 4 5 6 7 8 9 10 11 12 13	
University, technical, business or community college	1 2 3 4 5 6	
Other studies		

Have you ever worked for Canadian Tire Corporation or an Associate Store? Yes ☐ No ☐

Do you have any relatives employed with Canadian Tire Corporation or an Associate Store? Yes ☐ No ☐

WORK HISTORY

Start with present or last employer	Position Held	Wages	From month year	To month year	Reason for leaving
Employer: Address: Immediate supervisor:					
Employer: Address: Immediate supervisor:					
Employer: Address: Immediate supervisor:					
Employer: Address: Immediate supervisor:					

List social activities (sports, interests, etc.)

_____

List organizations of which you are a member, and office (past and present). Exclude those of religious, ethnic, racial or political nature.

_____

PLEASE READ
- I authorize the company to inquire as to my work record with any of my former employers or to check my credit status with no liability arising from such inquiries.
- I am legally eligible to work in Canada. (Persons legally eligible to work are Canadian citizens, landed immigrants and the holders of a valid work permit.) Documentary evidence of eligibility may be required.
- I understand that in case of employment any false statement may be sufficient cause for dismissal.
- Medical or bonding requirements may be necessary.

Date application filed _____ Signature _____

98-9028

14

Format
40-character line
Single spacing

■ Are you using a sharp, quick stroke?

Practise each line twice.
Practise as quickly as you can.

Use **A** finger.
Keep other fingers in home position.
Practise each line twice.

Use **J** finger.
Practise each line twice.

Practise each line twice.

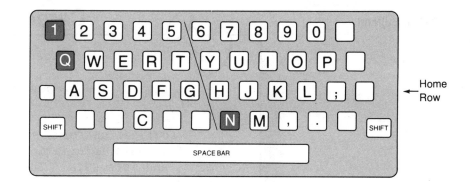

Review New Keys

1 s2 22 ju j7 jm ju jh jy j6 jh jy jyhj yy

2 ;p; ;p ;pp pp ;p0 ;0 ;0 00 dcd dc dc dcc

3 put cup depot cold patch copper pack cut

4 00 or 20 or 30 or 40 or 50 or 60 or 70 8

Reach to the Q Key

5 aaa aqa aqa aqq aqa qqa aq aq qa qa aqaq

6 aqa aq aq aqa qaq qaq qqa qqa qa qa qqaa

Reach to the N Key

7 jjj jnj jnj jnn jnj nnj jn jn nj nj jnjn

8 jnj jn jn jnj njn njn nnj nnj nj nj nnjj

Drill on the Q and N Keys

9 quit quick quiet pique cheque queue aqua

10 and men alien angle concur earn end find

11 Aspirin is a patented name for the drug.

12 I knit nylon squares for quilted aprons.

13 Caged animals squawk, squirm or quarrel.

· · · · 1 · · · · 2 · · · · 3 · · · · 4 · · · · 5 · · · · 6 · · · · 7 · · · · 8

Career Bulletin 5

CAREER PLANNING

The Application Form

Application forms vary in length and content, but all ask for basic information relating to education, employment, and interests. These details are included in your résumé. Have a copy with you when you visit a prospective company. The following points will help you to complete an application form:

· Read the complete form before you begin.

· Use pen. Do not use pencil unless requested.

· Follow all instructions carefully. Print if you are instructed to do so.

· Be neat. Think first so that you do not have to cross out.

· Do not leave blank spaces. If you do not understand a question, ask. If the question does not apply to you, draw a line or enter N/A (not applicable).

· Double check the application form to see that you have completed all sections correctly before signing it.

Listed below are a number of definitions of terms which are frequently used on application forms:

1. Surname: your last or family name

2. Given name: your first name in full

3. Longhand: handwriting

4. Bonding: an insurance policy on an employee that protects a company against losses through theft

5. Reference: someone who can vouch for your character or work habits

6. Post-Secondary Education: courses which you have taken which are beyond the high school level: business or technical school, college, university

7. Legally Entitled to Work in Canada: Canadian citizens, landed immigrants possessing authorized papers, and individuals with working permits are legally entitled to work in Canada.

Reach to the 1 Key

Use **A** finger.
Keep **F** finger on **F** key.
Practise each line twice.

14 aaa aqa aql aql aqla ala ala al al ala l

15 ala ala la la al al aqla lla alq alq qla

Drill on the 1 Key

Practise each line twice.

16 l quid. ll aprons. ll angles. l plant

17 lll colleges, ll clients. lll red coins

Drill and Practice

Practise each line once.
Repeat *or* take two
15-s timings on each line.

18 The queen quoted the name quite quickly.

19 Do not waste time. Send the cheque now.

20 He needs all the green and aqua squares.

21 Use white liquid ink for erasing errors.

22 The Faculty of Commerce has a new quota.

Number Drill and Practice

Practise each line once.
Practise each line again.

23 l noun; llO men; lO long quotes; l quilt

24 ll pink quills; l2 quiet engines; l quip

25 nail 6 squares; name l28 queens; 5l nets

· · · · 1 · · · · 2 · · · · 3 · · · · 4 · · · · 5 · · · · 6 · · · · 7 · · · · 8

Drill on Letter Combinations

Practise each line twice.
Do the underscored letters as
quickly as you can.

26 qu quit quote equal opaque request squad

27 en end cent client deny enter scene open

28 in inn infer pine citing coin final main

29 an and any gang jean giant hand organ an

30 ing trying going skiing issuing learning

· · · · 1 · · · 2 · · · 3 · · · 4 · · · · 5 · · · · 6 · · · 7 · · · 8

■ Are your fingers slightly curved?

Career Bulletin 4

```
CAREER PLANNING

Cold Contacts


     A large percentage of jobs available at a given
time are not advertised.  In many cases, these jobs are
given to people already within the organization.  In
others, however, companies use alternative methods to obtain
employees.

     Are there specific companies for which you would like to
work?  A personal visit or a telephone call to the human
resources department might be the step which could get
you considered as a future employee.

     Research the company before you make a cold contact.
Be prepared to explain why you believe this is a good
company to work for.

     Chance is part of the job search process.  You will
not be successful with each cold call you make, but you
might be in the right spot at the right time.  Do not be
afraid to take some risk!
```

15

Z / V / '

Format
40-character line
Single spacing

■ Are you sitting correctly at your keyboard with your feet flat on the floor?

Practise each line twice.
Practise as quickly as you can.

Use **A** finger.
Keep other fingers in home position.
Practise each line twice.

Use **F** finger.
Practise each line twice.

Practise each line twice.

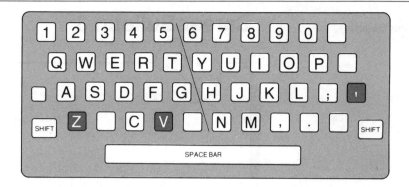

Review New Keys

1 aqa aq aqq qq aql al ll jnj jn nn jnn nj

2 de de dc dc dec dec d3c jy jy j6 jm jy6m

3 ll 22 33 44 55 66 77 88 99 00 0987654321

4 quit end quirk equal run aqua squat near

5 10 to 20 spoons; 107 quotas; 209 quills;

Reach to the Z Key

6 aaa aza aza azz aza zza az az za za azaz

7 aza az az aza zaz zaz zza zza za za zzaa

Reach to the V Key

8 fff fvf fvf fvv fvf vvf fv fv vf vf fvfv

9 fvf fv fv fvf vfv vfv vvf vvf vf vf vvff

Drill on the Z and V Keys

10 zeal jazz gaze fizz hazel plaza cozy zed

11 vast very civic dove envy love give oval

12 Very few invest their savings in silver.

13 In the arctic zone, many freeze quickly.

14 Vicky viewed eleven TV variety programs.

· · · · 1 · · · · 2 · · · · 3 · · · · 4 · · · · 5 · · · · 6 · · · · 7 · · · · 8

Career Bulletin 3

CAREER PLANNING

The Letter of Application

One way to contact a potential employer is by sending a letter of application. Try to send the letter to a specific person by name.

The application letter has three aims:

· to create a favourable impression on the prospective employer
· to introduce your résumé
· to help you to obtain an interview with the employer.

An effective letter of application will look attractive, be well written, and free of errors.

Production Practice

Production 1

Input the following application letter. Include all missing parts.

Ms. Vouly Tabas
Homestead Realty Ltd.
9428-121 Avenue
Grande Prairie, Alberta
T8V 6H9

Please consider me an applicant for the part-time position of office clerk which was advertised in the Daily Herald-Tribune on April 22, 19--.

Enclosed is my résumé which describes my background and qualifications. I am presently in my second year at St. Joseph's Composite High School. The business courses which I have taken have provided me with an understanding of the operation of a small business, as well as with good keyboarding skills. I enjoy working with people and am interested in the real estate field.

I would appreciate the opportunity of having an interview with you at your convenience. My telephone number is 483-9151 I look forward to hearing from you.

Yours very truly/Lars Gustafsson

Note: Lars lives at 9233 - 111 Avenue, Grande Prairie, Alberta T8V 3L7

Reach to the ' Key

`[; → ']`

15 ;;; ;'; ;'; ;'' ;'; ''; ;' ;' '; '; ;';'

Drill on the ' Key

16 it's don't can't we're they're won't all

17 Jody's car. Tony's camera. Ardis' kite

18 That's not George's card. It's Tracy's.

Drill and Practice

19 Victor analyzed and solved five quizzes.

20 Hazel's prize is five live jazz records.

21 Every citizen gazed at the crazy ravens.

22 Mrs. Van plays the zither and the viola.

23 The novel's vivid images were inspiring.

Number Drill and Practice

24 7 cozy vans; 71 lazy doves; 17 vast zoos

25 77 velvet zippers; 87 even zones; 7 vats

26 7 zodiac signs; move 973 prizes; 7 veins
    · · · · 1 · · · · 2 · · · · 3 · · · · 4 · · · · 5 · · · · 6 · · · · 7 · · · · 8

Drill on Letter Combinations

27 ze zero daze dozen size zeal gazelle zed

28 iz fizz horizon seize whiz lizard pizzas

29 iv civil fives waives ivory privy trivia

30 ev even devise eleven every levy reviews
    · · · · 1 · · · · 2 · · · · 3 · · · · 4 · · · · 5 · · · · 6 · · · · 7 · · · · 8

Spacing Reminder: The Apostrophe '

• No space before or after an apostrophe.

Use ; finger.
Practise each line twice.

Practise each line twice.

■ Do not space before or after an apostrophe in a word.

Practise each line once.
Repeat *or* take two
15-s timings on each line.

Practise each line once.
Practise each line again.

Practise each line twice.
Do the underscored letters as quickly as you can.

■ Are you reading the underscored letters as groups?

Career Planning — Application Letters/Forms

Format

60-character line
Single spacing

Practise each line twice.
Practise as quickly as you can.

Skill Building

Practise at a controlled rate.
Circle your errors. Do Speed
Improvement if you had three
errors or less. Do Accuracy
Improvement if you had four
errors or more.

Alternate-Hand Words

1 go pair town rush whale visitor laugh half bus signal enrich

2 us fork with clay bowls turkey social visual element auditor

Evaluate Your Progress

3   Always attempt to be relaxed when working on a machine.

When you feel tense, briefly slow down and relax. This will

be helpful in producing error-free copy. Begin each task at

an easy pace and gradually increase your speed. Many errors

are caused by feeling rushed when starting a task. Accuracy

is achieved through maintaining a controlled rate.

• • • • 1 • • • • 2 • • • • 3 • • • • 4 • • • • 5 • • • • 6 • • • • 7 • • • • 8 • • • • 9 • • • •10• • • •11• • • •12

Think **accuracy**. Take two 15-s
timings on each line. Take two
30-s timings on the complete
set of lines.

Accuracy Improvement

4 off feel good full class accept better effect address collar

5 by tow city half sicken profit bicycle icy ambush land firms

6 cat base fade debt water waste decade better terrace retreat

7 According to the book, we must edit rough draft essays well.

Try to do each timing faster.
Take two 15-s timings on each
set of two lines. Take two 30-s
timings on the complete set of
lines.
■ Do Evaluate Your Progress
and determine if you have
improved.

Speed Improvement

8 I am interested in this project, but I cannot help them now.

9 When we know the exact costs, we will make a definite offer.

10 Most workers like to take holidays during the summer months.

11 We waited for several days, but the painters did not appear.

Practise each line once.
Practise each line again.

Number Practice

12 Accounts beginning with 1, 2, 4, 7, 9, or 36 have rate 0.58.

13 Ken, flight 642 leaves at 14:10, so please be here by 12:35.

• • • • 1 • • • • 2 • • • • 3 • • • • 4 • • • • 5 • • • • 6 • • • • 7 • • • • 8 • • • • 9 • • • •10• • • •11• • • •12

16

X / B / /

Format
40-character line
Single spacing

■ Are both hands in home position?

■ Are your fingers slightly curved?

Practise each line twice.
Practise as quickly as you can.

Use **S** finger.
Keep other fingers in home position.
Practise each line twice.

Use **F** finger.
Keep **A** finger on **A** key.
Practise each line twice.

Practise each line twice.

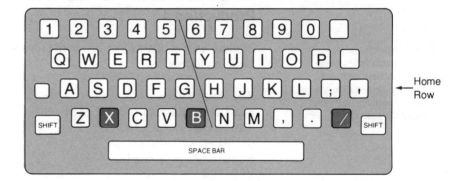

Review New Keys

1 jmj jnj jm jn jmn jmn ju j7 aq pp cc 001

2 aza az azz zz fvf fv fvv vv it's 's s' '

3 envy every amaze zero jazz vivid lazy VV

4 Hazel's topaz; Ed's pizza; it's is it is

Reach to the X Key

5 sss sxs sxs sxx sxs xxs sx sx xs xs sxsx

6 sxs sx sx sxs xsx xsx xxs xxs xs xs xxss

Reach to the B Key

7 fff fbf fbf fbb fbf bbf fb fb bf bf fbfb

8 fbf fb fb fbf bfb bfb bbf bbf bf bf bbff

Drill on the X and B Keys

9 wax six text index extra Xerox apex onyx

10 bad debt cube fibre habit job libel obey

11 Six excited foxes exit behind the annex.

12 We painted the balcony with latex stain.

13 Birds perch in birches and sing ballads.
· · · · 1 · · · · 2 · · · · 3 · · · · 4 · · · · 5 · · · · 6 · · · · 7 · · · · 8

Production 4

Prepare a list of names that you might use as references when applying for a job. Use the following format:

```
Mr. Max Weiss                    - full name
Business Education Director      - title
Mimico High School              - company/school
95 Mimico Avenue               - address
Etobicoke, Ontario
M8V 1R4                        - postal code
(416) 394-7630                 - area code/telephone
                                 number
```

* choose people from different occupations
* do not include relatives, boyfriends, or girlfriends
* ask for permission before using the names

Assess Your Progress

Set for double spacing. Take two 3-min or two 5-min timings. Circle all errors. Calculate Gross Words Per Minute (GWPM). Record your best timing on your personal progress chart.

SI 1.35

Three- or Five-Minute Timing

	1	CW	3
Layers of thinly sliced wood glued together are used to	12	12	4
make plywood. The grain of each ply runs at an angle to the	24	24	8
grain of its neighbours. This cross-graining equalizes much	36	36	12
of the strength along the length and width. This allows all	48	48	16
sheets of plywood to expand and contract without the fear of	60	60	20
splitting apart. This is a benefit to many builders.	70	70	23
The use of this wood dates back many years. It did not	12	83	28
become widely used until entire methods of modern production	24	95	32
were introduced. In the early days, plies were cut from the	36	107	36
flat surface of a split log, and no plies wider than the log	48	119	40
itself could be produced. Today smooth peeler logs are used	60	131	44
in a huge lathe against a long cutter blade. The blade cuts	72	143	48
off a continuous sheet of wood of various thicknesses.	82	153	51
The sheets are cut to size, and the required number are	12	165	55
glued together. Modern methods of manufacture use synthetic	24	177	59
plastics to hold the sheets together. Plastic-bonded sheets	36	189	63
are able to remain intact even after continuous soaking in a	48	201	67
vat of water. Plywood can be made even stronger by adding a	60	213	71
type of heat-setting plastic to the wood.	68	221	74

```
• • • • 1 • • • • 2 • • • • 3 • • • • 4 • • • • 5 • • • • 6 • • • • 7 • • • • 8 • • • • 9 • • • •10• • • •11• • • •12    1 min
              1                    2                    3                    4          3 min
```

Use ; finger.
Practise each line twice.

Reach to the / Key

14 ;/; ;/; ;;; ;/; /// ;/; ;/ ;/ ;//; ;/ /;

15 ;/; ;// /;/ /;/ ;// ;/; ;//; ;/ /; /; /;

Practise each line twice.
■ Do not space before or after a diagonal.

Drill on the / Key

16 2/10, n/30; either/or; is/are; 2/15; 4/8

17 are/hour; shall/should; will/would; n/60

Practise each line once.
Repeat *or* take two
15-s timings on each line.

Drill and Practice

18 Bob will fix the next barbell for Betty.

19 Xerox six extra copies of the blue text.

20 New terms as of next week are 2/5, n/30.

21 Both mixes use a milk and/or water base.

22 Taxes on the deluxe taxi were expensive.

Practise each line once.
Practise each line again.

Number Drill and Practice

23 9 boxes; 28 busy foxes; 57 axles; 4 bets

24 42 onyx bells; 34 bombs; 65 bins; 1 lynx

25 burn 8 boxes; buy 649 oxen; wax 25 boats
· · · · 1 · · · · 2 · · · · 3 · · · · 4 · · · · 5 · · · · 6 · · · · 7 · · · · 8

Practise each line twice.
Do the underscored letters as quickly as you can.

Drill on Letter Combinations

26 ax tax hoax maxim galaxy relax axle coax

27 ex text exit flex index Texas latex apex

28 bl able emblem humble blue table blanket

29 ib rib bribe legible libel exhibit fibre
· · · · 1 · · · · 2 · · · · 3 · · · · 4 · · · · 5 · · · · 6 · · · · 7 · · · · 8

■ Do you keep your eyes on the copy?

Spacing Reminder: Diagonal /

• No spaces before or after a diagonal.

Identification Section
- name
- address
- area code / telephone number

JEANETTE LE BLANC

DS

3584 Granville Avenue
Richmond, British Columbia
V9B 7A4
(604) 275-1933

TS

Education Section
- schools attended (in reverse chronological order if more than one)
- special skills

EDUCATION

DS

High School
Presently attending Grade 10 at Richmond Secondary School. Subjects include English, French, science, keyboarding, accounting, and mathematics.

DS

Special Skills
Keyboarding (45 words per minute)
Fluent in French

TS

Experience Section
- previous work experience and job function in reverse chronological order

EXPERIENCE

DS

Summer

DS

Cashier, 19--
Operated cash register at Dairy Queen on Anderson Road. Assisted store manager in preparing typewritten reports.

DS

Child Care, 19--
Babysat two preschool children for a neighbour.

DS

Part-Time

DS

Stock Clerk, 19--
Presently stocking shelves at Shoppers Drug Mart, Richmond Square, two evenings a week.

TS

Additional Information Section
- activities
- interests
- special awards

ADDITIONAL INFORMATION

DS

Honour Roll, Grades 9 and 10
Member of school basketball team
Student Council representative
Member of Richmond Tennis Club
Interests include photography, sports, reading

TS

References Section
- although not included on the résumé, a separate list should be prepared

REFERENCES

DS

Available on request

17

Review

Format
40-character line
Single spacing

■ Do you set a positive attitude to build **speed** or **accuracy**?

Practise each line according to your teacher's directions *or* practise each line twice.

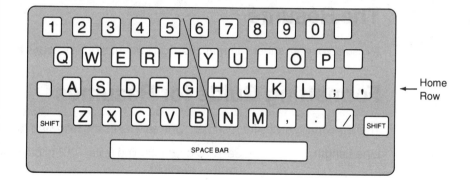

← Home Row

SPACE BAR

Keyboarding Review

B 1 fbf fb fb fbf bfb bfb bbf bbf bf bf bbff
  2 bad beats before cable comb doubt forbid

C 3 dcd dc dc dcc cdc cdc ccd ccd cd cd ccdd
  4 cue each echo came check cache coach ace

N 5 jnj jn jn jnj njn njn nnj nnj nj nj nnjj
  6 nag inn new none rent sense since things

P 7 ;p; ;p ;p ;p; p;p p;p pp; pp; p; p; pp;;
  8 pet put par play gripe group oppose pope

Q 9 aqa aq aq aqa qaq qaq qqa qqa qa qa qqaa
  10 quad quip quest equal squad aqua request

V 11 fvf fv fv fvf vfv vfv vvf vvf vf vf vvff
  12 van valve avoid curve divide ever eleven

X 13 sxs sx sx sxs xsx xsx xxs xxs xs xs xxss
  14 axe next flex latex sex exact excel exit

Z 15 aza az az aza zaz zaz zza zza za za zzaa
  16 zag zip zero lazy czar dazed fuzz seizes

· · · · 1 · · · · 2 · · · · 3 · · · · 4 · · · · 5 · · · 6 · · · 7 · · · 8

The Résumé

A résumé or data sheet summarizes an applicant's qualifications and interests.

Formatting Guide for Résumés

There are many styles for résumés. One style uses the following format:

Line Length:
- Set a 70-character line (elite — 12-pitch) or a 60-character line (pica — 10-pitch).

Tab:
- Set two tabs: five characters from the left margin and ten characters from the left margin.

Top Margin:
- Page one   Input your name on line 7.
- Page two   Input the page number on line 7.

Bottom Margin:
- Leave 6-10 blank lines.

Page Numbering:
- Page one   No page number.
- Page two   Pivot page number on line 7, followed by a triple space.

Title (Name):
- Capitalize and centre on line 7.

Subtitle (Address and Phone Number):
- Capitalize the first letter of each main word and centre each line, double spaced below the title (name).

Side Headings:
- Capitalize at the left margin.

Subheadings:
- Indent five from the left margin and underscore.

Secondary Headings:
- Indent ten from the left margin and underscore.

Spacing:
- Single space descriptive areas.
- Double space between descriptive areas.
- Triple space between side headings.

■ If it is necessary to spread your résumé to fill the page, vary the spacing appropriately.

Production 3

Using the following sample résumé as a guideline, input a rough draft of your own personal résumé. Edit your work and then prepare a good copy.

```
 017 ;0;  ;0;  0;  0;  ;0  ;0  ;p0 00;  ;0p  ;0p p0;0
  18 0  10  101  20  200  30  303  40  400  50  505  600

1 19 ll  l2  l3  l4  l5  l6  l7  l8  l9  l0  lll  l2l  ll

' 20 ;;;  ;';  ;';  ;''  ;''  ';'  '';  ';  ';  ;';  ';
  21 it's you're can't we're; Mr. Chang's hat

/ 22 ;/;  ;//  /;/  /;/  ;//  ;/;  ;//;  ;/  /;  /;  /;
  23 and/or yes/no 23/32 n/60 is/are them/him
      · · · · 1 · · · · 2 · · · · 3 · · · · 4 · · · · 5 · · · · 6 · · · · 7 · · · · 8
```

Letter Review Practice

```
24 aqa aza qqa zza fvf vfv frf fvf fgf fvfv
25 sws sxs sww sxx sas sws ssa wws xxs swxs
26 vim vet zip zero bit bat bad bore ox axe
```

Number Review Practice

```
27 lll 222 333 444 555 666 777 888 999 0000
28 1 car and/or 2 pots and/or 3 rats or not
29 45 lazy boys; 78 blue vests; 90 hot tips
   · · · · 1 · · · · 2 · · · · 3 · · · · 4 · · · · 5 · · · · 6 · · · · 7 · · · · 8
```

Editing Practice

```
30 We made made a rong turn down the back road.
31 We beggged joan to stop singing the song.
32 Roy didall his homework in re cord time.
33 Check to see if Ed broght all the gear
   · · · · 1 · · · · 2 · · · · 3 · · · · 4 · · · · 5 · · · · 6 · · · · 7 · · · · 8
```

Take two 30-s timings on each line *or* practise each line twice.

Take two 30-s timings on each line *or* practise each line twice.

Edit each line by correcting two errors.
Practise each line once with the corrections. If you completed lines 30-33 correctly, all lines will be even at the right margin.

Career Bulletin 2

■ If you are using a computer to prepare your résumé, read your software manual to determine if there is a spell check and/or grammar check.

```
          CAREER PLANNING

          The Résumé


     A résumé or data sheet is a brief summary of your
qualifications and interests.  Most employers prefer a
typewritten résumé which is no shorter than one full page
and no longer than two.

     Résumés take time to prepare.  Several rough copies
may be necessary.  Also, someone else should proofread
your résumé; spelling and grammatical errors are not
business-like.

     When preparing your résumé, put yourself in the
reader's place.  What impression does your résumé give?
The résumé is often used to screen applicants.
Hard, thoughtful work will prevent your résumé from
being thrown aside.  A carefully-planned, well-prepared
résumé will earn you an interview!
```

Graduated Speed Practice

15 s 12 s 10 s

		15s	12s	10s
34	I said it.	8	10	12
35	Do it soon.	9	11	13
36	We are back.	10	12	14
37	Use his note.	10	13	16
38	We were to go.	11	14	17
39	Give it to him.	12	15	18
40	Be a good loser.	13	16	19
41	The game was fun.	14	17	20
42	He wants that dog.	14	18	22
43	Their car is ready.	15	19	23
44	Put the top back on.	16	20	24
45	Do not ask about her.	17	21	25
46	She likes the red one.	18	22	26
47	He said that she knows.	18	23	28
48	Be sure to vote for him.	19	24	29
49	The girls liked the cake.	20	25	30

· · · · 1 · · · · 2 · · · · 3 · · · · 4 · · · · 5

One-Minute Timings

1 min

50	A rock concert will be held in the park.	8
51	The team did well and the party was fun.	16
52	The job must be one that you want to do.	8
53	Striped zebras were in the grassy plain.	16

· · · · 1 · · · · 2 · · · · 3 · · · · 4 · · · · 5 · · · · 6 · · · · 7 · · · · 8

Composition

Answer the following questions with a one word response.
1. What is your middle name?
2. How many people are there in your immediate family?
3. In what year were you born?
4. What is your favourite sport?
5. In what month of the year were you born?

Production 2

Where you look for a job will be determined by the type of career or position in which you are interested.

The more complex the position, the more detailed your list of contacts will be.

Input the following list of areas to research when looking for a job. Set a 60-character line. Vertically centre on a full sheet.

```
                    THE JOB MARKETPLACE


1.  Family, Friends, Relatives, Former Employers--Make a
    list of all the people you know personally who might
    be helpful in finding a job for you.  Let them know
    you are looking for work in your chosen field.

2.  Bulletin Boards--Check student services and super-
    market bulletin boards, as well as store windows.

3.  Classified Advertisements--Help Wanted Ads in newspapers
    should be checked regularly (especially local area
    papers).  Follow up as soon as you see a suitable
    position.

4.  Professionals--Your doctor, dentist, clergyman, or
    teachers might be able to provide you with the names of
    individuals to contact.

5.  Canada Employment Centres--The Job Information Centre
    (JIC) will list openings on notice boards.  Each job is
    given a number.  To find out more about the jobs that
    interest you, write down the numbers and bring them to the
    JIC counsellor.

6.  Government Services--The municipal, provincial, and
    federal government agencies (such as Hire-A-Student) offer
    many seasonal and permanent positions.

7.  Personnel Agencies--Check the newspapers and Yellow
    Pages for names of agencies.  These agencies charge the
    employers a commission fee--no charge is made to the
    applicant.

8.  School Programs--If you are eligible, participate in
    co-operative education and work experience programs.
    Part-time and permanent employment is often offered to
    program participants.

9.  Other Potential Employers--Prepare a list of companies
    you would like to work for.  Even though they may not
    have advertised, these companies may have openings now
    or in the near future.
```

? / : / !

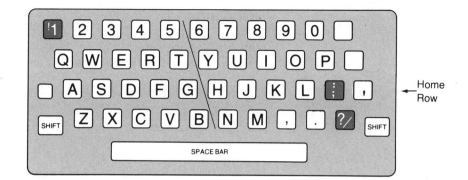

18

Format
40-character line
Single spacing

Practise each line twice.
Practise as quickly as you can.

Review New Keys

1 aqa aqa aqza zqa fvf fbf fv fb fvb fr f5

2 aa bb cc dd ee ff gg hh ii jj kk ll mm n

3 oo pp qq rr ss tt uu vv ww xx yy zz ,;/.

4 fix next six baby extras blue bombs both

5 2/10, n/40; and/or; either/or; 2/20 n/60

Use left shift key and ; finger.
Keep other fingers in home
position.
Practise each line twice.

■ Leave two spaces after a
question mark to indicate the
end of a sentence.

Reach to the ? Key

6 /// /?/ /?/ /// /?/ ?/? ?/? /// /?/ ???/

7 It is? Yes? No? Either? Never? Yes?

Use left shift key and ; finger.
Practise each line twice.

■ Leave two spaces after a
colon within a sentence. Do
not space before or after a
colon when expressing time.

Reach to the : Key

8 ;;; ;:; ;:; ;:; ;:; ;:; ;:; ;;; ;: ;: ::

9 The times are: 11:25, 09:30, and 13:50.

Practise each line twice.

Drill on the ? and : Keys

10 Can you meet us at the station at 11:30?

11 Does that movie start at 18:00 or 19:00?

12 Did you watch the game on TV last night?

13 When is Canada Day? What month and day?

14 Are you able to go on Monday? Yes? No?

• • • • 1 • • • 2 • • • 3 • • • 4 • • • 5 • • • 6 • • • 7 • • • 8

Production 1

The first step in getting the job or career you want is to know yourself and to know what you have to offer an employer. Taking a self-assessment will help you to analyze your potential.

No one else needs to see your personal assessment. Take your time and be honest in answering each question.

Answer in sentence form.

SELF-ASSESSMENT

1. What are your favourite school subjects?

2. What challenges you?

3. What would you like to know more about?

4. What personal qualities do you possess that would make you a good employee?

5. Describe something you have done that made you proud of yourself.

6. Do you prefer working with people, data, or things?

7. In what extra-curricular activities have you participated? Did you enjoy them? Why?

8. What are your weak points? How can you improve them?

9. What machines/equipment can you operate?

10. What work experience have you had?

11. Have you done any volunteer work? If so, where?

12. What are your hobbies and favourite leisure activities?

13. In what type of work would you be the happiest and most productive?

14. What kind of tasks bore or frustrate you?

15. Name three careers that you think would suit you in the future. Which one would be your first choice? Why?

Know your keyboard.
The exclamation mark is
usually the shift of the **1** key on
the number row.
Practise each line twice.

■ Leave two spaces after an
exclamation mark to indicate
the end of a sentence.

Practise each line twice.

Practise each line once.
Repeat *or* take two
15-s timings on each line.

■ What is your best timing on
each set of lines?

Reach to the ! Key

15 aaa aqa a!a qqq a! q! a!a aaa a!q a! a!!

16 Yes! No! Either! Never! Yes! It is!

Drill on the ! Key

17 Yes, I do! Oh, really! Not so! It is!

18 You really did that! Oh, no! Too bad!!

19 I am very surprised! That is that! No!

Drill and Practice

20 Were both black belt buckles on the peg?

21 Do you expect to stay here without food?

22 Will Marc return my books within a week?

23 Have you ever skied at Jasper and Banff?

24 Really! Show me 17:30 on the new clock.

25 Well! You ought to buy a map of Quebec!

· · · · 1 · · · · 2 · · · · 3 · · · · 4 · · · · 5 · · · 6 · · · · 7 · · · · 8

Composing Practice

Think and answer as quickly
as you can without hesitating.

Composition

Complete the following sentences, supplying all missing letters.

1. Th—ee m—nth— —s a l—ng t—me t— wa—t.

2. M—et m— —t th— sh—w t—n—ght.

3. W— a—e gl—d th—t y—u c—n co—e.

4. S—m—er j—b— a—e h—rd —o f—nd.

5. H—ve y—u bo—gh— y—ur t—ck—t y—t?

Career Bulletin 1

CAREER PLANNING

Whether you are searching for a part-time job, a permanent career, or a new job, the process requires planning.

The applicant and the position must be properly matched. Successful career and job selection is a step-by-step process:

1. A thorough self-assessment must be done to determine personal strengths, abilities, and future goals.

2. The job marketplace must be researched to find available positions.

3. A résumé should be prepared.

4. Contacts with potential employers are made by:

    · letters of application
    · telephone calls
    · personal visits (cold contacts)

5. Application forms must be completed.

6. Interviews are arranged with select companies.

7. Employment tests may be administered by an employer.

8. A follow-up to each interview should be done.

9. A final interview may be necessary before the actual hiring takes place.

Spacing Reminder: Question Mark ?

- Two spaces after a question mark as it ends the sentence.
- No space before a question mark.

Spacing Reminder: Colon :

- Two spaces after a colon within a sentence.
- No space before a colon.
- No space before or after a colon used to express time.

Spacing Reminder: Exclamation Mark !

- Two spaces after an exclamation mark as it ends the sentence.
- No space before an exclamation mark.

Career Planning— Résumés

Format

60-character line
Single spacing

Practise each line twice.
Practise as quickly as you can.

Skill Building

Practise at a controlled rate.
Circle your errors. Do Speed
Improvement if you had three
errors or less. Do Accuracy
Improvement if you had four
errors or more.

Right-Hand Words

1 hum jump polo pull nylon unhook plump limp kilo lull join up

2 him pump link only union million puppy loop ploy hymn in lip

Evaluate Your Progress

3   An inventor may have a brilliant idea for something new

but be quite unable to put that idea into effect. When it's

built, the item must work as planned. The concepts might be

perfectly sound but the finished product could be a failure.

Perhaps the materials used are not strong enough or the ways

of holding all the pieces together are not correct. Details

for all aspects of the invention must be carefully outlined.

• • • • 1 • • • • 2 • • • • 3 • • • • 4 • • • • 5 • • • • 6 • • • • 7 • • • • 8 • • • • 9 • • • •10 • • • •11 • • • •12

Accuracy Improvement

Think **accuracy**. Take two 15-s
timings on each line. Take two
30-s timings on the complete
set of lines.

4 tax ease fear trade beaver cassette draft were deeds ace ear

5 keep mill door appear process written carried follow proceed

6 oil pink join lion pupil monopoly limp hook link pin ink hop

7 All classes will visit the gallery to see the space missile.

Speed Improvement

8 If it rains Tuesday, we can always go shopping in the plaza.

Try to do each timing faster.
Take two 15-s timings on each
set of two lines. Take two 30-s
timings on the complete set of
lines.
■ Do Evaluate Your Progress
and determine if you have
improved.

9 Take care of this plant and it will bloom five times a year.

10 He gave us the directions, but we could not find the street.

11 According to the announcement, class pictures will be taken.

Number Practice

Practise each line once.
Practise each line again.

12 In clause 74-309, the 25-year policy states 15% for 9 years.

13 We have enclosed invoices 103297 and 53973 for the 680 cars.

• • • • 1 • • • • 2 • • • • 3 • • • • 4 • • • • 5 • • • • 6 • • • • 7 • • • • 8 • • • • 9 • • • •10 • • • •11 • • • •12

19

Paragraph Indentation / Margin Release

Practise each line twice.
Practise as quickly as you can.

Review New Keys

1 ;:; ;:; ::: ;;; a;s;d;f;g; j;k;l; :: ;;;

2 Did he go? Will we come? Are you glad?

3 Never! Go! Put that down! Sure thing!

4 oo qq ww vv xx mm nn bb dd ll xx qq pp ;

5 15 ribbons and/or 21 robins and/or none;

• • • • 1 • • • • 2 • • • • 3 • • • • 4 • • • • 5 • • • • 6 • • • • 7 • • • • 8

Tabulation

Tabulation means that the print indicator or cursor will stop where you have set *tabs*. This allows you to set up material in columns and to indent for paragraphs. You need to know how to use the:
• tab key • tab clear key or option • tab set key or option

■ Electronic typewriters and computers using word processing software frequently have preset tabs. To reset or clear these tabs, ask your teacher or read the software manual.

Tab Key

1. Locate your tab key.
2. Depress the tab key. This will move the print indicator or cursor to any previously set tab.

Tab Clear Key or Option

1. Depress the tab key to locate previously set tabs.
2. Depress the tab clear key or option to clear the tab.
3. Repeat steps 1 and 2 until each tab is cleared.

To clear all tabs:
1. If your machine has a total tab clear key, depress it to clear all previously set tabs.

If your machine does *not* have a total tab clear key:
1. Move the print indicator to the extreme right margin.
2. Depress the tab clear key and hold.
3. Return.
4. Release the tab clear key.

Tab Set Key or Option

1. Move your print indicator to the position where you want to have a tab set.
2. Depress the tab set key or option.
3. Repeat steps 1 and 2 to set each tab.

Assess Your Progress

Set for double spacing. Take two 3-min *or* two 5-min timings. Circle all errors. Calculate Gross Words Per Minute (GWPM).
Record your best timing on your personal progress chart.

SI 1.48

Three- or Five-Minute Timing

	1	CW	3
The fiery brilliance of the diamond makes it one of the	12	12	4
very favourite jewels in the world. The name comes from the	24	24	8
Greek term adamas, which is unconquerable. All diamonds are	36	36	12
extremely hard, the strongest natural substance found on the	48	48	16
earth. Tools tipped with this jewel can cut through granite	60	60	20
as easily as a steel blade saws through a piece of old wood.	72	72	24
The gem is composed of crystals of pure carbon that are	12	84	28
subjected to tremendous heat and pressure. The slow process	24	96	32
involved is believed to have occurred deep inside the earth.	36	108	36
Humans have been unable to make this gem until this century.	48	120	40
General Electric Company was the first company to subject an	60	132	44
amount of graphite to great heat and pressure to make a gem.	72	144	48
Diamonds were probably created millions of years ago in	12	156	52
molten lava. As the lava flowed to the surface of the earth	24	168	56
through vents known as pipes, it cooled and became solid. A	36	180	60
blue rock was formed containing the precious jewels. Mining	48	192	64
these jewels occurs on many continents. Africa mines larger	60	204	68
amounts of diamonds than any other country in the world.	71	215	72

```
• • • • 1 • • • • 2 • • • • 3 • • • • 4 • • • • 5 • • • • 6 • • • • 7 • • • • 8 • • • • 9 • • • 10 • • • • 11 • • • • 12    1 min
          1                    2                    3              4              3 min
```

Margin Release Drill and Practice

6 Did you watch the hockey game last night?

7 I saw most of the game, but I fell asleep.

8 Some of the games are boring; others aren't.

9 I learned to ski when I was very young.

10 I can't believe I ate the whole thing!

11 Are you going to go on Monday or Tuesday?

■ Locate the margin release key on your typewriter.

In some of these lines it will be necessary to press the margin release key to finish the sentence on the same line.

Practise each line once.

Postal Codes

The Canadian Postal Code is called the *ANA NAN* code. This means that the format of the postal code is:
Alpha Numeric Alpha (Space) *Numeric Alpha Numeric.*
No other characters, periods, commas, hyphens, etc., should be included as part of the postal code. The postal code is preferred as the last line of the address.

Endorsement Recruiters Inc.
150 Consumers Road
Willowdale, Ontario
M2J 1P9

Drill on Postal Codes

Practise each line twice.

12 M9R 1Z5 and M9R 1Z5 and M9R 1Z5

13 P1R 3C5 and P1R 3C5 and P1R 3C5

14 K2A 9Y7 and K2A 9Y7 and K2A 9Y7

Drill and Practice

Practise each line once.
Repeat *or* take two
15-s timings on each line.

15 Barbara played in the yard with her pal.

16 Our French poodle enjoys eating noodles.

17 We appoint you to pinpoint the problems.

18 Can Willy assist them to gain 25 points?

19 Exercise 25 on page 4 is easier than 24.

20 Note this: 107 boys, 81 girls, 190 men.

. . . . . 1 . . . . 2 . . . . 3 . . . . 4 . . . . 5 . . . . 6 . . . . 7 8

Production 1

Input the following list of books as a bibliography. Use correct format. Use the same margins that were used for reports. Remember to listen for the right margin signal if you are using a typewriter as the production uses a different line length.

BIBLIOGRAPHY

Black, Gayle. The Sun Sign Diet. New York: Macmillan Publishing Company,
        1986.

Grant, Russell. Your Sun Signs. London, England: Virgin Books Ltd.,
        1984.

Goodavage, Joseph F. Write Your Own Horoscope. New York: New American
        Library, Inc., 1968.

Gettings, Fred. The Book of the Zodiac. London,
    England : Ward Ltd., 1972.

Goodman, Linda. Linda Goodman's Sun Signs. New York:
    Taplinger Publishing Co., Inc., 1968.

■ Did you arrange in alphabetical order?

Production 2

Input a title page for the report, ''The Signs of the Zodiac.''

Paragraph Indentations

Set a tab five spaces from the left margin for paragraph indentations. Your machine or word processing program may have preset tabs. Know your machine.

Practice

Set a tab. Return to the left margin. Make an exact copy of each line.

5 Thank you for your invitation to attend the party. We will be sure to come!

⁊ Our principal is going to run in a marathon race. One must be very fit to run that distance.

⁊ I can't wait until Thanksgiving weekend. We are going up to a cottage to visit friends.

⁊ Do you own a compact disc player? I would really like to buy a good one, but my parents say they are too costly.

⁊ I want my friends to be honest, dependable, and courteous. If someone is rude to me, it is very annoying and sometimes hurtful.

⁊ I try to have the same qualities that I respect in my friends. I know these qualities are valued at home and at work as well.

· · · · 1 · · · · 2 · · · · 3 · · · · 4 · · · · 5 · · · · 6 · · · · 7 · · · · 8

Composition

Create as many words as you can to describe each of the following items. Allow one minute for each item.

pizza hamburger spaghetti French fries

Common Words

1 jetliner back adept copy eagle digit frank hand great invite

2 series laser kick oath none margin quest paint ratio trouble

Evaluate Your Progress

3   Students are learning how to use a keyboard as early as

kindergarten or elementary school. Microcomputers have been

introduced in the classrooms of many schools in the country.

These students usually use the hunt and peck method which is

a slow way of locating each letter and number to be input on

the keyboard. Students who learn to type by touch can input

information more quickly and efficiently on the micros.

• • • • 1 • • • • 2 • • • • 3 • • • • 4 • • • • 5 • • • • 6 • • • • 7 • • • • 8 • • • • 9 • • • •10• • • •11• • • •12

Accuracy Improvement

4 beautiful allure balcony announce abolish banana carrot ugly

5 tribute ulcer umbrella rabbit queasy publish justify lateral

6 keynote quarrel legislate initially edict drummer victor wad

7 wallet yogurt plastic zipper seniority terrain census diesel

Speed Improvement

8 Snowdrops were the first sign of spring after a long winter.

9 Edmonton hosted Universiade '83, the world university games.

10 The scent of the purple and white lilacs filled this office.

11 A ball of fire lit the sky as the meteor fell to the ground.

• • • • 1 • • • • 2 • • • • 3 • • • • 4 • • • • 5 • • • • 6 • • • • 7 • • • • 8 • • • • 9 • • • •10• • • •11• • • •12

Graduated Speed Practice

1. Turn to Lesson 81, page 264.
2. Drill on the appropriate Graduated Speed Practice.

20 Analytical Practice

Format

40-character line
Single spacing

Practise each line twice.
Practise as quickly as you can.

Analyze Your Practice

Take two 1-min timings on
each sentence.
Each sentence contains the
alphabet.
Circle all errors.

Alternate-Hand Words

1 go cut nap yam both torn fish pang slept

2 man dig disk worn cork handy signs audit

Alphabetic Sentences

3 A number of zinnias grow in this meadow,
but quite often excited children like to
jump and play volleyball here.

4 Jack said it was a crazy quilt because a
few patches were very strangely matched;
you might say the mixture was flashy.
· · · · 1 · · · · 2 · · · · 3 · · · · 4 · · · · 5 · · · · 6 · · · · 7 · · · · 8

Selected Letter Practice

1. Circle all errors in the Alphabetic Sentences.
2. From your errors, choose the letter or letters which gave you difficulty.
3. Select the appropriate drill lines in the Selected Letter Practice.
4. Practise each line twice concentrating on accuracy.
5. If you had no errors in the Alphabetic Sentences, or if you complete the accuracy lines before your teacher calls **time**, start at line A and **push** for speed. Practise each line once.

After Selected Letter Practice,
take two 1-min timings on each
Alphabetic Sentence and
determine if you have
improved.

A 5 an as at am and all any can may had area
6 After that alarm, many planes were late.

B 7 by be but big bus bank rib debt box baby
8 A branch of my blueberry bush is broken.

C 9 can cap ice act cow scar each copy cubic
10 Each coach carefully checks score cards.

D 11 and did day add sad ride held deal would
12 Dad adds the dairy and field data daily.
· · · · 1 · · · · 2 · · · · 3 · · · · 4 · · · · 5 · · · · 6 · · · · 7 · · · · 8

Three- or Five-Minute Timing

		1	CW	3
The fungus belongs to the family of plants which do not		12	12	4
have roots, stems, leaves, and flowers. They do not contain		24	24	8
chlorophyll, the green pigment used by most plants to supply		36	36	12
their own food. Fungus can live on various types of organic		48	48	16
matter. Slime molds feed on decaying matter. Ergot attacks		60	60	20
the grain rye. Other fungus will cause white rust on trees.		72	72	24
The more common members of this big group of plants are		12	84	28
mushrooms, puffballs, yeasts, molds, and rust. Some are now		24	96	32
used by humans: mushrooms are edible, and yeasts are always		36	108	36
found in beer and wine. Several kinds of molds are used for		48	120	40
making chemicals and processed cheese. Other fungi help the		60	132	44
decomposition of plants and animals present in the soil.		71	143	48
Many fungi are harmful to living plants and animals. A		12	155	52
fungus can cause Dutch elm disease and other kinds of mildew		24	167	56
in plants. Human beings suffer from athlete's foot or ring-		36	179	60
worm. Many types of fungi, such as yeasts, have one cell; a		48	191	64
puffball, on the other hand, can reach 30 cm in diameter. A		60	203	68
number of fungi are colourless, but some may be red, yellow,		72	215	71
orange, etc.		74	217	72

```
· · · ·1· · · ·2· · · ·3· · · ·4· · · ·5· · · ·6· · · ·7· · · ·8· · · ·9· · · ·10· · · ·11· · · ·12    1 min
         1                2                3                4              3 min
```

Composition

* Many companies use identification symbols on their letterhead and in their advertisements. These symbols are called logos. How many popular logos can you list, using the enumeration method? Briefly describe each logo and the company it represents. Use sentence format.

■ *flavours* or *flavors*

Know the preference in your area of Canada.

E 13 be we me he the end eye age red are edge
14 Everyone else entered the meeting early.

F 15 if for far off fit free from refer after
16 Fix a few more different fancy flavours.

G 17 go get ago gas beg gift gang going given
18 George suggested green luggage as gifts.

H 19 he the she his has hush high thigh hitch
20 Her harp hung by the hearth in the hall.

I 21 in is it if him ill lie tip ice ink iris
22 Crisis is still a time for civic spirit.

J 23 jar jet jaw jam jog jail ajar jazz eject
24 Joanne has a jean jacket just like mine.

K 25 ask milk bike know think kind kite knife
26 Kay likes to bake cakes and make snacks.

L 27 low all ill lay let play lose will legal
28 Lillian laughed at the little log cabin.

M 29 my am man aim met him map made some them
30 Many members will miss the May meetings.

N 31 an no on not and end fun nine once linen
32 Send one apron and nine new napkins now.

O 33 on to so out too now off only also motor
34 We took a photo of a baboon on the post.

· · · · · 1 · · · · 2 · · · · 3 · · · · 4 · · · · 5 · · · · 6 · · · · 7 · · · · 8

Scorpio the Scorpion (October 24 to November 22)

Scorpio is the only sign with three symbols: the scorpion, the serpent, and the eagle. Scorpions have total command of themselves and their emotions. They are able to size up situations at a glance. A Scorpion is intensely loyal to friends and never forgets a gift or a kindness.

Taurus the Bull (April 21 to May 21)

The Taurean is solid and practical. It is difficult to change the Taurean's mind once it has been set. Worrying or fretting isn't part of the bull's nature. The average Taurean is healthy, with a strong constitution, and has an excellent appetite.

Virgo the Virgin (August 24 to September 23)

Worry comes naturally to the Virgo. Virgos are very dependable, sincere, and hard-working. An orderly mind causes the Virgo to form habits which are not easily broken. People born under this sign usually find more satisfaction in serving others than in satisfying their own personal ambitions.

P 35 pay lip pig nap pump pipe paper pour tap
36 People put pumpkin and apples into pies.

Q 37 aqua quart squad quick quiet quill equip
38 The queen questioned the quick decision.

R 39 or our for are red real very order ruler
40 Raja prefers rock records for the party.

S 41 ask say use she has best same says basis
42 Sue saw several styles of summer slacks.

T 43 it to ten the tent ate three tenth state
44 They often take trips to study the past.

U 45 us but you buy our unit must usual uncle
46 Guy found the ukulele under the counter.

V 47 van vow every velvet very love even save
48 Vera loves velvet vests and mauve veils.

W 49 we saw new was few away walk where crowd
50 We want to know why Walter was with Wes.

X 51 six fix wax mix extra exam text box lynx
52 Fix that axle before Rex waxes the taxi.

Y 53 my bye yet sky you type your loyal youth
54 You are a year younger than Guy and Roy.

Z 55 zip zoo buzz zero zone dozen fuzzy seize
56 Ezra watched the lazy zebras at the zoo.
· · · · 1 · · · · 2 · · · · 3 · · · · 4 · · · · 5 · · · · 6 · · · · 7 · · · · 8

Gemini the Twins *(May 22 to June 21)*

Eagerness and energy mark the Gemini. Geminians are clever, quick-witted, and charming, but they lack persistence and patience. A Gemini is very good at disguising true motives. Many people born under this sign are found in occupations relating to the communications field.

Leo the Lion *(July 24 to August 23)*

Leo is a natural leader and loves to give free advice. A Leo will give money to almost anybody. The lion's roar is often not indicative of his true feelings. Leo is a fiercely loyal friend.

Libra the Scales *(September 24 to October 23)*

The Libran's goal in life is to achieve harmony--the balancing of the scales. The Libran character is a curious mixture of kindness, gentleness, fairness, stubbornness, logic and indecision. Most Librans have a good ability to concentrate, and they generally like books.

Pisces the Fish *(February 20 to March 20)*

Very few of the people born under the Pisces sign can stand being confined for long in one place. Pisces people are charming and have a relaxed nature. They are very kind and sympathetic and cannot stand to see others suffer. While Aries represents birth in the zodiac, Pisces represents death and eternity. The fish is the twelfth sign, a composite of all others.

Sagittarius the Archer *(November 23 to December 21)*

Sagittarians are known for their direct honesty and disregard for conventional behaviour. The archer loves animals. The typical Sagittarian is attracted to danger--in sports, occupation, or hobby. Freedom and independence are valued highly. The archer also tends to have a violent temper.

Sentences with Numbers

Take two 1-min timings on each sentence.
Circle all errors.

57 In 1989 they visited 106 villages and 23

cities.   The entire trip lasted 47 days.

58 We went 2 958 km in 10 busy winter days.
. . . . 1 . . . . 2 . . . . 3 . . . . 4 . . . . 5 . . . 6 . . . . 7 8

Selected Number Practice

1. Circle all errors in the Sentences with Numbers.
2. From your errors, choose the number or numbers which gave you difficulty.
3. Select the appropriate drill lines in the Selected Number Practice.
4. Practise each line twice concentrating on accuracy.
5. If you had no errors in the Sentences with Numbers, or if you complete the accuracy lines before your teacher calls **time**, start at line 0 and **push** for speed. Practise each line once.

After Selected Number Practice, take two 1-min timings on the Sentences with Numbers and determine if you have improved.

0 59 0 and 00 and 000 or 0 or 00 or 000 and 0

1 60 1 and 11 and 111 or 1 or 11 or 111 and 1

2 61 2 and 22 and 222 or 2 or 22 or 222 and 2

3 62 3 and 33 and 333 or 3 or 33 or 333 and 3

4 63 4 and 44 and 444 or 4 or 44 or 444 and 4

5 64 5 and 55 and 555 or 5 or 55 or 555 and 5

6 65 6 and 66 and 666 or 6 or 66 or 666 and 6

7 66 7 and 77 and 777 or 7 or 77 or 777 and 7

8 67 8 and 88 and 888 or 8 or 88 or 888 and 8

9 68 9 and 99 and 999 or 9 or 99 or 999 and 9

Drill on Postal Codes

Practise each line twice.

69 J2X 4L1 and J2X 4L1 and J2X 4L1

70 G5C 1R5 and G5C 1R5 and G5C 1R5

71 A1E 3X1 and A1E 3X1 and A1E 3X1
. . . . 1 . . . . 2 . . . . 3 . . . . 4 . . . . 5 . . . . 6 . . . . 7 8

Production

The following are the signs of the zodiac listed in alphabetical order. Rearrange the information, listing by date rather than by sign. Start the list with March 21 to April 20 (Aries). Arrange the information attractively in report form. The report should be titled "The Signs of the Zodiac." Single space the body. Listen for the right margin signal if you are using a typewriter as the production does not use the standard report line length. Add the following paragraph as an introduction:

What zone of the zodiac was the sun in when you were born? For centuries people have studied the effect of the sun and other celestial bodies in shaping the personalities of individuals. Many people believe that it is possible to achieve a better understanding of individuals by knowing what sign of the zodiac they were born under.

Aquarius the Water Bearer *(January 21 to February 19)*

Aquarians are always analyzing situations, friends, and strangers. This sun sign is known as the sign of genius. Aquarians are inclined to be scientific, unpredictable, honest, and usually cheerful.

Aries the Ram *(March 21 to April 20)*

Aries is the first sign of the zodiac. It represents birth. People born under the sign of the ram are very frank and honest. They are likely to be strong, tough, and optimistic. Aries people are inclined to go right to the point, even if it means being blunt.

Cancer the Crab *(June 22 to July 23)*

The Cancerian has many moods and changing emotions. The life-of-the-party will be a Cancer--with a keen sense of humour. Sensitive feelings and crankiness are also characteristic. You'll often find the Cancerian on the water--swimming, water-skiing, etc.

Capricorn the Goat *(December 22 to January 20)*

The goat is a climber, striving to get to the top. A quietly ambitious person, the average Capricorn can look and act quite harmless but can be very tough. A good mind and reasoning ability often mark the Capricorn.

Production

Input the following paragraphs using a 40-character line. Set a tab for paragraph indentations.

¶ Put all of your books away when you are
given the order to do so. The exam will
begin after you have your books in the desk.

¶ When you start the exam, you cannot visit
and chat with your friends. This exam must
be done by you without help from anyone.

¶ Lastly, you must remain in the room until
all exams are handed in. There are no rewards
for you if you finish early.

Difficulty of Timed Writings

SI or *syllabic intensity* indicates the average number of speech syllables per actual word in the timed writing. The lower the SI, the easier is the timed writing.

Two-Minute Timing

Timed writings are calculated in gross words per minute (GWPM). For a 2-min timing, the total words completed would be divided by two. A 2-min scale is given with each timing for your convenience. Therefore, it is not necessary to divide the total words completed by two.

Set for double spacing. Take two 2-min timings. Circle all errors. Calculate Gross Words Per Minute (GWPM). Record your best timing on your personal progress chart.

SI 1.1

	1	2
The green grass was thick and high.	8	4
In the morning, the front lawn was moist	16	8
with dew. The leaves had curled and lay	24	12
on the ground. All the trees were bare.	32	16
The air was crisp and clear. Winter was	40	20
on its way.	42	21

· · · · 1 · · · · 2 · · · · 3 · · · · 4 · · · · 5 · · · · 6 · · · · 7 · · · · 8   1 min
          1   2   3   4   2 min

Reports

Format

60-character line
Single spacing

Practise each line twice.
Practise as quickly as you can.

Skill Building

Practise at a controlled rate.
Circle your errors. Do Speed
Improvement if you had three
errors or less. Do Accuracy
Improvement if you had four
errors or more.

Think **accuracy**. Take two 15-s
timings on each line. Take two
30-s timings on the complete
set of lines.

Try to do each timing faster.
Take two 15-s timings on each
set of two lines. Take two 30-s
timings on the complete set of
lines.
■ Do Evaluate Your Progress
and determine if you have
improved.

Practise each line once.
Practise each line again.

Alternate-Hand Words

1 by both when turn shrub hand surname profit ivory field owns

2 air bowl land usual signal giant Henry coal sight turkey map

Evaluate Your Progress

3　　　Not all roots are under the ground. Some plants have a

life system in water. Others have aerial roots which absorb

moisture from the air. There are plants whose lengthy roots

branch out for several hundred feet. These stretch out long

distances to get necessary food and water. Tiny projections

called root hairs allow the plant to soak up the much-needed

water and minerals from the soil.

　• • • •1• • • •2• • • •3• • • •4• • • •5• • • •6• • • •7• • • •8• • • •9• • • •10• • • •11• • • •12

Accuracy Improvement

4 too been well loss carry office cannot issue account meeting

5 vex fact read swat after street beverage cataract data weave

6 key dial them Nancy fish chairman panels firms men their rot

7 Mary Anne ate three egg rolls and seventeen fortune cookies.

Speed Improvement

8 Vacuum the hallway floor and wash the green glasses by noon.

9 We suggest that you correct the grammar and spelling errors.

10 The bookkeeper will not allow accounts to fall into arrears.

11 By this time next month, we should have the correct balance.

Number Practice

12 It took 15 months and 27 days to complete the 824 km voyage.

13 She sold 4 758 in May, 3 675 in July, and 10 587 in October.

　• • • •1• • • •2• • • •3• • • •4• • • •5• • • •6• • • •7• • • •8• • • •9• • • •10• • • •11• • • •12

21

Shift Lock

Format
40-character line
Single spacing

Practise each line twice.
Practise as quickly as you can.

Common Words

1 fair high sale grow sour tale stay years

2 away pair past best cook hour them plays

3 with seem very both must dart pork yards

4 torn part word page read yawn rain girls

Practise each line once.
Repeat *or* take two
15-s timings on each line.

Drill and Practice

5 Inform him of the new rules of the game.

6 She was hired to solve all the problems.

7 I was absent for four days with the flu.

8 Be sure the car is in top running order.
· · · · 1 · · · · 2 · · · · 3 · · · · 4 · · · · 5 · · · · 6 · · · · 7 · · · · 8

Spacing Review

Space **once** after:	comma	,
	semi-colon	;
Space **twice** after:	period (end of sentence)	.
	question mark	?
	colon (exception 10:45)	:
	exclamation mark	!

Spacing Drill and Practice

Practise each line once.
Repeat *or* take two
15-s timings on each line.

9 Joyce, Silvana, and Eri agreed to speak.

10 Bring these items: cups, plates, forks.

11 Frank went to Italy; Kim went to France.

12 Please help us. Send your cheque today.

13 Is my car fixed? We hope to leave soon.

14 Hurry! The others will not wait for us.
· · · · 1 · · · · 2 · · · · 3 · · · · 4 · · · · 5 · · · · 6 · · · · 7 · · · · 8

Three- or Five-Minute Timing

	1	CW	3
The cattle business is old and proud. It was the first	12	12	4
money—making business on this continent. Opinions differ on	24	24	8
whether cattlemen attach as much importance to horses as the	36	36	12
saddles. Each rider does have a preference in horses. Most	48	48	16
cow hands do not own their own horses, but many of them have	60	60	20
their own saddle. The horses are the property of the boss.	71	71	24
Cattle raising is an industry first associated with the	12	83	28
west. Industrial manufacturing developed in the east, where	24	95	32
land areas were limited. The great years of the cattle were	36	107	36
in the west, while the range land was still open. No barbed	48	119	40
wire fences blocked the well—used trails. Herds were driven	60	131	44
where there was plenty of good, clean water and tall grass.	71	142	47
The purpose of driving herds to distant shipping points	12	154	51
was profit. Cattle were and still are identified with large	24	166	55
or small brands. Nowadays branding is done in a chute. One	36	178	59
ear is usually tattooed with a registration number. A quick	48	190	63
slice in the other ear lets an owner's identification tag be	60	202	67
attached. After a run and some head shaking, all is well.	71	214	71

```
• • • • 1 • • • • 2 • • • • 3 • • • • 4 • • • • 5 • • • • 6 • • • • 7 • • • • 8 • • • • 9 • • • •10• • • •11• • • •12
          1                    2                    3                    4
```
1 min
3 min

SI 1.46

Reach to the Shift Lock Key

To input a word or words in upper case (all capital letters):
1. Depress the shift lock key with the **A** finger.
2. Input the characters, word, or words in upper case.
3. Release the shift lock by depressing **either** the right or left shift key on your typewriter **or** the shift lock (caps lock) key on your computer.

Drill on the Shift Lock Key

15 This area is PERFECT for flying my kite.

16 We expect you to be ON TIME for classes.

17 Make the APPOINTMENT with the agent now.

18 We would be GLAD to give you the REFUND.

19 Come to our SPECIAL SALE this WEDNESDAY.

· · · · 1 · · · · 2 · · · · 3 · · · · 4 · · · · 5 · · · · 6 · · · · 7 · · · · 8

Practise each line twice.

■ *Note:* Remember to release the shift lock key if some of the characters are **not** in upper case.

■ Most word processing programs have a default for single spacing.

■ To reset the line spacing on your computer, ask your teacher or read the software manual.

Single Spacing ss

When single spacing paragraphs, the line space regulator on your typewriter is set on 1. This means the print indicator or cursor returns to every line leaving **no** blank lines between the lines of text. Before beginning a new paragraph, strike the return or enter key **twice**. This leaves one blank line or a double space.

Double Spacing ds

When double spacing paragraphs, the line space regulator on your typewriter is set on 2. This means the print indicator or cursor returns to every second line leaving **one** blank line between the lines of text. Before beginning a new paragraph, strike the return or enter key **once**. This leaves a double space.

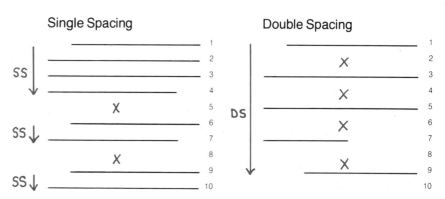

The airspace that falls under Canadian defence control is monitored by ROCC. Every plane that enters this space must be immediately identified. This is done by comparing the computer data with the flight plans of known aircraft. ¶ If the intruder cannot be identified as "friendly," it is classified as "unknown." The aircraft is then challenged using ground-to-air radio communication. If necessary, Canadian CF-18's may be used to intercept the unknown aircraft. The CF-18's photograph the planes, particularly the door numbers to establish the identification of the aircraft. Once identified, the aircraft is escorted along a flight path which leads it away from Canadian defence airspace. ¶ Using the latest electronic devices, the aircraft interceptors can be controlled from the time they become airborne, throughout flight, including the firing of weapons, if necessary, and the return to home base.

The Canadian NORAD Region ROCCs hold a key defensive position because they block the polar routes to vital industrial complexes and population centres of Canada and the United States.

1½

Right Margin Signal on Your Typewriter

A signal (e.g. a bell or beep) will sound as the print indicator approaches the right margin. *Know your typewriter*. This signal may indicate as few as 5 characters or as many as 15 characters before the right margin setting. Set the right margin beyond the line length (e.g. 40-character line) so that the signal will give advance warning and time to decide to either return at the end of the word or complete the word using the margin release key.

Some electronic typewriters and word processing programs on computers have automatic word wrap at the right margin. This is a system or program default. A right margin signal will not sound. Ask your teacher if the word wrap default should be changed to *off*?

Production Practice

Production 1

Set a 40-character line. Input the following paragraphs using single spacing. Listen for the right margin signal on your typewriter.

```
     Our yearbook, URSUS, is now being organized
for this year.  The book was a great success
last year.

     The new edition will feature eight pages of
full colour.  We are looking forward to producing
an even better yearbook than last year.

¶     URSUS is sold to our students at well below
the actual cost of the book.  Funds must be
raised to make up the difference between the
actual cost and the selling price. sp|¶ Please
give us your support by placing an ad in our
yearbook.  The attached page gives further
details about cost.  ¶  We would be glad to
issue a tax receipt upon payment.  URSUS needs
your support.
```

■ Did you double space between paragraphs?

Production 2

Set a 40-character line. Input the paragraphs in Production 1 using double spacing. Listen for the right margin signal on your typewriter.

Construction

When the underground excavation began in August, 1959, an unusual swedish mining technique, "smooth wall blasting," was used for the first time in North America. This involved the use of special blasting powder which produced a clean shearing effect and reduced the need for scaling to smooth the walls after blasting. More than 228 000 m³ of rock were excavated from the site over an 18-month period. The cavern was then ready for construction of the building which now houses the Canadian NORAD Region.

The Facility

At first glance, the interior of the underground facility looks like other modern business buildings. The offices are air-conditioned, bright, and the furniture is modern and efficient. The building is a free-standing structure but only a few short distance from the walls are the grey faces of rock.

Basically, the three-storey building is situated in 2 huge chambers 120 m long, connected by three cross-caverns 60 metres long. All are 18 metres high and 13.5 metres wide. To assure that the site can be self-sufficient under attack, there are kitchen and dining facilities capable of feeding about four hundred people, a hospital and infirmary, large washrooms and showers, and space for personnel to rest or sleep.

The Basic Concept of ROCCs

The peacetime mission for the Canadian ROCCs is the detection and identification of all aircraft flying into the regions. In wartime, the Canadian norad Region also is responsible for engaging aircraft in combat. The brain of the ROCC system is a state-of-the-art, HUGHES H5118ME computer, which receives data, memorizes, calculates, records, and presents answers simultaneously on console screens (similar to a television screen). STET

Timing

Set for double spacing. Take two 2-min timings. Circle all errors. Calculate Gross Words Per Minute (GWPM). Record your best timing on your personal progress chart.

SI 1.1

Two-Minute Timing

			1	2
We want to go on a long trip. Last			8	4
summer, it was too wet for camping. All			16	8
our friends want to come with us. There			24	12
will be many places to visit. We have a			32	16
new tent and sleeping bags. The car has			40	20
been fixed and is ready to go.			46	23

· · · · 1 · · · · 2 · · · · 3 · · · · 4 · · · · 5 · · · · 6 · · · · 7 · · · · 8   1 min

1 .... 2 .... 3 4   2 min

Composing Practice

Think and answer as quickly as you can without hesitating.

Composition

How many of the following traffic signs can you identify? Explain each sign in three words or less. Use a separate line for each explanation.

Example: traffic signals ahead

1

2

3

4

5

6

7

8

9

10

11.

12

Production 1

Input the following report using one and one-half spacing rather than double spacing. Use correct format. Remember to listen for the right margin signal if you are using a typewriter as the production does not use the standard report line length.

THE CANADIAN NORAD REGION ROCCS

One of the largest contributions to the North America ~~Air~~ *& aerospace* Defence (norad) has been the construction and operation of the complex which now houses two Region Operations Control Centres (ROCCs), which together make up the Canadian Norad Region.

The underground complex is located at the Canadian Forces Base in North Bay. The site was completed in 1963 for 51 million dollars (it was originally called SAGE). The two ROCCs, Canada East and Canada West, play a vital role in the air defence of north america.

The North Bay ROCCs are unique in two ways: they are the only rocc centres outside the United States, and they are the only ROCC centres located underground.

Why North Bay?

Four criteria led to the choice of North Bay as the site of the underground installation:

1. A good rock formation. North Bay is located in the southern portion of the Precambrian Shield, a hard and stable rock formation covering roughly 50% *(spell out)* of Canada. This rock is estimated to be two billion years old and has the characteristics of a fine grained granite.

2. Administrative support. An existing Canadian Forces Base provides administrative support.

3. Water. Nearby Trout Lake provides fresh water for the complex.

4. Good communications. North Bay is approximately 330 km north of Toronto and about the same distance from Ottawa. Major road and rail networks come together in this area, and telecommunications are also well established. *In addition, there is a microwave system located at the Canadian Forces Base, connecting it with all radar stations in Northern Ontario and Quebec.*

22

Format
40-character line
Single spacing

Practise each line twice.
Practise as quickly as you can.

Practise each line once.
Repeat *or* take two
15-s timings on each line.

Practise each line once.
Practise each line again.

Common Words

1 man map mat may mad mail made make masks
2 cry fry try diary worry sorry bury dairy
3 ink drink think pink sink rink mink wink
4 word worn world worst worm worth workman

Drill and Practice

5 I played the record over and over again.
6 Put those boxes in the trunk of the car.
7 The new policy is explained in the memo.
8 The history papers are due in two weeks.

Shift Lock Drill and Practice

9 to DO to GO to COME to SAY to PLAY to BE
10 as a PART as a WHOLE as a MATTER OF FACT
11 if NOT if YOU WILL if I GO if SO if I AM
12 for US for THEM for HIM for YOU for MANY
· · · · 1 · · · · 2 · · · · 3 · · · · 4 · · · · 5 · · · · 6 · · · · 7 · · · · 8

Reach to the ° Key

1. Locate the degree sign symbol on the keyboard.
2. If there is no degree sign symbol on the keyboard, the letter **o** is used as a superior figure.*
3. Do not space before or after the degree sign symbol when giving temperatures, e.g. 21°C.
   *A superior figure is one half space above the line.

Practise each line twice.

■ If your keyboard does not have a degree sign key, did you turn your cylinder knob a half space? OR Did you ask your teacher or read the software manual?

P   °   O
    :   OR   L

Drill on the ° Key

13 Water freezes at 0°C and boils at 100°C.
14 Bake the pie at 175°C for about an hour.
15 Body temperature is normally about 37°C.
16 The air temperature is a cool 9°C today.
· · · · 1 · · · · 2 · · · · 3 · · · · 4 · · · · 5 · · · · 6 · · · · 7 · · · · 8

Reports

Format
60-character line
Single spacing

Practise each line twice.
Practise as quickly as you can.

Skill Building

Practise at a controlled rate.
Circle your errors. Do Speed
Improvement if you had three
errors or less. Do Accuracy
Improvement if you had four
errors or more.

Left-Hand Words

1 art were race deaf great creased bazaar savage better awards

2 web date safe tear react breeze excess aged dear weds freeze

Evaluate Your Progress

3   The microscope is a great instrument that focuses light

or other radiation through one or more lenses to produce the

magnified image of a specimen. It has affected the study of

biology and medicine, revealing the tremendous quantities of

activity that could never have been determined otherwise. A

microscope is also helpful in other scientific and technical

areas. Simple lens magnification has been known for years.
•••1••••2••••3••••4••••5••••6••••7••••8••••9•••10•••11•••12

Accuracy Improvement

Think **accuracy**. Take two 15-s
timings on each line. Take two
30-s timings on the complete
set of lines.

4 bar vet raft fade award decade retread scared crazed streets

5 fee less sell book happy little assure manner between access

6 dot disk down shoe cycle island quench cubicle penalty quite

7 A traffic accident can occur when a driver becomes careless.

Speed Improvement

Try to do each timing faster.
Take two 15-s timings on each
set of two lines. Take two 30-s
timings on the complete set of
lines.
■ Do Evaluate Your Progress
and determine if you have
improved.

8 He rushed to catch his plane, but he did not arrive on time.

9 We will have to use these copies even if they are not clear.

10 We are having problems, but we feel we will solve them soon.

11 It is doubtful if he will be able to go back for his cheque.

Number Practice

12 See pages 122, 130, and 274 for the data on the 25 new dogs.

13 In 1989, 536 invoices were issued with the 274 form letters.
•••1••••2••••3••••4••••5••••6••••7••••8••••9•••10•••11•••12

Triple Spacing ts

When triple spacing (e.g. after a title), set the line space regulator on your typewriter on 1, and return three times. This leaves a triple space or **two** blank lines between the lines of text.

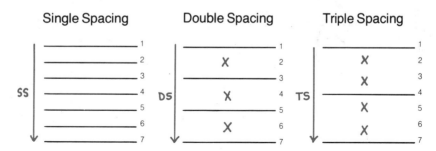

Single Spacing   Double Spacing   Triple Spacing

Production

Input the following paragraphs using a 40-character line. Observe the symbols for correct spacing. Listen for the right margin signal on your typewriter.

```
The Name CANADA
        TS

¶    Several theories exist about the origin of
the name CANADA.  However, it is generally
accepted that the name CANADA comes from the
Iroquois KANATA or KANADA, meaning a cabin or
lodge.  The word first appeared in Jacques
Cartier's records of his second voyage to Canada
in 1535.
        TS

What is ARVIDA?
        TS

¶    ARVIDA is the site of one of the world's
biggest aluminum smelters.  It is also the
largest planned city in Canada.  This Quebec city
was built in 1926 and named for ARthur VIning
DAvis, a president of the Aluminum Company of
Canada.
        TS

Where is ALERT?
        TS

¶    ALERT is the most northerly settlement in
the world.  It was built by the Canadian
government in 1950.  ALERT is closer to Moscow
than to Montreal.
```

Assess Your Progress

Set for double spacing. Take two 3-min *or* two 5-min timings. Circle all errors. Calculate Gross Words Per Minute (GWPM).
Record your best timing on your personal progress chart.

Three- or Five-Minute Timing

	1	CW	3
Nipper is the world's most famous dog. He is the black	12	12	4
and white terrier of "his Master's Voice." His trademark is	24	24	8
older than this century and is found all over the world. He	36	36	12
began life as a happy puppy in England in 1884. The theatre	48	48	16
was his home, as he belonged to a scene designer. Many dark	60	60	20
corners were explored in a long busy day of the young puppy.	72	72	24
In those days the scene director would often answer the	12	84	28
curtain call with the cast. Whenever his master appeared on	24	96	32
stage, so did the puppy. After the death of his first owner	36	108	36
Nipper belonged to a commercial artist. The dog enjoyed his	48	120	40
new life of meeting more people and running in a big garden.	60	132	44
He would pose for illustrations if a dog was required.	71	143	48
It was Nipper's habit to sit in the studio and keep his	12	155	52
master company, especially while the phonograph was playing.	24	167	56
The dog sat close to the phonograph, with his head cocked to	36	179	60
one side. A painting of him was done in this position. The	48	191	64
original phonograph was replaced by the tulip-horn type.	59	202	67

`· · · ·1· · · ·2· · · ·3· · · ·4· · · ·5· · · ·6· · · ·7· · · ·8· · · ·9· · ·10· · ·11· · · ·12`   1 min

       1   2   3   4   3 min

SI 1.41

Composition

Choose one of the following topics. Using the enumeration method, list the steps involved in performing the task you have chosen. After editing and making corrections on your rough copy, input a good copy.

Topics: How to Ride a Bicycle
            Skateboarding
            How to Bake a Cake
            Washing a Car
            How to Grow Plants

SI 1.22

Two-Minute Timing

		1	2
A cat washing her face, sparks from		8	4
a wood stove flying to the floor, a fork		16	8
or knife falling, signal a good visit by		24	12
a stranger. Looking at a new moon first		32	16
over the left shoulder, seeing two black		40	20
crows flying, picking up a coin, are but		48	24
omens of good luck. These have roots in		56	28
our folklore.		59	29

```
· · · · 1 · · · · 2 · · · · 3 · · · · 4 · · · · 5 · · · · 6 · · · · 7 · · · · 8      1 min
         1              2              3              4                   2 min
```

Composing Practice

Think and answer as quickly as you can without hesitating.

Composition

How many of the following phobias can you identify from the list below? Input each answer on a separate line.

zoophobia	claustrophobia	triskaidekaphobia
agoraphobia	bacteriophobia	acrophobia
hemophobia	hypnophobia	photophobia
pyrophobia		

1. fear of confined spaces *cl*
2. fear of the number 13 *t*
3. fear of blood *it*
4. fear of animals *zoo*
5. fear of heights *ac*
6. fear of fire *py*
7. fear of germs *bac*
8. fear of light
9. fear of open spaces
10. fear of falling asleep

Production 1

Input the bibliography for the report "Dungeons & Dragons." Use correct format.

Bibliography

Gygax, Gary. *Advanced Dungeons & Dragons, Player Handbook*. Lake Geneva, Wisconsin: TSR Games, 1978.

Langone, John. "Dungeons and Dragons Craze." *Discover* (January, 1981), 33-34.

Gygax, Gary. *Dungeon Master Guide*. Lake Geneva, Wisconsin: TSR Games, 1979.

Gygax, Gary. *Advanced Dungeons & Dragons, Monster Manual*. Lake Geneva, Wisconsin: TSR Games, 1978.

Ross, Phillip. "A D & D Decade." *Games* (December 1984), 7.

Remember to alphabetize your list.

Production 2

Input a title page for the report, "Dungeons & Dragons."

- / **Vertical Centring**

Format
40-character line
Single spacing

Practise each line twice.
Practise as quickly as you can.

Common Words

1 full add seek ask rule lots king bag yet

2 four each class space fuss more rose wet

3 back iron such easy make job man tar raw

4 girl near rule just spell age say credit

Practise each line once.
Repeat or take two
15-s timings on each line.

Drill and Practice

5 We took out five books from the library.

6 Jo Anne lost her cheque on the way home.

7 Add up the last four columns of figures.

8 He hopes to visit Calgary in the spring.

Drill on Postal Codes

Set tab stops 16 and 32 spaces from the left margin.

9	T5J 0B3	M5K 1E9	T2P 0J4
10	R3B 0B6	S7K 1J5	P6A 5P2
11	V8A 2Z2	H3C 2H2	E1C 1E7
12	B3J 3C4	N1H 6L7	B0K 1S0

        ↑   ↑
       Tab   Tab

Reach to the - Key

13 ;p; ;0; ;-; ;-; -;- --; ;;- ;p; ;0; ;-;-

14 mid-term exams; well-to-do; right-handed

Drill on the - Key

Practise each line twice.

■ Use periods without
spacing when abbreviating
compass points.
Example: S.W.

15 a one-way street; three well-known books

16 Drop me off at The Regency, 53 - 183 St.

17 They lived at 9 - 39 Ave. S.W., Calgary.

· · · · 1 · · · · 2 · · · · 3 · · · · 4 · · · · 5 · · · · 6 · · · · 7 · · · · 8

Bibliographies / Title Pages

Format

60-character line
Single spacing

Practise each line twice.
Practise as quickly as you can.

Left-Hand Words

1 tea stress baggage water sweeter greets verse cases exact as

2 raw best face card extra drawer street grease average regret

Evaluate Your Progress

Skill Building

Practise at a controlled rate.
Circle your errors. Do Speed
Improvement if you had three
errors or less. Do Accuracy
Improvement if you had four
errors or more.

3   For untold centuries people have kept track of the days

by the march of daylight and darkness. The changing seasons

indicated when to plant crops and get ready for winter. One

way to keep a record of time was to notch a stick or to knot

a cord once every day. The movement of the sun and stars, a

change in the moon, and the habits of plants and animals can

indicate the passage of time. Today we have our calendars.

· · · ·1· · · ·2· · · ·3· · · ·4· · · ·5· · · ·6· · · ·7· · · ·8· · · ·9· · · ·10· · · ·11· · · ·12

Accuracy Improvement

Think **accuracy**. Take two 15-s
timings on each line. Take two
30-s timings on the complete
set of lines.

4 been carry offends vaccine smaller accurate written arrivals

5 aid fight icicle problem profit Pamela formal fog theory big

6 act east west edge tease average agree gates faded bread wet

7 Sherri called to assure us that a bigger wedding is planned.

Speed Improvement

8 If this matter cannot be settled, it will be referred to me.

9 Our costs of production have increased more than our output.

10 Our production costs have steadily increased in three years.

11 In the first place, we told them that we would arrive later.

Try to do each timing faster.
Take two 15-s timings on each
set of two lines. Take two 30-s
timings on the complete set of
lines.
■ Do Evaluate Your Progress
and determine if you have
improved.

Number Practice

12 They ate 24 pieces of pie with a 10 cm arc and 11 cm radius.

13 A little car may use 8 L of gas per 100 km on a 15 997 trip.

· · · ·1· · · ·2· · · ·3· · · ·4· · · ·5· · · ·6· · · ·7· · · ·8· · · ·9· · · ·10· · · ·11· · · ·12

Vertical Centring

Vertical centring means that the blank space at the top and bottom of a page is equal.

To Calculate the Starting Line:

1. Count the total number of lines and blank spaces to be used.

```
HOW TO TELL A LOON FROM A DUCK          1
                                        2
TS                                      3
                                        
        Loons have larger and longer bodies    4
    than ducks.  The loon's bill is sharply     5
    pointed; the duck's is round-tipped and     6
    flat.  There's no confusing the sounds:     7
    ducks quack, but the loon's cry can be      8
    a lonely wail, a frenzied laugh, or an      9
    eerie yodel.                                10
```

2. Subtract this total from the number of lines on a full sheet *or* on a half sheet of paper.
   Note: A full sheet of paper contains 66 lines, and a half sheet of paper contains 33 lines.

Full Sheet	Half Sheet
66 − 10 = 56	33 − 10 = 23

3. Divide your answer by two, dropping any fraction.
   56 ÷ 2 = 28   23 ÷ 2 = 11

4. Add 1 to your answer to calculate the starting line.
   28 + 1 = 29   11 + 1 = 12

Note: The status line on your computer monitor indicates the line number and character position at which the cursor is positioned on a sheet of paper.

Read your software and printer manuals to determine the defaults for the top and bottom margins. This could change your calculations.

Three- or Five-Minute Timing

Assess Your Progress

Set for double spacing. Take two 3-min *or* two 5-min timings. Circle all errors. Calculate Gross Words Per Minute (GWPM).
Record your best timing on your personal progress chart.

	1	CW	3
When duties on the job are performed well and please an	12	12	4
employer, one can expect to earn respect and esteem. It can	24	24	8
be a special feeling to be a valuable member of a successful	36	36	12
business team. The business world provides many chances for	48	48	16
personal growth as well as career advancement. One can move	60	60	20
to positions that offer increased salaries and challenges.	71	71	24
In this modern world, a good education is required. An	12	83	28
employer will require that young people write and speak very	24	95	32
fluently, read for meaning and understanding, and work under	36	107	36
stress. In addition, it is necessary to have enough general	48	119	40
knowledge to engage in various conversations. Remember, the	60	131	44
business world welcomes people who can meet these standards.	72	143	48
Graduates from business programs are lucky to have both	12	155	52
general knowledge and special skills. These skills are very	24	167	56
much in demand and are readily saleable to employers. It is	36	179	60
important to have the "tools of the business world." It may	48	191	64
be helpful to secure a minor position in an office and learn	60	203	68
on the job. Advancement comes with experience.	69	212	71

SI 1.55

· · · ·1· · · ·2· · · ·3· · · ·4· · · ·5· · · ·6· · · ·7· · · ·8· · · ·9· · · ·10· · · ·11· · · ·12   1 min

       1   2   3   4   3 min

Production

Set a 40-character line. Vertically centre an exact copy of the following paragraphs. Observe the symbols for correct spacing.

KOREAN SPORTS
                    TS
¶   Spectator and player sports are very

popular in Korea. Baseball, volleyball,

and judo are the most popular. Many are

also attracted to basketball, table tennis,

swimming, soccer, tennis, archery, shoot-

ing, skating, skiing, boxing, wrestling,

golf, and judo, which is called yudo in

Korea.
                    DS
¶   Ssirum and taekwondo, native sports

of Korea, also have many followers. The

Korean government has taken a keen interest

in fostering sports to promote physical

fitness and participation at international

events. In 1988, the 24th Summer Olympic

Games were held in Seoul, South Korea.

Two-Minute Timing

		1	2
Try to be pleasant to everyone that		8	4
you meet. Being kind to others does not		16	8
take extra time. It takes only a little		24	12
effort to smile, even if you are feeling		32	16
low. Each of us has days when things go		40	20
wrong, but we do not have to take it out		48	24
on the next person. Smiling makes you a		56	28
happier person.		59	29

· · · · 1 · · · · 2 · · · · 3 · · · · 4 · · · · 5 · · · 6 · · · · 7 · · · · 8   1 min
            1   2   3   4   2 min

■ Did you ask your teacher if the word wrap should be *off*?

Timing

Set for double spacing. Take two 2-min timings. Circle all errors. Calculate Gross Words Per Minute (GWPM). Record your best timing on your personal progress chart.

SI 1.27

The Game

  Each participant acquires imaginary characteristics by rolling a number of six-sided dice. This procedure establishes such qualities as strength, intelligence, dexterity, and charisma.

  A referee (Dungeon Master) oversees the playing of the game. With dungeon map, handbooks, combat tables, and monster lists, the DM creates the fantasy world in which all action takes place. Only the Dungeon Master knows where treasure is buried and where danger lies.

  As the game progresses, players proceed through the dungeon, trying to accumulate treasure, grow in power and skill, and stay alive. In the course of their travels, players may be confronted by monsters with such names as Gorgon, Purple Worm, and Barracuda.

  D & D is not usually played at one sitting—it is an ongoing campaign with each playing session linked to the next. As players build the experience level of their characters, they face stronger monsters and more difficult problems.

  Rules are not cut and dried. Books and manuals only suggest guidelines and methods. The game is limited only by the inventiveness and imagination of the players. "Swords and sorcery best describe what this game is all about, for those are the two key fantasy ingredients."[2]

---

[2] Gary Gygax, _Advanced Dungeons & Dragons_ (Lake Geneva, Wisconsin: TSR Games, 1978), p. 7.

■ Do you have a bottom margin of 6-10 lines?

Unit Review

Format
40-character line
Single spacing

Take two 30-s timings on each line. Do each phrase as quickly as you can.

Common Phrases

1 of the/to it/from them/at home/of course/

2 in it/from this/at once/on time/of every/

3 more than/for one/if possible/not always/

4 on end/to avoid/as they are/all the time/

Practise each line once.
Repeat or take two
15-s timings on each line.

Drill and Practice

5 Buy butter and bread if you go shopping.

6 Will you play soccer with us on Tuesday?

7 The sponsors will buy the team sweaters.

8 Our order should be sent in a day or so.

Number Drill and Practice

Practise each line once.
Practise each line again.

9 Call him today before 12:00 at 239-0702.

10 Does he need the 57 cases by October 13?

11 Liz's code is V5H 3Z7; Rob's is V6B 4A8.

12 Meet us at 10476 Jasper Avenue at 18:00.
····1····2····3····4····5····6····7····8

Spacing Review

No space before or after: apostrophe in a word   '
diagonal   /
degree sign for temperature   °
hyphen   -

Spacing Drill and Practice

Practise each line once.
Repeat or take two
15-s timings on each line.

13 Cam's guitar needs a new set of strings.

14 They changed the speed limit to 80 km/h.

15 The child's temperature dropped to 38°C.

16 These man-made fabrics are quite strong.
····1····2····3····4····5····6····7····8

Steps for Planning Footnotes

1. Use a backing sheet (extended to right of the page) with the numbers in reverse order at the bottom of the page.
2. Start the report.
3. After the first footnote reference, calculate four blank lines (ruling line plus first footnote).
4. Add this number to six (bottom margin).
   6 + 4 = 10
   If there is only one footnote, stop the body of the report ten lines from the bottom of the page. Use the backing sheet as a guide.
5. If there is more than one footnote on a page, add three lines for each additional footnote.

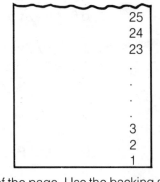

Example: two footnotes 6 + 4 + 3 = 13
Stop 13 lines from the bottom of the page.
Note: Calculate the allowance for the bottom margin as you input your report.

Production

Input the following using report format and footnoting at the bottom of the page. Remember to listen for the right margin signal as the production does not use the standard report line length.

```
                    DUNGEONS & DRAGONS


     Dungeons & Dragons is a fantasy game of role playing.  Players are
adventurers who take on character roles which enable them to explore a
world of monsters and dungeons.


The Background
     D & D was created by E. Gary Gygax, of Lake Geneva, Wisconsin in
1974.  Gygax started his company, "TSR Hobbies, with a $2000
investment."1  Currently, TSR sales of D & D products are in the
millions.  These products include books and booklets which contain
rules, lists of possible roles, battle strategies, etc.  Other
related products include colouring books, action figures, jigsaw
puzzles, videos, and a Saturday morning cartoon show.
                 SS↓
                _____
                 DS↓
                   1John Langone, "Dungeons & Dragons Craze," Discover (January,
1981), p. 34.
```

■ Did you start to calculate for the bottom footnote?

■ Did you input the reference number as a superior number?

■ This reference is from a magazine.

■ Put the title of the article in quotation marks.

Editing Practice

17 Brennan plans to go by buss to North bay.

18 The taxes on the porperty are very high

19 Try to finisih the program by nooon today.

20 is the air show on Tuesday or Wenesday?

Production Practice

Production 1

Set a 40-character line. Input the following paragraphs.

CAMPING ETIQUETTE

            TS

¶ Care, cleanliness, and courtesy are important
when camping. By being careful, you reduce the
hazards and discomforts of outdoor living. Keeping
your camp clean discourages insects and animal pests.
By being courteous, you allow others to enjoy
themselves.

            DS
¶ Be especially careful with fire and fuel. Put
out a campfire with water. A courteous camper does
as little damage to the environment as possible and
leaves the campsite clean for others.

↓ SS

↓ SS

■ Did you read the symbols
for spacing?

■ Did you listen for the
right margin signal on your
typewriter?

Composition

Composing Practice

Think and answer as quickly
as you can without hesitating.

How many words can you list which describe the shades of a
primary colour? Begin your list using the colour red, followed
by blue and yellow.

Example: red: rose, scarlet, etc.
          blue: navy, sapphire, etc.
          yellow: lemon, gold, etc.

Footnotes

There are many styles of recognizing material which has been quoted or paraphrased in a report. The reference or footnote may be placed at the bottom of the page where the reference occurs, on a separate page at the back of the report, or within the text (APA style).

Superior Figures

In the body of the report, footnotes are indicated by a superior figure after the reference. No space is left between the word and the superior figure.

In the footnote reference at the bottom of the page, the footnote number is input as a superior figure before the reference. No space is left between the superior figure and the reference.

Placing the Footnote at the Bottom of the Page

1. Separate the body of the report and the footnotes by a horizontal line 18 characters (elite) or 15 characters (pica).
2. Leave one space above and one space below the horizontal line.
3. Leave a bottom margin of 6-10 lines after the last footnote on the page.
   - Single space the reference. Indent the first line of the footnote by five spaces. The second and subsequent lines begin at the left margin.
   - Double space between references.

Formatting Guide for Footnotes

(Know the preference in your area of Canada.)

Style 1

```
This is the last line of text.
    SS
    _____
    DS
   5   Author, Book Title (City of Publication:  Publisher, Date of
Publication), page number.
```

Format:

Example:

```
   1Steven N. Spetz, Take Notice, Third Edition (Toronto: Copp Clark
Pitman, 1989), page 264.
```

Style 2

```
This is the last line of text.
    SS
    _____
    DS
   5   Author, Book Title, Publisher, City of Publication, Date of
Publication, page number.
```

Format:

Example:

```
   1Steven N. Spetz, Take Notice, Third Edition, Copp Clark Pitman,
Toronto, 1989, p. 264.
```

Production 2

Set a 40-character line. Vertically centre an exact copy of the following paragraphs.

HIKING

TS

¶   To some, a hike is an easy stroll along a well-marked trail. To others, it is a vigorous trek up a mountain.

DS ¶   All you need to enjoy the sport is a sturdy pair of boots and a healthy respect for the wilderness. Light walking boots or ankle-high sneakers are good for hiking along clearly marked trails. Heavier boots will protect the feet and support ankles when hiking over rough areas or when carrying a heavy load.

Two-Minute Timing

1 2

Many are learning to count by using an old method for counting. This method uses the hands. Each of the fingers has a value. Many can add and subtract, but do not know the basis of computing. The modern term is fingermath.

	1	2
	8	4
	16	8
	24	12
	32	16
	40	20
	45	23

. . . 1 . . . 2 . . . 3 . . . 4 . . . 5 . . . 6 . . . 7 . . . 8   1 min

    1   2   3   4   2 min

Timing

Set for double spacing. Take two 2-min timings. Circle all errors. Calculate Gross Words Per Minute (GWPM). Record your best timing on your personal progress chart.

SI 1.4

Reports with Footnotes

Format
60-character line
Single spacing

Practise each line twice.
Practise as quickly as you can.

Right-Hand Words

1 joy moon mink pulp lymph kimono opinion link kiln hill on my

2 you join milk phony minimum oily plum link pin hip ink union

Evaluate Your Progress

3   Coal is the wood of the ancient forests which once grew

on almost all of the earth, long before humans appeared. It

is the result of the decay of plants in the long-ago swamps.

Forests died and fell. New growth appeared and slowly layer

upon layer of decayed plants were built up. The upper areas

pressed more and more heavily on the ones underneath. Years

later, after many changes in the earth, coal was formed.

• • • •1• • • •2• • • •3• • • •4• • • •5• • • •6• • • •7• • • •8• • • •9• • • •10• • • •11• • • •12

Skill Building

Practise at a controlled rate.
Circle your errors. Do Speed
Improvement if you had three
errors or less. Do Accuracy
Improvement if you had four
errors or more.

Accuracy Improvement

4 wax gave cast brew aware feet regret straw axe raw wart drew

5 ink pony lily honk pumpkin imply poll poppy plumk Phillip up

6 key lamb gown risk them height bicycle divine right worn eye

7 Ella offered vanilla pudding and ginger cookies for dessert.

Think **accuracy**. Take two 15-s
timings on each line. Take two
30-s timings on the complete
set of lines.

Speed Improvement

8 It was difficult for him to say no to her when she returned.

9 Take out the six papers that were returned to you yesterday.

10 Sooner or later she will have to learn how to relate to him.

11 Most students enjoy the two happy summer months best of all.

Try to do each timing faster.
Take two 15-s timings on each
set of two lines. Take two 30-s
timings on the complete set of
lines.
■ Do Evaluate Your Progress
and determine if you have
improved.

Number Practice

12 They received his letter dated 1989 08 17 with invoice 5B27.

13 This milk can be purchased in 3 L, 4 L, and 18 L containers.

• • • •1• • • •2• • • •3• • • •4• • • •5• • • •6• • • •7• • • •8• • • •9• • • •10• • • •11• • • •12

Practise each line once.
Practise each line again.

Evaluate Your Progress

Format
40-character line
Single spacing
Practise each line twice.
Practise as quickly as you can.

Common Words

1 went much your stay rest clean tame cake

2 blew side much jobs rate play brave kick

Practise each line once.
Repeat *or* take two
15-s timings on each line.

Drill and Practice

3 We must try to mail the cheques on time.

4 Many of us want to take this new course.

Number Drill and Practice

5 Our SIDEWALK SALE will be held on May 9.

6 Kurt's temperature rose to 40.5°C today.

7 Drive to The Sheraton at 135 Bay Street.

8 I must call Pietro at 432-9871 by 15:00.

9 Terms for these invoices are 2/10, n/30.

· · · · 1 · · · · 2 · · · · 3 · · · · 4 · · · · 5 · · · · 6 · · · · 7 · · · · 8

Production Practice

Production 1

Set a 40-character line. Input the following paragraphs.

QUICK DECORATING IDEAS

TS

¶   Do you need a laundry bag? Use an old pair
of jeans. Place darks in one leg and lights in the
other. Tie off or sew the bottom of the legs so that
laundry won't tumble out. Add a belt for lugging
to the laundry room.

DS

¶   Stack your art or hobby supplies on a
plastic turntable. It can be spun around to find
what you need in just a few seconds.

DS

¶   Glue together several disposable cardboard
milk cartons, after removing the pouring spout
area. Decorate the outside with gift-wrap,
wallpaper, etc. Use to store shoes or winter
gloves and scarves.

■ Did you listen for the right margin signal on your typewriter?

Set for double spacing. Take two 3-min *or* two 5-min timings. Circle all errors. Calculate Gross Words Per Minute (GWPM).
Record your best timing on your personal progress chart.

■ *Colors* or *colours*. Know the preference in your area of Canada.

SI 1.33

Three- or Five-Minute Timing

		1	CW	3

People who study the meaning of choice of color and the | 12 | 12 | 4

effect color has upon us state we do not select our favorite | 24 | 24 | 8

color as we grow up. They say we are born with a preference | 36 | 36 | 12

that stays with us for a long time. Colors often change our | 48 | 48 | 16

moods, making us happy, sad, tired, or relaxed. | 57 | 57 | 19

People who like yellow, orange, or red look on the good | 12 | 69 | 23

side of life. They are active people who are often leaders. | 24 | 81 | 27

People who like grey and blue are often quiet and shy. They | 36 | 93 | 31

would rather follow than lead others. People who like brown | 48 | 105 | 35

or green are said to prefer things that are plain and basic. | 60 | 117 | 39

Light and bright colors seem pleasant to us and make us | 12 | 129 | 43

happy and more active. Factory workers work harder and have | 24 | 141 | 47

fewer accidents on machines painted orange rather than black | 36 | 153 | 51

or dark grey. A yellow room makes most people more cheerful | 48 | 165 | 55

and relaxed than a dark green one. A red dress or shirt can | 60 | 177 | 59

bring warmth and laughter to a freezing winter day. | 70 | 187 | 62

· · · 1 · · · 2 · · · 3 · · · 4 · · · 5 · · · 6 · · · 7 · · · 8 · · · 9 · · · 10 · · · 11 · · · 12   1 min

1   2   3   4   3 min

Production 2

Set a 40-character line. Vertically centre an exact copy of the following paragraphs.

MOTORCYCLING

TS

Motorcycling is one of the fastest growing sports and means of transportation. Unfortunately, the number of motorcycle drivers and passengers killed and injured has also been increasing at a

DS

rapid rate.

As a motorcyclist, you must drive defensively at all times. A motorcycle is one of the smallest vehicles on the road, which makes it harder for truckers and motorists to see it.

Timing

Set for double spacing. Take two 2-min timings. Circle all errors. Calculate Gross Words Per Minute (GWPM). Record your best timing on your personal progress chart.

SI 1.2

Two-Minute Timing

	1	2
She ran to the front window and sat	8	4
down. She jumped up and wagged her long	16	8
thin tail. Squeals of joy were heard as	24	12
she danced about. She paused and rested	32	16
her nose on the sill. The grey squirrel	40	20
chattered and ran around an old oak tree	48	24
outside the window. It was a daily game	56	28
between two old friends, a black dog and	64	32
a grey squirrel.	67	34

```
. . . . 1 . . . . 2 . . . . 3 . . . . 4 . . . . 5 . . . 6 . . . . 7 . . . . 8     1 min
            1              2              3              4                2 min
```

Production 2

Set a 60-character line and double spacing. Remember to listen for the right margin signal if you are using a typewriter as the production uses a different line length. Input each of the following paragraphs including capitals according to the capitalization rules.

the peace tower forms part of the main entrance to the parliament buildings in ottawa and commemorates canada's contribution in people and treasure in world war i.

disney world is a theme amusement park located in central florida, between the cities of orlando and kissimmee. disney world is as large as the city of san francisco.

the canadian armed forces is canada's sixth largest employer. the following training plans are available through the canadian forces for high school graduates: the regular officer training plan (rotp), the officer candidate training plan (octp), the medical officer training plan (motp), the dental officer training plan (dotp), and the career trades plans.

on saturday, we have an appointment to have our pet dog, rags, vaccinated. our veterinarian, dr. richardson, has his animal clinic in brampton on king street.

puma has marketed a unique running shoe. the shoe, originally available in the u.s., has a built-in computer microchip that measures distance and calories used during a run. at home the runner plugs one end of a cable into the heel of the shoe and the other end into an apple iie or commodore 64 computer.

the resource centre in our school has just ordered a subscription for the magazine, discover, which is a monthly publication about science. it is published by time incorporated. time also publishes fortune, life, people, and sports illustrated.

george crum, an american indian, accidentally invented the potato chip in 1853 when he was working as a chef at an elegant resort in saratoga springs, new york. the french fried potatoes he made kept being sent back to the kitchen by someone who claimed that they were much too thick. crum decided to cut the slices so thin you could see through them. he then fried them to crispness in boiling fat. they became the specialty of the house.

Unit II

Objectives

By completing this unit *you* will:

1 Develop speed and accuracy on alphabetic and numeric copy.

2 Learn the use of editors' symbols.

3 Learn and apply the rules for metric expressions.

4 Learn and apply the rules for hyphenation.

5 Learn to format material on a page using horizontal centring, spread centring, block centring, and vertical centring.

6 Learn to format open tables without column headings.

7 Learn to format open tables with blocked column headings, *or* open tables with centred column headings, *or* both.

8 Learn to format programs.

9 Learn the use of leaders.

10 Work toward developing a minimum speed of 25 words per minute with four or fewer errors on a two-minute timing.

Note: Additional production practice for this unit may be found on page 332.

This includes practice using the numeric key pad, three production exercises for horizontal and vertical centring, three production exercises for tables, and one production exercise for programs.

Bibliographies

A bibliography is an alphabetic listing of all the works consulted by an author when writing a report. This includes all works cited in the footnotes.

Formatting Guide for Bibliographies

1. Alphabetize the list of books, articles, etc.
2. Input the bibliography on a full sheet of paper.
3. Use the same margins as were used in the report.
   - Centre the title in capital letters on line 13 followed by a triple space.
   - Single space each reference. Indent the second and subsequent lines of the reference five spaces.
   - Double space between references.

   Author's surname, first name and initials. <u>Book title.</u>   City of Publication: Publisher, Date of publication.

   Ubelacker, Sandra D., et al. <u>Keyboarding for Canadian Colleges.</u>
   [5] Toronto: Copp Clark Pitman, 1990.

Production Practice

Production 1

Input the following bibliography on a full sheet of paper. Use the same margins that were used for reports. Remember to listen for the right margin signal if you are using a typewriter as the production does not use the standard report line length.

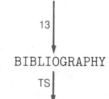

13

BIBLIOGRAPHY

TS

SS| Brown, Darrel R. "Ch-Ch-Ch-Change!?," <u>Drake Business Review</u>, Vol.
   [5] 3, No. 2 (May, 1988), 28.

Cake, Leslie and Daniel Stewart. <u>Problem Solving with Basic.</u>
   Toronto: Addison-Wesley Publishers Limited, 1986.

Crawford, Tim and Gail Hook. <u>Computer Literacy.</u> Toronto: McGraw-
   Hill Ryerson Limited, 1982.

Noonan, Larry. <u>The Age of Computer Literacy.</u> Toronto: Oxford
   University Press, 1983.

Horizontal Centring

Format
50-character line
Single spacing

Practise each line twice.
Practise as quickly as you can.

Skill Building

Practise each line once.
Repeat *or* take two
15-s timings on each line.

Practise each line once.
Practise each line again.

Practise each underlined word
four times. Practise each line
once concentrating on the
underlined words.

Metric Rules

Read the Metric Rules.
Practise each line twice,
concentrating on the Metric
Rules.

Alternate-Hand Words

1 if us end she tug and pep they soap alto half city

2 it by the aid cob for big dial both them cowl foam

Common-Word Sentences

3 I could see the giant corn fields in the distance.

4 As the invoice arrived late, it will be paid late.

5 I have a book that will help us with that problem.

Sentences with Numbers

6 Number these: 21, 28, 35, 38, 44, 47, 52, and 96.

7 Send 20 cakes, 61 hats, and 37 games to the party.

Spelling Practice

8 The length of the article depends on many factors.

9 His niece will be taking her holidays in February.

· · · · 1 · · · · 2 · · · · 3 · · · · 4 · · · · 5 · · · · 6 · · · · 7 · · · · 8 · · · · 9 · · · · 10

Metric Rules

Rule 1: Use symbols for the metric terms when units are expressed in numbers.

Example:

83 kg (not 83 kilograms)

Rule 2: Metric symbols remain the same to indicate singular or plural.

Example:

1 kg   8 kg

Rule 3: Leave one space between the quantity and the symbol (except when
expressing temperature).

Example:

90 km/h   but 30°C

10 23 mm in diameter; a mass of 250 g; the 100 m dash

11 a 150 mL tube of toothpaste; 180 cm tall; 100 km/h

12 a door 2 m high; a 40 km distance; 300 mL of juice

13 temperature of 19°C; a metre ahead; a 10 kg turkey

14 a gain of a kilogram; 65 km from Toronto; low 21°C

· · · · 1 · · · · 2 · · · · 3 · · · · 4 · · · · 5 · · · · 6 · · · · 7 · · · · 8 · · · · 9 · · · · 10

Bibliographies

Format
60-character line
Single spacing

Practise each line twice.
Practise as quickly as you can.

Skill Building

Practise at a controlled rate.
Circle your errors. Do Speed
Improvement if you had three
errors or less. Do Accuracy
Improvement if you had four
errors or more.

Think **accuracy**. Take two 15-s
timings on each line. Take two
30-s timings on the complete
set of lines.

Try to do each timing faster.
Take two 15-s timings on each
set of two lines. Take two 30-s
timings on the complete set of
lines.
■ Do Evaluate Your Progress
and determine if you have
improved.

Practise each line once.
Practise each line again.

Alternate-Hand Words

1 end the girl hair sleigh title shape wish dial melt hem when

2 or city pant world profit rich also make eight laugh duck if

Evaluate Your Progress

3   A piece of mica 250 mm thick can be further sliced into

nearly a thousand sheets, each as thin as tissue paper. Old

stove and furnace windows, lanterns, and lamp chimneys often

had mica in them. Today it is a necessary material for many

electronic and electrical industries. Mica is a single name

for nine silicate minerals. These minerals crystallize in a

book-like form with perfect cleavage or divisions.

· · · ·1· · · ·2· · · ·3· · · ·4· · · ·5· · · ·6· · · ·7· · · ·8· · · ·9· · · ·10· · · ·11· · · ·12

Accuracy Improvement

4 few draw vast ward start secret tweezer deserter rate exceed

5 sir lake duck sign eight chapel orient burlap apricot disown

6 free shall agreed fully school support allowed looking three

7 Green moss grew inside the fallen trees on the forest floor.

Speed Improvement

8 I am almost certain that I did mail those letters yesterday.

9 Turn on the lights in your backyard as soon as it gets dark.

10 Savings will result if the costs are kept to a bare minimum.

11 She told me that she had read four books in only two months.

Number Practice

12 On May 29, Cycle 74 had a $16.85 connect charge for 30 days.

13 Most small fruit comes in 2 L, 10 L, and 15 L boxes or bags.

· · · ·1· · · ·2· · · ·3· · · ·4· · · ·5· · · ·6· · · ·7· · · ·8· · · ·9· · · ·10· · · ·11· · · ·12

Basic English

can: ability or power
may: permission

15 (Can, May) I go to the game with Kathy tonight?

16 I'm not sure I (can, may) operate this machine properly.

17 (Can, May) you read that street sign from this distance?

Horizontal Centring

Horizontal centring means the blank space to the right and left of each line is equal.

To Horizontally Centre:

1. Determine the horizontal centre point on a sheet of paper which will be inserted in your typewriter OR Determine the horizontal centre point on your monitor which will be the centre point when your file is printed.

2. Tab to the centre point.

3. Backspace one for every two letters, numbers, and spaces in the word or phrase to be centred.

   Examples:

   ```
        M a t h
         ∪   ∪
      M a t h  10
       ∪   ∪   ∪ *
   ```

   *Do not backspace for any odd letter or number left at the end of the line.

4. Input the word(s).

   ```
        M a t h
      M a t h  10
   ```

5. Master the Backspace Method.

Production 1

Using the Backspace Method, centre each line of the display horizontally. Read the symbols.

```
TS ↓      SUN SIGNS

             Aries
             Taurus
             Gemini
             Cancer
              Leo
             Virgo
             Libra
            Scorpio
          Sagittarius
           Capricorn
           Aquarius
            Pisces
```

Production 2

Using the Backspace Method, centre each line of the display horizontally.

```
TS ↓       GAMES

          Backgammon
      trivial Pursuit
   ≡     Scrabble
         Balderdash
          Pictionary
    The Wall Street Game
           Monopoly
    Dungeons and Dragons
             Zodiac
            chess
             ≡
```

Production

Input the review of Capitalization Rules on a full sheet of paper. Set a 70-character line (elite — 12 pitch) or a 60-character line (pica — 10 pitch). Use the correct format for enumerated material. The title is on line 13. *Note:* This will not be vertically centred.

Capitalization Review

■ Do you have a top/bottom margin default?
■ Do you have an indent option?

Review of Capitalization Rules

1. Capitalize the first word in sentences, direct quotations, and complimentary closings.

2. Capitalize proper nouns such as names of people, places and geographic locations, days of the week and months of the year, holidays, animals, and trade names.

3. Capitalize departments, companies, organizations, historical events or documents, and specific courses in schools or colleges.

4. Capitalize the first word of a title (book, magazine, article, etc.) and all other words, except joining words such as of, to, the, etc.

5. Capitalize titles or degrees that come before or after proper nouns.

6. Capitalize nouns when they are followed by figures or letters indicating sequence. Do not capitalize nouns indicating minor divisions.

7. Capitalize nouns showing family relationship when they are used as specific names or when there is no possessive pronoun in front of mother, father, etc.

Production 3

Centre each line of the display horizontally.

Clubs and Activities

TS↓

Drama Club
Concert Band
Assembly Committee
Library Club
Film Club
Camera Club
Auditorium Technical Crew
Student Council Reps
Cheerleaders
Announcement Committee
Chess Club
Yearbook Staff

Timing

Set for double spacing. Take two 2-min timings. Circle all errors. Calculate Gross Words Per Minute (GWPM). Record your best timing on your personal progress chart.

SI 1.38

Two-Minute Timing

	1	2

From earliest times we have relied on forests
for shelter and trade. The first settlers came to
Canada in wooden ships. They cleared forests when
they built homes and farm areas. They built tools
from the wood and also used it to build houses and
barns. Fur traders, loggers, lumber merchants and
farmers were the first to enjoy all the benefits a
forest provides.

1	2
10	5
20	10
30	15
40	20
50	25
60	30
70	35
73	36

. . . . 1 . . . . 2 . . . . 3 . . . . 4 . . . . 5 . . . 6 . . . . 7 . . . . 8 . . . . 9 10   1 min
    1   2   3   4   5   2 min

Selected Number Practice

1. Circle all errors in the Sentence with Numbers.
2. From your errors, choose the number or numbers which gave you difficulty.
3. Select the appropriate drill lines in the Selected Number Practice.
4. Practise each line twice concentrating on accuracy.
5. If you had no errors in the Sentences with Numbers, or if you complete the accuracy lines before your teacher calls **time**, start at line 0 and **push** for speed. Practise each line once.

After Selected Number Practice, take two 1-min timings on the Sentences with Numbers and determine if you have improved.

1 59 1 not 11 or 12 like 111 as 1 but 1 211 for 11 now 1 then 111

2 60 the 22 and 2 as 12 for 212 not 22 or 2 212 but 2 of 222 as 2

3 61 all 3 of 333 and 31 my 33 a 3 on 3 233 for 3 not 33 or 3 313

4 62 4 of 44 the 41 for 4 414 a 4 not 14 is 44 but 444 as 4 of 44

5 63 a 5 or 55 by 525 for 51 and 5 in 5 155 but 55 like 15 and 55

6 64 6 will 61 for 6 626 not 66 as 16 and 6 but 616 as 62 then 66

7 65 but 7 or 77 as 17 for 7 177 and 7 717 all 7 a 77 in 727 of 7

8 66 8 for 8 and 828 as 88 in 818 will 82 an 8 but 8 818 by 8 281

9 67 the 9 in 99 for 919 as 9 not 9 991 is 99 but 9 929 as 9 a 99

0 68 0 and for 02 or 010 but 0 like 100 in 100 in 1 020 and 0 a 0

· · · ·1· · · ·2· · · ·3· · · ·4· · · ·5· · · ·6· · · ·7· · · ·8· · · ·9· · ·10· · · ·11· · · ·12

Assess Your Progress

Graduated Speed Practice

1. Turn to Lesson 81, page 264.
2. Drill on the appropriate Graduated Speed Practice

Vertical Centring Review

Format

50-character line
Single spacing
Practise each line twice.
Practise as quickly as you can.

One-Hand Words

1 in on mop tar wax milk art noon debt bet rear pill

2 as in tab fat lip pup set mink grew verb hill race

Skill Building

Practise each line once.
Repeat *or* take two
15-s timings on each line.

Common-Word Sentences

3 A lazy worker will be very bored most of the time.

4 The mouse watched as she set the trap with cheese.

5 Did you see the red fox behind a bush on the hill?

Sentences with Numbers

6 Par on hole 6 is 5, but he needed 3 extra strokes.

7 She reserved Room 927 at least 30 days in advance.

Edit each line by correcting
two errors.
Practise each line once with
the corrections.

Editing Practice

8 Are you sure? I thought the test was no Thursday.

9 Uranium isused as the fuell for the CANDU reactor.

10 Pembroke and Cobden are Located in renfrew County.

· · · · 1 · · · · 2 · · · · 3 · · · · 4 · · · · 5 · · · · 6 · · · · 7 · · · · 8 · · · · 9 · · · · 10

Metric Rules

Rule 4: Do not put a period after the metric symbol unless the symbol ends the sentence.

Example:

His sleeve length is 80 cm and his neck size is 40 cm.

Rule 5: Numbers less than one should be expressed in decimals, with a zero placed to the left of the decimal marker.

Examples:

0.75 kg   0.36 cm

Rule 6: Spaces are used to separate numbers into groups of three. Whole numbers below 10 000 may be input without the space.

Examples:

12 000 people   4 000 or 4000 people

T 43 ticket treat turtle not typist table trout tremendous better

44 The telephone is a vital instrument of verbal communication.

U 45 until usual ugly understand uncle bug upper unless universal

46 The university offered an unusual course on underwater life.

V 47 vane valve vapour ivory violin vowel vacant value volley ivy

48 Ava visited the villa very often because she loved the view.

W 49 window awake wall owe winter power worry aware western where

50 Wendy will work as a waitress for several weeks this summer.

X 51 text fox except index exhaust oxygen luxury expect tax exact

52 Explain these unexpected expenses for the roadway extension.

Y 53 yodel yarn young jolly yard yacht tyrant yoke yeast try yell

54 Many travel to Egypt to study the mysteries of the pyramids.

Z 55 zodiac zoo zone razor zero bazaar zoom jazz doze size amazed

56 Lizzy was amazed at the size of the zebras in the Metro Zoo.

• • • • 1 • • • • 2 • • • • 3 • • • • 4 • • • • 5 • • • • 6 • • • 7 • • • • 8 • • • • 9 • • • •10• • • •11• • • •12

Sentences with Numbers

Take two 1-min timings on each sentence. Circle all errors.

57 By 1997 they will have 430 varieties in their 1652 branches.

58 Are 123, 09, 654, and 78 the 4 sets of adjacent number keys?

Read the Metric Rules. Practise each line twice, concentrating on the Metric Rules.

11 The weather forecast predicts a snowfall of 30 cm.

12 Did that recipe call for 175 mL of flour or sugar?

13 The cereal contained 14.1 mg of iron and thiamine.

14 I believe that 17 500 people attended the concert.

15 Which form does Dr. Kimoto prefer: 4 000 or 4000?

· · · · 1 · · · · 2 · · · · 3 · · · · 4 · · · · 5 · · · · 6 · · · · 7 · · · · 8 · · · · 9 · · · · 10

Vertical Centring Review

To Calculate the Starting Line:

1. Count the total number of lines and blank spaces to be used.

```
              LESSON 27              1
          TS |                       2
             |                       3
             ↓
          One-Hand Words            4
      Common-Word Sentences         5
      Sentences with Numbers        6
         Editing Practice           7
           Metric Rules             8
```

2. Subtract this total from the number of lines on a full sheet *or* on a half sheet of paper.
   Note: A full sheet of paper contains 66 lines, and a half sheet of paper contains 33 lines.

Full Sheet	Half Sheet
66 − 8 = 58	33 − 8 = 25

3. Divide your answer by two, dropping any fraction.
   58 ÷ 2 = 29   25 ÷ 2 = 12

4. Add 1 to your answer to calculate the starting line.
   29 + 1 = 30   12 + 1 = 13

Note: The status line on your monitor indicates the line number and character position at which the cursor is positioned on a sheet of paper.

Read your software and printer manuals to determine the defaults for the top and bottom margins. This could change your calculations.

H 19 health half home ahead why hard heir hurray phony his height

20 Hugh was happy to help the three men with the heavy machine.

I 21 insist icing opinion itch imitate iron increase instruct ink

22 I am going to visit the International Institute next spring.

J 23 jaunt jazz join jangle junior object jump judge jester jumbo

24 Jennifer strongly objected to joining the junior jazz group.

K 25 Kodak remark truck kid take bake knife knock kangaroo karate

26 Kindly keep the kitten in the kitchen until Kiki comes home.

L 27 largely label public still loss align let lateral level will

28 The little league players learned the principle of the game.

M 29 memory music summer symptom make maximum major magician more

30 The motors must be moved to make room for the latest models.

N 31 noun cannon none lantern new nest knock many northern newest

32 I cannot name any of the new neighbours, but Nan knows them.

O 33 outdoor often monopoly ooze odour hollow onto apology honour

34 He gave his opponent the opportunity to oppose the decision.

P 35 plate pump plan happy pulp propel up proper people papa past

36 This spring Pamela planted petunias, pansies, and impatiens.

Q 37 quit quotes inquest queen quiz quarter inquire require quiet

38 Quincy requested that the questionnaire be returned quickly.

R 39 error radar rural raspberry ruin orchard respect reward rain

40 Rainy spring weather provided the grain farmers with orders.

S 41 sister spoils stirs sausages ship sinus his senseless spoons

42 Susan says she is sure she passed her summer school courses.

· · · · 1 · · · · 2 · · · · 3 · · · · 4 · · · · 5 · · · · 6 · · · · 7 · · · · 8 · · · · 9 · · · ·10· · · ·11· · · ·12

Production 1

Centre the following display horizontally and vertically on a half sheet of paper.

```
            COMPUTER COMPONENTS
       TS↕   keyboard
        central processing unit
             video monitor
                printer
            hard disk drive
              floppy disk
                modem
```

Production 2

Centre the following display horizontally and vertically on a half sheet of paper.

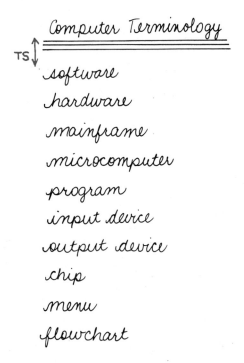

Computer Terminology

TS↕

software

hardware

mainframe

microcomputer

program

input device

output device

chip

menu

flowchart

Production 3

Centre the following display horizontally and vertically on a half sheet of paper.

Student Exchange Programs

TS↕ Japan

China

South Korea

Indonesia

(continued on next page)

Analytical Practice

Format

60-character line
Single spacing

Practise each line twice.
Practise as quickly as you can.

Analyze Your Practice

Take two 1-min timings on
each sentence. Each
sentence contains the
alphabet. Circle all errors.

One-Hand Words

1 gates jump sweater minimum bread nun fade lollipop dread ill

2 setter look eager poppy were hook Teresa link zest lip dress

Alphabetic Sentences

3 Very few phlox grow and bloom just back of that zinc quarry.

4 Baxter snorkels very quietly in the danger zone with jumping

  fish among the jagged coral.

  • • • • 1 • • • • 2 • • • • 3 • • • • 4 • • • • 5 • • • 6 • • • • 7 • • • • 8 • • • 9 • • • •10 • • • •11 • • • •12

Selected Letter Practice

1. Circle all errors in the Alphabetic Sentences.
2. From your errors, choose the letter or letters which gave you difficulty.
3. Select the appropriate drill lines in the Selected Letter Practice.
4. Practise each line twice concentrating on accuracy.
5. If you had no errors in the Alphabetic Sentences, or if you complete the accuracy lines before your teacher calls **time**, start at line A and **push** for speed. Practise each line once.

After Selected Letter Practice,
take two 1-min timings on each
Alphabetic Sentence and
determine if you have
improved.

A 5 area each an ahead actual yard was about alarm accident asks

  6 Alan amazed Adrienne by eating all the bananas and apricots.

B 7 bank baby barber bubble debt back bring bundle rubbed braves

  8 Bargain with the little boy before you buy the baseball bat.

C 9 can clock face coach hectic ice cream climb catch crack care

  10 It occurred to Cass that the coach's comments were accurate.

D 11 dodge diamond dark deduct ledge drill dew dreams door riders

  12 Muddy dirt roads and deep dark ditches dampened David's day.

E 13 enemy ever renew metre we each eagle erect escape meet every

  14 We agreed to meet with each member of the embassy committee.

F 15 fifteen off fluffy far effect affix four fresh fortify fifty

  16 Is Francesca flying to Florida on the fifteenth of February?

G 17 garage grey long going ignore eight singing game grin giants

  18 Gary agreed to give his geography notes on Germany to Gregg.

  • • • • 1 • • • • 2 • • • • 3 • • • • 4 • • • • 5 • • • 6 • • • • 7 • • • • 8 • • • 9 • • • •10 • • • •11 • • • •12

Malaysia
U.S.S.R.
Brunei
Philippines
Singapore
Thailand
Hong Kong
India

Timing

Set for double spacing. Take two 2-min timings. Circle all errors. Calculate Gross Words Per Minute (GWPM). Record your best timing on your personal progress chart.

CW means cumulative word count.

SI 1.32

Composing Practice

Think and answer as quickly as you can without hesitating.

Two-Minute Timing

1	CW	2

        Her favourite picnic spot was the island. It | 10 | 10 | 5 |
was always cool and peaceful there. Even the trip | 20 | 20 | 10 |
to the island was fun. The ferry boat took people | 30 | 30 | 15 |
from the mainland to the island every half hour. | 40 | 40 | 20 |
        A visit to the island was never dull. Of all | 10 | 50 | 25 |
the choices available, she liked to rent a bike to | 20 | 60 | 30 |
tour the island. A canoe trip was the best method | 30 | 70 | 35 |
of relaxing at the end of the long bike ride. The | 40 | 80 | 40 |
picnic lunch was last on the agenda. | 47 | 87 | 44 |

· · · · 1 · · · · 2 · · · · 3 · · · · 4 · · · · 5 · · · 6 · · · · 7 · · · · 8 · · · · 9 · · · · 10   1 min
         1   2   3   4   5   2 min

Composition

Complete the following sentences, supplying the proper canine breed from the list given.

Collies	Bulldogs	Boxers	Poodles
Greyhounds	Beagles	St. Bernards	Spaniels

1._____ are swift dogs with long heads.

2._____ get their name from Spain.

3._____ rescue people in the Swiss Alps.

4._____ are often named Lassie.

5._____ are often clipped in a fancy way.

Assess Your Progress

Set for double spacing. Take
two 3-min *or* two 5-min timings.
Circle all errors. Calculate
Gross Words Per Minute
(GWPM).
Record your best timing on
your personal progress chart.

Three- or Five-Minute Timing

	1	CW	3

The crocodile, which is found in many tropical zones of the world, is the most feared of all the giant reptiles. In comparison, its alligator cousin is a pussycat. The armour-plated body of the crocodile bends very easily, and it could grow to be around 3 m in length. Crocodiles can move with a lightning speed and can kill a human with a strong lash from the powerful tail.

It is the mouth of the crocodile that is really fright-ening. The jaws can snap shut with immense pressure. Large teeth are set like a row of deadly weapons. These 70 deadly teeth are endlessly replaced as they are lost. Any concerns about the failure of this natural arsenal are not necessary. The 70 huge teeth also intermesh, giving the reptilian mouth the look of a murderous zipper.

Although the teeth do serve the crocodile well, there's a dental problem. Unlike the alligator, this big saurian is without a tongue. This leads to trouble freeing debris from between the teeth. Some crocodiles solved this problem ages ago by forming a partnership with the Egyptian plover. This bird keeps the big reptile's teeth clean by feeding on what-ever food is lodged between the enormous teeth.

1	CW	3
12	12	4
24	24	8
36	36	12
48	48	16
60	60	20
72	72	24
75	75	25
12	87	29
24	99	33
36	111	37
48	123	41
60	135	45
72	147	49
78	153	51
12	165	55
24	177	59
36	189	63
48	201	67
60	213	71
72	225	75
81	235	78

• • • • 1 • • • • 2 • • • • 3 • • • • 4 • • • • 5 • • • 6 • • • 7 • • • • 8 • • • • 9 • • • •10 • • • •11 • • • •12   1 min

1   2   3   4   3 min

SI 1.48

Composition

Using the enumeration method, list detailed directions for one of the following:
1. The route you take to get to your school.
2. The route you take to get to the nearest bank or library.

Composing Practice

Think and answer as quickly
as you can without hesitating.

Spread Centring

Alternate-Hand Words

1 is am tie but air cow eye held then pair slap work

2 or do hen pay toe lay got bowl curl fork worm pans

Common-Word Sentences

3 Rene saw a deer on the hill and took two pictures.

4 The pony was thirsty and walked into the new pool.

5 A dish of milk and meat was prepared for the dogs.

Sentences with Numbers

6 Jody took 12 rock and 6 folk albums to 35 King St.

7 The 27 boys and 35 girls will buy 8 compact discs.

Spelling Practice

8 An athlete must exercise daily to maintain skills.

9 My mother is anxious to have the cabinet finished.

. . . . 1 . . . . 2 . . . . 3 . . . . 4 . . . . 5 . . . . 6 . . . . 7 . . . . 8 . . . . 9 10

Metric Rules

Rule 7: Numeric dating consists of the year, month, and day in descending order, with a space left between each component.

Examples:

1938 04 07   1991 12 30

Rule 8: Times in the day are expressed by four digits, commencing at midnight with 00:00, which is read as **zero hours**. The first two numbers represent the time in hours, followed by a colon. The other two digits represent the number of minutes.

Examples:

06:30   16:00   23:45

10 It took him approximately 0.5 h to climb the hill.

11 Bernice's reply to my letter was dated 1989 03 27.

12 Did Harold say the meeting is scheduled for 09:00?

13 The day train from Vancouver will arrive at 10:23.

14 Our sales conference should last only about 1.5 h.

. . . . 1 . . . . 2 . . . . 3 . . . . 4 . . . . 5 . . . . 6 . . . . 7 . . . . 8 . . . . 9 10

J U N I O R   A C H I E V E M E N T | THE HISTORY OF CANDY AND CHOCOLATE

From Ancient to Modern Times

Prepared for
Your Teacher

Prepared by
Your Name

Your Name
Your School

Date

Date

```
*
*
*
*
*
*
*
*
*
*                                       WEST EDMONTON MALL
*
*
*
*   HOW TO PASS EXAMINATIONS                        X
*
*                                               X   X   X
*
*                                           X   X   X   X   X
*
*                                               X   X   X
*
*   Your Name                                        X
*
*   Subject
*
*
*
*
*                                               Your Name
*                                               Your School
*
*   Date                                            Date
*
*
```

Spread Centring

Spread centring means that **one** blank space is left between each letter in a word and **three** blank spaces are left between words. This is a form of horizontal centring.

Steps for Spread Centring One Word Only

1. Tab to the centre point of your paper.
2. Backspace **once** for each letter in the word. *Ignore the last letter.

c o m p u t i n g

3. Input the word, leaving one space between every letter.

c o m p u t i n g

Production Practice

Production 1

Using the Backspace Method, centre the following display horizontally and vertically on a half sheet of paper. Spread centre the first line.

A T T E N T I O N

TS ↓

Peppi Piccininni
is proud to announce
the grand opening
of
PEPPI'S PIZZA PARLOUR
2647 Islington Avenue
Toronto
Phone 741-8654

14 kkk k8k k*k k** k*k k* k* ki* ki* *k *k **k k** k8*k *k*k k*

15 *one and **two and ***three and ****four and *****five and *

16 *This data is taken from the Canadian Government statistics.

•••••1••••2••••3••••4••••5••••6••••7••••8••••9••••10•••11•••12

Title Pages (Cover Pages)

A title page is the first page of a report. It usually states the report title, author's name, and date. The information is attractively centred using a variety of display techniques. Some display techniques use:

1. Vertical centring
2. Horizontal centring
3. Spread centring
4. Underscoring
5. Designs
6. Borders

General Principle

The title page is blocked or centred with top and bottom margins of at least six lines, and left and right margins of at least six to ten spaces.

Production 1

Select and prepare at least three of the sample title pages.

Production 2

Prepare a title page for the report in Lessons 77-78.

Production 2

Using the Backspace Method, centre the following display attractively on a full sheet of paper.

SKIING TECHNIQUES

TS↓
3 enters

(NOVICE) *spread centre*
Climbing Side-Step
Herring Bone
Snowplow
Snowplow Turns
Traversing

DS↓
(INTERMEDIATE) *spread centre*
Side Slipping
Plow Christie
Stem Christie

DS↓
2 enters
(ADVANCED) *spread centre*
Parallel Christie
Wedeln
Compression Turns

Basic English

access: freedom to approach, enter, or use
excess: more than usual

Read the definition of each word.
Practise each sentence once using the correct word in parentheses.

15 Our school has (access, excess) to the public tennis courts.

16 Airlines charge a fee for any (access, excess) baggage.

17 Only the store manager has (access, excess) to the vault.

· · · · 1 · · · · 2 · · · · 3 · · · · 4 · · · · 5 · · · · 6 · · · · 7 · · · · 8 · · · · 9 · · · · 10

Two-Minute Timing

Timing

Set for double spacing. Take two 2-min timings. Circle all errors. Calculate Gross Words Per Minute (GWPM). Record your best timing on your personal progress chart.

	1	CW	2
Growing plants in the home is not a new idea,	10	10	5
but it has become more popular in recent years. A	20	20	10
large number of people enjoy the feeling of warmth	30	30	15
and brightness that greenery brings to a home. To	40	40	20
others, plant growing is a pleasant hobby.	48	48	24
Plants require very little care. Most plants	10	58	29
need water and light to make them grow, but others	20	68	34
will grow in places that have very little light.	30	78	39

· · · · 1 · · · · 2 · · · · 3 · · · · 4 · · · · 5 · · · · 6 · · · · 7 · · · · 8 · · · · 9 · · · · 10   1 min

1   2   3   4   5   2 min

SI 1.37

* / Title Pages

Format
60-character line
Single spacing

Practise each line twice.
Practise as quickly as you can.

Skill Building

Practise at a controlled rate. Circle your errors. Do Speed Improvement if you had three errors or less. Do Accuracy Improvement if you had four errors or more.

Think **accuracy**. Take two 15-s timings on each line. Take two 30-s timings on the complete set of lines.

Try to do each timing faster. Take two 15-s timings on each set of two lines. Take two 30-s timings on the complete set of lines.
■ Do Evaluate Your Progress and determine if you have improved.

Practise each line once.
Practise each line again.

Alternate-Hand Words

1 he paid turns half land rich worm busy forms lake town works

2 it may when lamb downtown keys blame elbow handy quake theme

Evaluate Your Progress

3   Office productivity has risen by approximately four per

cent in recent years. The costs of operating an office have

increased many times more than productivity. To narrow this

broad gap, word processing is being utilized. The aim is to

produce high quality output at rapid speeds and with reduced

costs. Word processing involves the transformation of ideas

into forms of communication quickly and efficiently.

· · · ·1· · · ·2· · · ·3· · · ·4· · · ·5· · · ·6· · · ·7· · · ·8· · · ·9· · · ·10· · · ·11· · · ·12

Accuracy Improvement

4 in lumpy pumpkin phony minimum up milk lull hop you plump on

5 zoo tree occurred cannot yellow carriage fall arrange better

6 created caves cedar facts carve gate war trades affects wade

7 signal social antique flame whale eighty nap turns snap wipe

Speed Improvement

8 From your statement, it would appear that she paid the bill.

9 For the next few days, he will have to take the bus to work.

10 It occurred to him that the missing address was in the book.

11 Business needs efficient workers who will accept challenges.

Number Practice

12 Some tables are listed on pages 5 and 27; others on page 31.

13 Barb's report states the diameter of the earth is 12 470 km.

· · · ·1· · · ·2· · · ·3· · · ·4· · · ·5· · · ·6· · · ·7· · · ·8· · · ·9· · · ·10· · · ·11· · · ·12

29

Format
50-character line
Single spacing
Practise each line twice.
Practise as quickly as you can.

Format
50-character line
Single spacing
Practise each line twice.
Practise as quickly as you can.

Skill Building

Practise each line once.
Repeat or take two
15-s timings on each line.

Practise each line twice.

Practise each line once.
Practise each line again.

Practise each underlined word
four times. Practise each line
once concentrating on the
underlined words.

Alternate-Hand Words

1 he go fir tub die rib cow dock glow tick slap form

2 us by fox men rob ham dot goal land slam town clay

Common-Word Sentences

3 He opened the books and we looked at the drawings.

4 The ball went to the side that has four big holes.

5 Ken will audit the books of the new branch office.
· · · · 1 · · · · 2 · · · · 3 · · · · 4 · · · · 5 · · · · 6 · · · · 7 · · · · 8 · · · · 9 · · · · 10

Reach to the Dash Key

Strike two hyphens. (Do not space before, after, or in between the hyphens.)

Example:

All large items--desks, chairs, cabinets--must be

moved before the floor can be waxed.

Drill on the Dash Key

6 We need results--instant results--or we must fold.

7 Practice is necessary--daily practice--to improve.

8 Pennies, quarters, dollars--any amount is helpful.

9 The book is out of date--it was published in 1921.

Sentences with Numbers

10 It is 59 - 39 Ave. S.W., Calgary, Alberta T6E 6M7.

11 Bring 36 apples, 18 pears, and 12 plums to school.

Spelling Practice

12 Mr. Rose had to attend an <u>urgent</u> <u>business</u> meeting.

13 The <u>signature</u> <u>appeared</u> across the top of the page.
· · · · 1 · · · · 2 · · · · 3 · · · · 4 · · · · 5 · · · · 6 · · · · 7 · · · · 8 · · · · 9 · · · · 10

Three- or Five-Minute Timing

	1	CW	3
A tapestry is a textile with a woven pattern, and it is	12	12	4
generally used for wall hangings and some carpets. Patterns	24	24	8
are woven right into the textiles, rather than being applied	36	36	12
after the cloth has been woven. Tapestry weavings have been	48	48	16
around for many years, and the industry is still thriving.	59	59	20
The weaving is done on a frame or loom. Original plans	12	71	24
or designs (called cartoons) are worked out in exact detail.	24	83	28
The weaver follows these designs very closely. Most designs	36	95	32
are not the work of the weaver; they are likely commissioned	48	107	36
from a famous artist. Raphael and Goya have many well-known	60	119	40
designs on display in various countries around the world.	71	130	43
Early works used a limited number of colours. Today, a	12	142	47
piece could contain several hundred colours. Subjects range	24	154	51
from Biblical scenes to coats of arms. Mythology, heraldry,	36	166	55
sport, and hunting are popular subjects. French artists had	48	178	59
factories where they designed many tapestries and supervised	60	190	63
the workers. These factories now produce some modern works.	72	202	67

```
• • • •1• • • •2• • • •3• • • •4• • • •5• • • •6• • • •7• • • •8• • • •9• • • •10• • • •11• • • •12      1 min
        1                 2                 3                 4                    3 min
```

SI 1.54

Composition

Compose a short descriptive paragraph on one of the following people. Edit and make any necessary corrections in pen or pencil. Then, do a good copy of the paragraph.

Terry Fox, Alexander Graham Bell, Wayne Gretzky, Stephen Leacock,

Karen Kain, Sir John A. Macdonald, Michael J. Fox, Rick Hansen,

Farley Mowat, W. O. Mitchell, or Diane Jones-Konihowski

Basic English

clothe: to dress
cloth: fabric

14 What type of (clothe, cloth) will you buy for the skirt?

15 I would like you to (clothe, cloth) the baby after his bath.

16 A bright checkered (clothe, cloth) was placed over the trunk.
· · · · 1 · · · · 2 · · · · 3 · · · · 4 · · · · 5 · · · · 6 · · · · 7 · · · · 8 · · · · 9 · · · · 10

Hyphenation (Word Division)

It is best to avoid hyphenating words at the ends of lines whenever possible. Excessive hyphenation takes away from the neat appearance of the copy. It increases the possibility of hyphenating words incorrectly. It also distracts the reader's attention.

However, it is sometimes necessary to hyphenate words. The lessons in this unit contain hyphenation rules which will assist you to hyphenate or divide words correctly.

Hyphenation

Rule 1: Hyphenate words between speech syllables.

Examples:
pic-ture truth-ful pur-pose pre-cede por-tion
con-den-sa-tion

17 breakfast cautious comprise pancakes portable

18 treatment traction display prevails greetings

19 headings sawdust produced fearful performing

20 passport pension sickness scouting northbound

21 matchless ointments sulphur kindness outright

2. Be sure of the exact time and location of the exam -- be there at least ten minutes ahead of the starting time.

3. At the beginning of the exam, estimate the length of time each question should take, according to its size and value.

4. Read the questions carefully. Underline key words. Be sure you understand clearly the meaning of each question.

5. Always select the easiest question first while you are fresh -- avoid the frustration of not being able to do a difficult question at the very beginning.

6. Before answering an individual question, it is often a good idea to make a rough outline first, with headings. This helps to make your answers orderly, systematic, and neat.

7. Answer what is asked. Do not pad your answer with unnecessary details, but be sure that you answer all that is asked, not just part of the question.

8. Try to leave a few minutes at the end of the exam to read and correct your answers. Additional information will often come to mind and can be added if you have left space between the questions.

Spread Centring Review

Steps for Spread Centring More than One Word

1. Tab to the centre point of your paper.
2. Backspace **once** for each letter in each word and **once** for each space between words. Ignore the last letter*.
3. Input the line leaving one space between every letter in each word and three spaces between words.

```
m a t h      1 0
ᴜ ᴜ ᴜ ᴜ ᴜ ᴜ *
m a t h      1 0
```

Production Practice

Production 1

Centre the following display attractively on a full sheet of paper.

THE BUSINESS STUDIES DEPARTMENT

of

T H I S T L E T O W N   C O L L E G I A T E

invites

parents and students

to it's

(OPEN HOUSE) — spread

on Wednesday, October 28

from 19:00 to 21:00

The symbol ℘ means delete.

Production 2

Centre the following display attractively on a half sheet of paper.

THINGS TO REMEMBER / in / K E Y B O A R D I N G   C L A S S /

sit up straight / keep your eyes on the copy /

keep your feet flat on the floor / curve your

fingers on the home row / *read and listen to*

instructions carefully / edit your work /

The symbol / means the end of a line.

Production 2

Input the following report which contains enumerated material. The enumerations are at the left margin not indented. Use correct report format. Remember to listen for the right margin signal if you are using a typewriter as the production does not use the standard report line length.

HOW TO PASS EXAMINATIONS

While students rarely look forward to examinations, they are a very necessary part of the learning process. Examinations require a complete review of the subject as a whole, which is essential to final understanding. They test the student's ability to learn and to remember. The students are able to gauge their ability to think rapidly and accurately under stress.

How to Prepare for Examinations

1. Overcome examination-anxiety by being prepared--if you have done a reasonable amount of work and have average learning capacity, you are going to pass.

2. Make a timetable of available hours of study (study should begin two or three weeks before the actual exam). Allow yourself 20 to 40 minutes for each study session, depending upon the subject difficulty. Stick to this timetable.

3. Review the subject as a whole immediately prior to the exam. The learning should have been done previously.

4. Know exactly what work is to be covered by the examination. Review main facts, general rules, and principles of the subject.

5. During your study and examination period, get plenty of sleep.

6. Get some relief from the strain of studying by exercise and relaxation.

The Examination Day

1. Before going to an examination, be sure you have your pens, pencils, eraser, and any other instruments needed.

Set for double spacing. Take
two 2-min timings. Circle all
errors. Calculate Gross Words
Per Minute (GWPM). Record
your best timing on your
personal progress chart.

SI 1.36

Two-Minute Timing

	1	CW	2

Weather plays an important part in what we do | 10 | 10 | 5

and how we feel. Winter storms keep us indoors; a | 20 | 20 | 10

spring sunshine raises our spirits. Summer is the | 30 | 30 | 15

time for outdoor fun; rain cancels many sports and | 40 | 40 | 20

can ruin a holiday. | 44 | 44 | 22

In winter we talk about how cold it is. When | 10 | 54 | 27

summer comes, we forget our winter gripes and soon | 20 | 64 | 32

are complaining about the heat. | 26 | 70 | 35

• • • 1 • • • • 2 • • • • 3 • • • • 4 • • • • 5 • • • 6 • • • • 7 • • • • 8 • • • • 9 • • • • 10   1 min

    1   2   3   4   5   2 min

Production 1

Set a 70-character line (elite — 12 pitch) or a 60-character line (pica — 10 pitch). Input the following as enumerated material. Remember to listen for the right margin signal if you are using a typewriter as the production uses a different line length. These sentences illustrate the Metric Rules.

■ Do you have an indent option?

1. The distance from Ottawa to Toronto is 400 km; from Halifax to Vancouver, 5 960 km; and from the North Pole to the Equator, it is 10 000 km.

2. Roger drove at 80 km/h, but the speed limit along that highway was only 60 km/h.

3. Even though I tried to stick to my diet, I gained a kilogram.

4. Han's temperature went up to 39°C. His mother called the doctor.

5. The fastest speed anyone has travelled is 39 897 km/h or 11.08 km/s. This was accomplished by Cernon, Young, and Stafford in Apollo X.

6. Time after midnight, such as 00:15, might be stated as "zero fifteen."

7. In Canada, toothpaste comes in sizes such as 25 mL, 50 mL, 100 mL, and 150 mL.

8840 *or* 8 840

8. The height of Mt. Everest is 8 840 m; the length of the river Nile is 6 670 km.

9. In numeric dating, April 7, 1995 is expressed as 1995 04 07.

10. Someone has said: "Metric makes it 10 times easier, 100 times faster, 1 000 times better."

30

Skill Building / __ /
Block Centring

Format
50-character line
Single spacing

Practise each line twice.
Practise as quickly as you can.

Skill Drives

Practise each line once.
Repeat *or* take two
15-s timings on each line.

Practise each line once.
Repeat *or* take two
15-s timings on each line.

Use the left shift key and
the ; finger.
Practise each line twice.

Practise each line once.
Practise each line again.

Take two 30-s timings on each
line. Do each phrase as
quickly as you can.

One-Hand Words

1 at up plum car jump bet ill him west saw oily fade

2 we at pin deaf hill seed you dress pink dear wears

Alternate-Hand Words

3 by owl fix pen jam work name gown soap cycle rigid

4 is rod bye cut wit fury pale both auto their shape

5 of bus the dig men town band sign with usual laugh

Alternate-Hand Sentences

6 Their big fight by the lake kept the six men busy.

7 He is to pay for the malt and the corn on the cob.

8 Six owls nap in the old oak tree near the cut hay.

Reach to the __ Key

9 ;;; ;p; ;p;_ ;p_; ;_; ;__ ;;; ___ ;_ ;_p ;_p _; _;

10 Elvis also sang in Blue Hawaii and Jailhouse Rock.

11 Stephen King authored Carrie and then The Shining.

Sentences with Numbers

12 In 1989, our 27 teams made 38 to 40 points a game.

13 They live 396.2 km from you and 718.5 km from her.

Common Phrases

14 of it/of the/of their/of his/of hers/of my/of them/

15 and she/and it/and they/and get/and then/and their/

16 the man/the fee/the girl/the sum/the order/the end/
  · · · · 1 · · · · 2 · · · · 3 · · · · 4 · · · · 5 · · · · 6 · · · · 7 · · · · 8 · · · · 9 · · · · 10

Reports with Enumerations

Format
60-character line
Single spacing

Practise each line twice.
Practise as quickly as you can.

Skill Building

Practise at a controlled rate.
Circle your errors. Do Speed
Improvement if you had three
errors or less. Do Accuracy
Improvement if you had four
errors or more.

Left-Hand Words

1 wax zest verb facts rear tar attracts face date feed sad was

2 act beg edge waste greed scare target effect swears act fare

Evaluate Your Progress

3   An afternoon stroll on that summer day made everyone as

happy and relaxed as they had ever been. The bright sun and

warm breeze helped to remove troubled thoughts and concerns.

The cheerful songs of the birds and radiant smiles of active

children reduced stress and tension in those who had thought

they would not survive the fighting. Peace had finally been

achieved, and there would be no more violence in their town.

• • • • 1 • • • • 2 • • • • 3 • • • • 4 • • • • 5 • • • 6 • • • • 7 • • • • 8 • • • • 9 • • • •10• • • •11• • • •12

Think **accuracy**. Take two 15-s
timings on each line. Take two
30-s timings on the complete
set of lines.

Accuracy Improvement

4 lily look million Phillip jump noon join up mono lip opinion

5 go pal they height sleigh shriek snake end slant problem eye

6 age grab vest after grease tweezers averages dead Fred cares

7 cherry filling immature matter account immediate hood wheels

Speed Improvement

8 Elliott finally arrived at noon when the meetings had ended.

9 The current offer for cutting tobacco tariffs will not pass.

10 The bank returned the cheques after she closed the accounts.

11 It was not necessary for them to check all the old invoices.

Try to do each timing faster.
Take two 15-s timings on each
set of two lines. Take two 30-s
timings on the complete set of
lines.
■ Do Evaluate Your Progress
and determine if you have
improved.

Number Practice

Practise each line once.
Practise each line again.

12 Air Canada Flight 807 from Banff arrived at Gate 9 at 15:40.

13 Has the order for 200 envelopes (10.1 cm x 22.8 cm) arrived?

• • • • 1 • • • • 2 • • • • 3 • • • • 4 • • • • 5 • • • 6 • • • • 7 • • • • 8 • • • • 9 • • • •10• • • •11• • • •12

Alphabetic Sentence

17 The temperature quickly fell below zero, and every
grape vine and fruit blossom froze--it was exactly
five months until the July harvest days.

Skill Building

Your teacher will select one of
the time intervals indicated at
the right of the drill lines.
Select the line that you think you
can complete in that interval.

If you complete the line, try the
next line which is longer. If not,
try again or adjust your goal to
a shorter line.

If your objective is speed,
concentrate on speed by
pushing to complete the line
in the time limit. Errors should
not be a concern.

If your objective is accuracy,
concentrate on accuracy by
attempting to complete the line
with one error or less in the
time limit.

Graduated Speed Practice

15 s 12 s 10 s

18 He has it.	8	10	12
19 It is late.	9	11	13
20 He was here.	10	12	14
21 She took one.	10	13	16
22 Bring it back.	11	14	17
23 Take four more.	12	15	18
24 They need paper.	13	16	19
25 Date their order.	14	17	20
26 Visit there later.	14	18	22
27 Issue him six more.	15	19	23
28 Maria has a red car.	16	20	24
29 June is a fine month.	17	21	25
30 Pour her a cup of tea.	18	22	26
31 They have a new kitten.	18	23	28
32 Marcel gave five to her.	19	24	29
33 We went to the late show.	20	25	30
34 Fill the pails with water.	21	26	31
35 One cup of flour is enough.	22	27	32
36 Tom took the dog for a walk.	22	28	34
37 Ingrid wore a new blue dress.	23	29	35
38 Liz made a cake for the party.	24	30	36
39 He might have a plant for them.	25	30	36
40 She has gone to mail the letter.	26	31	37
41 They should read the books today.	26	33	40
42 She put all of the tests in there.	27	34	41

· · · · 1 · · · · 2 · · · · 3 · · · · 4 · · · · 5 · · · · 6 · · · · 7

Santa Maria Ship

The Santa Maria Ship is an exact replica of Columbus' ship. It was hand carved and hand painted at False creek in Vancouver, British Columbia. It was then transported in flat-bed trucks across the Rocky Mountains to Edmonton, where it was reconstructed.

Assess Your Progress

Set for double spacing. Take two 3-min *or* two 5-min timings. Circle all errors. Calculate Gross Words Per Minute (GWPM).
Record your best timing on your personal progress chart.

SI 1.44

Three- or Five-Minute Timing

		1	CW	3
All of the stars, including our Sun, are gigantic balls		12	12	4
of very hot gas. They maintain these temperatures by atomic		24	24	8
reactions. In our Sun, this reaction is hydrogen fusion: a		36	36	12
helium atom formed from four hydrogen atoms. It is about 20		48	48	16
million degrees centigrade at the centre of our Sun, and the		60	60	20
surface area temperature is six thousand degrees centigrade.		72	72	24
There is really no surface on the Sun since it is a big		12	84	28
ball, but it has large layers. The layer which is innermost		24	96	32
is the photosphere. The next layer is the chromosphere. It		36	108	36
is in steady motion. Enormous sections of it that break off		48	120	40
are sometimes visible in space. The corona lies outside the		60	132	44
chromosphere. It makes a total eclipse a magnificent sight.		72	144	48
Our Sun moves in two directions in space. One of these		12	156	52
appears to be a straight line towards a constellation of the		24	168	56
Milky Way. Our Sun also is part of the Milky Way. This big		36	180	60
system rotates slowly around its own centre as well. During		48	192	64
this straight-line motion, the Sun rotates on its axis. The		60	204	68
rotation speed is much greater than the straight-line speed.		72	216	72

```
• • • 1 • • • • 2 • • • • 3 • • • • 4 • • • • 5 • • • 6 • • • 7 • • • • 8 • • • 9 • • • •10• • • •11• • • •12     1 min
        1                2                3                4        3 min
```

Block Centring

Block centring means that the longest line in a group of lines is horizontally centred. The other lines are aligned (or blocked) with the left margin. This is a form of horizontal centring.

Steps for Block Centring

1. Select the longest line which is called the *key line*.

```
              REFERENCE MATERIALS


              Books
              Encyclopaedias
              Newspaper Clippings
              Almanacs and Year Books*
              Directories
              Magazines
```

* This is your key line.

2. Tab to the centre point of your paper.
3. Backspace **once** for every two letters, numbers, and spaces in the key line.
4. Set a left margin where you stopped backspacing.
5. Input all lines beginning at this left margin.

Production 1

Using the Backspace Method, centre the following display on a half sheet of paper. Use block centring.

```
              PUBLIC LIBRARY SERVICES
         TS ↓
              Books
              Information and Reference ~~Services~~  Sources
              Periodicals and Newspapers
              Discs and Tapes
              8 mm Silent Movies
              16 mm Sound Movies
              Language Labs
              Video Equipment
              Art Rental collection
              Bookmobile ≡
              Adult and Children's programmes
              Meeting Rooms          ≡
              Photocopying Machines
```

Production Practice

■ *programs* or *programmes*

Know the preference in your area of Canada.

■ Did you centre the key line?

Fifteen thousand employees work in the Mall, servicing the following areas:

- over 800 stores and services
- 19 movie theatres
- 110 eating establishments
- 5 amusement areas
- 1 night club
- 1 bingo hall
- 1 chapel
- animal environments
- bird aviaries
- fish aquariums
- works of art
- parking for 20 000 cars
- RV and trailer day parking

*horizontally centre*

Special Amusement Areas

Fantasyland Amusement Park

Fantasyland is the world's largest indoor amusement park. It contains 24 rides and attractions, including "Mindbender," a triple-loop roller coaster that is 14 storeys high.

Ice Palace

Ice Palace, an NHL-size rink, is the second home to the Stanley Cup Champions, the Edmonton Oilers, who practise there 20 times per year.

Deep Sea Adventure

West Edmonton Mall has four submarines, capable of reaching a depth of approximately 45 m. Each is large enough to hold 24 passengers and a captain. The Deep Sea Adventure ride takes place in a lake approximately 122 m long, where 200 different types of marine life can be seen, including barracudas and sharks.

World Water Park

West Edmonton Mall has the world's largest indoor wave pool called "Blue Thunder." It is a 2 ha park, whose temperature is a constant 30°C. Twenty-two slides and attractions are featured in the park.

Production 2

Using the Backspace Method, centre the following display attractively on a full sheet of paper. Use block centring.

The symbol ⌐ means move to the left.

CANADA IS

Words by Steve Hyde
Music by Eric Robertson
Recorded by Roger Whittaker

```
Canada is the Rocky Mountains,
Canada is Prince Edward Island,
Canada is a country made for love.

Canada is the prairie cowboy,
Canada is the Yukon miner,
Canada is a country full of love.

We have love for our neighbours
of whatever creed or colour,

We have love for our cities
and our valleys and our plains,

We have a voice that is calling
telling all the world we're willing
```

To welcome them to this great land,
and that's what Canada is.

■ Did you consider both the handwritten and printed lines when determining the key line?

Two-Minute Timing

		1	2
Many people like the fall. It is the time of		10	5
the year to think about some of the good times one		20	10
had in the summer. New plans for the winter might		30	15
be made. In the fall, the air is crisp and clear.		40	20
Walks in the woods are fun. The sounds of walking		50	25
carry quite far. Everything seems to be at peace.		60	30

```
· · · 1 · · · 2 · · · 3 · · · 4 · · · 5 · · · 6 · · · 7 · · · 8 · · · 9 · · · 10    1 min
        1           2           3           4           5                        2 min
```

Timing

Set for double spacing. Take two 2-min timings. Circle all errors. Calculate Gross Words Per Minute (GWPM). Record your best timing on your personal progress chart.

SI 1.15

Production 1

Input the Review of Metric Rules on a full sheet of paper. Set a 70-character line (elite — 12 pitch) or a 60-character line (pica — 10 pitch). Use the correct format for enumerated material. The title is on line 13. *Note:* This production will not be vertically centred.

Metric Review

■ Do you have an indent option?

Review of Metric Rules

1. Use symbols for the metric terms when units are expressed in numbers.

2. Metric symbols remain the same to indicate singular or plural.

3. Leave one space between the quantity and the symbol (except when expressing temperature).

4. Do not put a period after the metric symbol unless the symbol ends the sentence.

5. Numbers less than one should be expressed in decimals, with a zero placed to the left of the decimal marker.

6. Spaces are used to separate numbers into groups of three. Whole numbers below 10 000 may be input without the space.

7. Numeric dating consists of the year, month, and day in descending order, with a space left between each component.

8. Times of the day are expressed by four digits, commencing at midnight with 00:00, which is read as "zero hours." The first two numbers represent the time in hours, followed by a colon. The other two digits represent the number of minutes.

Production 2

Input the following as a report. Use correct format. Remember to listen for the right margin signal if you are using a typewriter as the production does not use the standard line length.

WEST EDMONTON MALL

According to the Guinness Book of World Records, West Edmonton Mall is the largest shopping mall in the world. It is the size of 115 American football fields. The mall was built in three phases: Phase 1 opened in 1981; Phase 2 in 1983; and Phase 3, in 1985. Total cost of the Mall was approximately 1.1 billion dollars.

31

Open Tables without Column Headings

Format
50-character line
Single spacing

Practise each line twice.
Practise as quickly as you can.

Skill Building

Practise each line once.
Repeat or take two
15-s timings on each line.

Practise each line once.
Practise each line again.

Hyphenation Rule

Read the Hyphenation Rule.
Practise each line once,
hyphenating the words
according to the Hyphenation
Rules.
Each line will end evenly at the
right margin when the rules
are applied correctly.

Edit each line by correcting
two errors.
Practice each line once with
the corrections.

One-Hand Words

1 as my ear mop fed hip rag fact east milk gave junk

2 Outdoor plants need sun and rain in order to grow.

Common-Word Sentences

3 Bring your report card back here when he signs it.

4 The warm sun helps most things grow free and easy.

5 If they handle the work right, they make a profit.

Sentences with Numbers

6 Bank rates went from 9 to 14 per cent in 23 weeks.

7 Take the 54 flat parcels to 27 Yonge St. by 16:45.

· · · · 1 · · · · 2 · · · · 3 · · · · 4 · · · · 5 · · · · 6 · · · · 7 · · · · 8 · · · · 9 · · · · 10

Hyphenation

Rule 2: Hyphenate words between double letters of speech syllables.

Examples:

gram-mar suc-cess rob-ber jog-gers rib-bons with-hold

Note: spell-ing toss-ing drill-ing

8 shudder letter commerce winner borrow cannot

9 swimming shipper correct dropping commission

10 smallest telling dressing sleepless stainless

11 luggage colleagues druggist splitting baggage

12 massive challenge comment deepest marvellous

Editing Practice

13 Be sure to vist the calgary Stampede this summer.

14 The NHL hockey season will finishish in about a weak.

15 Nanaimo and Trial are located British Columbia.

· · · · 1 · · · · 2 · · · · 3 · · · · 4 · · · · 5 · · · · 6 · · · · 7 · · · · 8 · · · · 9 · · · · 10

Reports

Format
60-character line
Single spacing

Practise each line twice.
Practise as quickly as you can.

Skill Building

Practise at a controlled rate.
Circle your errors. Do Speed
Improvement if you had three
errors or less. Do Accuracy
Improvement if you had four
errors or more.

Right-Hand Words

1 oily pony hook pin minimum Honolulu upon plum join mill link

2 pup hulk lollipop lip him moon nylon monk mummy no pink junk

Evaluate Your Progress

3   A promise should be carefully made and should always be

kept. Try not to let anything let you break a promise. The

best advice is to promise to do something only if it is very

likely that it can be fulfilled. After a promise is broken,

explain the reason, and then attempt to honour your word. A

true friend rarely breaks a promise, and this occurs only in

extremely special situations.

· · · ·1· · · ·2· · · ·3· · · ·4· · · ·5· · · ·6· · · ·7· · · ·8· · · ·9· · · ·10· · · ·11· · · ·12

Think **accuracy**. Take two 15-s
timings on each line. Take two
30-s timings on the complete
set of lines.

Accuracy Improvement

4 sea ebb tact bazaar far after agree drawer recess tree sweet

5 off ladder attend cheerful proof summary install room adding

6 is town blame fox form title element blend quit widow island

7 joy lion Johnny pulp puppy hill only opinion union moon plum

Try to do each timing faster.
Take two 15-s timings on each
set of two lines. Take two 30-s
timings on the complete set of
lines.
■ Do Evaluate Your Progress
and determine if you have
improved.

Speed Improvement

8 Unless his staff assists us, we shall need to get more help.

9 The terms set forth in the original contract must be quoted.

10 It would have been easier if she had left the books at home.

11 In the business world, good manners and grooming are needed.

Practise each line once.
Practise each line again.

Number Practice

12 A big car may use 20 L of gas per 100 km on a 7 540 km trip.

13 The 1988 12 31 cash dividend dropped from $126.24 to $97.83.

· · · ·1· · · ·2· · · ·3· · · ·4· · · ·5· · · ·6· · · ·7· · · ·8· · · ·9· · · ·10· · · ·11· · · ·12

Open Tables without Column Headings

HOLIDAYS

```
          January        New Year's Day
          April          Good Friday
          April          Easter Monday
          May            Victoria Day
          July           Dominion Day
         *September      Labour Day
          October        Thanksgiving Day*
          November       Remembrance Day
          December       Christmas Day
```

*The key line is: September ⌐6⌐ Thanksgiving Day

Steps

1. Horizontally centre and capitalize the title. Triple space.

2. • Select the longest item in each column (the key words).
   • Decide the number of spaces you wish to leave between columns. In the example, there are six spaces. *Note:* It is convenient to choose an even number of spaces between columns.

Backspace Method

3. • Move the print indicator or cursor to the horizontal centre of your paper.
   • Backspace **once** for every two letters and spaces in the key line.

   ```
   September123456Thanksgiving Day
   ⌣ ⌣ ⌣ ⌣ ⌣ ⌣ ⌣ ⌣ ⌣ ⌣ ⌣ ⌣ ⌣ ⌣ ⌣
   ```

   Note: Be sure to include the spaces between the columns.
   • Note the character or cursor position.
4. Set a left margin where you stopped backspacing.
5. • Clear all tabs.
   • Space forward on the space bar **once** for each letter or space in the longest item of column 1, plus **once** for each of the spaces between the two columns.
   • Note the character or cursor position.
   • Set a tab.

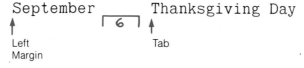

6. You are now ready to continue with the table.

Three- or Five-Minute Timing

		1	CW	3

By cutting, tearing, and grinding food and then helping
to mix this food with saliva, teeth carry out the first step
of digestion. This is known as mastication. Our teeth also
help us to form the sounds of speech and to determine facial
expressions. We grow two sets of these tough structures. A
first set serves us during childhood. Our second set should
last a lifetime if it receives proper care and attention.

Teeth of different shapes do different tasks during the
process of eating. Incisors have sharp chisel-shaped edges.
They are used to bite and cut food. Cuspids are pointed and
are useful for tearing and shredding. Bicuspids are double-
pointed teeth which tear and grind. Molars have broad, flat
surfaces used for grinding and crushing food.

The structure of teeth differs according to the type of
food that the animal eats. Plant eaters usually have strong
incisors for biting grasses and grains. They also have huge
molars for grinding and softening food. Cuspids for tearing
and piercing are well-developed in beasts of prey. They may
not have molars. Humans have teeth of all four varieties.

1	CW	3
12	12	4
24	24	8
36	36	12
48	48	16
60	60	20
72	72	24
81	81	27
12	93	31
24	105	35
36	117	39
48	129	43
60	141	47
69	150	50
12	162	54
24	174	58
36	186	62
48	198	66
60	210	70
71	221	74

• • • 1 • • • • 2 • • • • 3 • • • • 4 • • • • 5 • • • • 6 • • • • 7 • • • • 8 • • • • 9 • • • • 10 • • • • 11 • • • • 12   1 min

1   2   3   4   3 min

SI 1.42

Composition

Compose an announcement for an upcoming school event. Use horizontal, vertical, and spread centring to create an attractive notice.

Production 1

Using the Backspace Method, centre the following two-column table on a half sheet of paper. Leave eight spaces between columns.

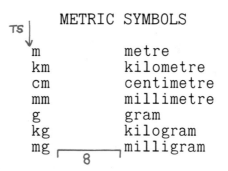

METRIC SYMBOLS

TS

m	metre
km	kilometre
cm	centimetre
mm	millimetre
g	gram
kg	kilogram
mg	milligram

8

Production 2

Using the Backspace Method, centre the following two-column table attractively on a half sheet of paper.

Commonly Used Foreign Words and Expressions

TS

a la mode	served with ice cream
au revoir	till we meet again
bona fide	genuine, in good faith
bravo	shout of applause
caveat emptor	let the buyer beware
connoisseur	a critical expert
cum laude	with highest honours
faux pas	social blunder, mistake
kudos	glory, prestige
re	in the matter of
résumé	summary
status quo	current state

10

6

Graduated Speed Practice

No.	Line	20s	15s	12s
14	Dirt bikes roared up the hill.	18	24	30
15	The water was chilly and dirty.	19	25	31
16	An award was also given to them.	19	26	32
17	Put the yellow book on the shelf.	20	26	33
18	Place his presents under the tree.	20	27	34
19	Make pencil marks on the last page.	21	28	35
20	Compose and write two short stories.	22	29	36
21	It is easier to study from our notes.	22	30	37
22	They went camping on the long weekend.	23	30	38
23	Thank you very much for the gold chain.	23	31	39
24	When they return home, we will ask them.	24	32	40
25	It took their band three hours to set up.	25	33	41
26	Their new lamp lay in pieces on the floor.	25	34	42
27	Letters mailed today should reach you soon.	26	34	43
28	Do good work and you will be praised for it.	26	35	44
29	Kelvin played the drums for the school dance.	27	36	45
30	High above, huge black clouds joined together.	28	37	46
31	A tall red rose bloomed in the golden sunlight.	28	38	47
32	Icy roads caused trucks to slide into the ditch.	29	38	48
33	The blinds were drawn to keep out the bright sun.	29	39	49
34	She went to the store after she mailed the letter.	30	40	50
35	The song on the radio reminded them of last summer.	31	41	51
36	Wooden boxes will be better for those heavier items.	31	42	52
37	The girls chose the material and cut out the pattern.	32	42	53
38	We were told we would be paid for painting the fences.	32	43	54
39	Tell me about yourself and the places you have visited.	33	44	55
40	Last night they listened to the new album several times.	34	45	56
41	Forget the faults of others and you will be much happier.	34	46	57
42	Work on that page until you finish all of these questions.	35	46	58
43	Finish doing your third paper before you go out for dinner.	35	47	59
44	I will never forget my visit here with you and your friends.	36	48	60

` • • • •1• • • •2• • • •3• • • •4• • • •5• • • •6• • • •7• • • •8• • • •9• • • •10• • • •11• • • •12`

SI 1.23

Two-Minute Timing

	1	CW	2

Netting a fish is easy if you learn the right method. It can be very disappointing to lose that prize fish that took you hours to hook.

If you are fishing from shore or from a boat, lower the net with one hand so that it is half way underwater. Position the fish so that it swims to the net head first. Lower the tip of your fishing rod just enough to provide slack. Then, scoop the fish into the net.

	1	CW	2
	10	10	5
	20	20	10
	28	28	14
	10	38	19
	20	48	24
	30	58	29
	40	68	34
	50	78	39
	53	81	41

1 min
2 min

• • • 1 • • • 2 • • • 3 • • • 4 • • • 5 • • • 6 • • • 7 • • • 8 • • • 9 • • • 10
    1   2   3   4   5

Formatting Guide for Tables

Line Length	• Determine by horizontally centring the key line.
Tab	• Set a tab at the beginning of the second and subsequent columns.
Spaces between Columns	• Leave an even number of spaces e.g. 4, 6, or 8 between columns.
Spacing	• The body can be single spaced, double spaced, or variable spaced.
Top and Bottom Margins	• Usually equal as tables are vertically centred.
Title	• Capitalize and horizontally centre. Then, triple space to the body of the table.
Subtitle (when used)	• Capitalize the first letter of each main word in the subtitle and horizontally centre it double spaced below the title. Then, triple space to the body of the table.
Column Heading	• Capitalize the first letter of each main word. • Either blocked or horizontally centred over each column. *Note:* If the title, subtitle, or the column headings are more than one line, they are single spaced.

Skill Building

Alternate-Hand Words

1 of sir auto rock burial enamel height shake male oak air end

2 by with Norman ornament dish fuel soak rush eight rigid girl

Evaluate Your Progress

3   Music plays an important part in everyone's life. This

begins when a parent holds a baby and sings a lullaby. Many

families are drawn closer together by music. Happy memories

of singing and family bands can deepen personal feelings. A

creative spirit may be discovered in children, leading to an

exciting sense of fulfillment. All of these joyous memories

will likely remain with one for a lifetime.

· · · ·1· · · ·2· · · ·3· · · ·4· · · ·5· · · ·6· · · ·7· · · ·8· · · ·9· · · ·10· · · ·11· · · ·12

Accuracy Improvement

4 imply kin onion inn my you ink null pool up pin loon in kink

5 or lap both usual handle laughs ornament rod aid tight signs

6 egg call jogged still tanned village cabbage passing hurries

7 axe data race garter waste beverage fee eat fade average gas

Speed Improvement

8 It will be impossible for them to finish in time to go home.

9 Please give her some money and she will pay for the tickets.

10 He must be taken to their office before this letter is sent.

11 The error in Bill's business address was processed annually.

Spelling Practice

12 The surprised look on Lee-Anne's face was genuine.

13 He earns an equitable salary for the work he does.

· · · ·1· · · ·2· · · ·3· · · ·4· · · ·5· · · ·6· · · ·7· · · ·8· · · ·9· · · ·10· · · ·11· · · ·12

Open Tables without Column Headings

Format
50-character line
Single spacing

Practise each line twice.
Practise as quickly as you can.

Skill Building

Practise each line once.
Repeat *or* take two
15-s timings on each line.

Practise each line once.
Practise each line again.

Alternate-Hand Words

1 or he fit rid tie bid pen down clay dusk pale maid

2 sick soap lap fix hem bit risk make coal wish rush

Common-Word Sentences

3 Run to the top of the hill and see if she is back.

4 The old man loved to go for a long walk every day.

5 I went to the travel agency to pick up my tickets.

Sentences with Numbers

6 Take my 39 books, 71 covers, 48 tops, and 56 pens.

7 There will be 27 parents here for the 16:30 class.

. . . . 1 . . . . 2 . . . . 3 . . . . 4 . . . . 5 . . . . 6 . . . . 7 . . . . 8 . . . . 9 10

Hyphenation Rule

Hyphenation

Rule 3: Divide only after the hyphen in a compound word.

Examples:

twenty-one sugar-coated son-in-law old-time left-hand

Read the Hyphenation Rule.
Practise each line once,
hyphenating the words
according to the Hyphenation
Rules.
Each line will end evenly at the
right margin when the rules
are applied correctly.

8 low-grade co-author eighty-six run-down up-to-date

9 one-way vice-president set-up by-play safe-keeping

10 self-employed earphones gallons dictate gossip

11 stiffness collect tailor-made chipmunk biggest

12 subtracting non-profit dislike mid-day build-up

Spelling Practice

Practise each underlined word
four times. Practise each line
once concentrating on the
underlined words.

13 We expect to <u>acquire</u> a <u>mortgage</u> for this property.

14 Ron had an <u>adverse</u> reaction to the cough <u>medicine</u>.

. . . . 1 . . . . 2 . . . . 3 . . . . 4 . . . . 5 . . . . 6 . . . . 7 . . . . 8 . . . . 9 10

World War I. A candy maker accidentally launched what was to prove one of the most popular confections of all: the candy bar. Candy bars were first mass produced for military use.

More than eighty of the world's agricultural products are candy ingredients. Today, the average Canadian consumes about eight kilograms of candy annually from a choice of 1500 varieties.

Assess Your Progress

Set for double spacing. Take two 3-min *or* two 5-min timings. Circle all errors. Calculate Gross Words Per Minute (GWPM).
Record your best timing on your personal progress chart.

SI 1.29

Three- or Five-Minute Timing

		1	CW	3
Our paper one dollar bill has been replaced by the gold		12	12	4
coin which most people call the loonie. Some people collect		24	24	8
the coins because of their beauty or novelty value. Another		36	36	12
reason for saving loonies could be the belief that the coins		48	48	16
from the first year will be worth more than one dollar.		59	59	19
It is not known how many loonies are being saved. Some		12	71	23
coin experts say that millions of loonies are not being used		24	83	27
and that it will be a long time before the loonies are worth		36	95	31
more than one dollar. Only loonies with a minting flaw will		48	107	35
be worth more than their face value. Some loonies have been		60	119	39
found to have a minor flaw in the name of our country.		71	130	43
Also, there is little reason to expect one dollar bills		12	142	47
to be worth more as there are too many of them around. Even		24	154	51
dollar bills issued for very special events are not worth as		36	166	55
much as it was thought they would be. It can be fun to save		48	178	59
both coins and paper money, whether they are new or old.		59	189	62

• • • 1 • • • • 2 • • • • 3 • • • • 4 • • • • 5 • • • 6 • • • 7 • • • • 8 • • • • 9 • • • 10 • • • • 11 • • • • 12   1 min

1   2   3   4   3 min

between: refers to two
among: refers to more than two

15 The will divided the money (between, among) the two sons.

16 We could not find John (between, among) all the people.

17 Bev planted the onions (between, among) the peas and corn.

Production Practice

■ Did your teacher show you how to triple space on your computer?

Production 1

Using the Backspace Method, centre the three-column table on a half sheet of paper. Triple space after the title and double space the body.

```
                    CAMPING EQUIPMENT

sleeping bag        backpack           air mattress
tent                hiking boots       compass
matches             first-aid kit      insect repellent
flashlight          suntan lotion      cooking supplies
                 [ 6 ]               [ 6 ]
```

Production 2

Using the Backspace Method, centre the following four-column table attractively on a half sheet of paper.

CARS

                              H
Ford / Pontiac / Honda / Mercedes-Benz

                                        Volkswagen
Chevrolet / Dodge / Plymouth / Audie

                         Lada
Nissan / Toyota / Mazda / Subaru

Chrysler / Mazda /Jeep / Cadillack

                                  Volvo
Lincoln / Fiat / Renault / Velvet

"chocolatl". In the early 16th century, Cortez, the conqueror, brought cocoa beans back to his native Spain where a thriving industry started. Spain planted cacao trees in its overseas colonies and kept the industry a secret from the rest of Europe for a hundred years. It was the Spanish monks who carried the drink beyond Spain. The first of the historic English Chocolate Houses appeared in 1657.

TS

Special Varieties

DS

The 17th and 18th centuries brought new sweets. In 1671, a German doctor asked his cook, Franz Marzip, to make an almond dessert. Marzip's creation was in such demand that he returned to his native town and founded a marzipan factory.

The nougat was first heard of in the 18th century in France. It was made of honey, sugar, eggs, nuts, and fruits. According to the legend, the word "nougat" comes from the story of Tante Manon, an elderly woman who made sweets and gave them to the youngsters. The children used to say, "Tante Manon, tu nous gates"--you spoil us.

The North American Industry

The first candy makers in the New World were the Dutch bakers of New York, who in the 17th century made sugar wafers, macaroons, and other sweets for celebrations.

The commercial candy industry in America dates back to at least 1712. That year the first known candy advertising was carried on by a Boston shop. Thus, the industry in America is at least 270 years old.

The most recent major development came just before

Two-Minute Timing

She ran home to play the new album. She felt
so good. It had finally come to the store. Eight
days had been so long to wait for it. All the way
home, she sang the song. She had first heard much
of the album at the class party. She was going to
invite some friends over to hear this choice album
tonight or tomorrow afternoon. If the rest of the
family were not home, she would hear it very soon.

	1	2
	10	5
	20	10
	30	15
	40	20
	50	25
	60	30
	70	35
	80	40

· · · · 1 · · · · 2 · · · · 3 · · · · 4 · · · · 5 · · · 6 · · · · 7 · · · · 8 · · · · 9 · · · · 10   1 min

1　　　　2　　　　3　　　　4　　　　5   2 min

Composition

Answer each of the following questions, using one word or a phrase, not a sentence. Put each answer on a line by itself.

1. Where were you born?
2. Name three cities you have visited, not including the one you live in or the one in which you were born.
3. What was the last movie you saw at the theatre?
4. What is your favourite rock group?
5. Do you have a part-time job? If so, what is it?
6. What radio station do you listen to?
7. Name two television shows that you enjoy watching.

Production 2

Input the following report which uses both subheadings and side headings. Use correct format. Remember to listen for the right margin signal if you are using a typewriter as the production does not use the standard report line length.

Title:

Subtitle:

Subheading:

Side Heading:

THE HISTORY OF CANDY AND CHOCOLATE

DS↓

From Ancient to Modern Times

TS↓

The earliest recorded history of candy dates back 4 000 years. Ancient writings show that Egyptians sold sweetmeats in the market place in 1566 B.C. Paintings in Egyptian tombs pictured candy makers using rough moulds to form confections. Honey was used as a sweetener in those days and was mixed with nuts, chopped fruits, sweet herbs, and spices.

TS↓

Origins of the Ingredients

DS↓

Sugar

Sugar was first produced in India and later introduced into Persia and Arabia. In the Middle Ages, the Arabs developed a sugar refining process. The Crusaders, who had acquired a taste for sugar in the Far East, are given credit for making candy popular and for starting a demand for the sugar plant in Europe. Venice became the sugar capital of Europe in the 13th century. Explorers carried the sugar plant with them on their voyages, and sugar cane soon became an important item of world commerce.

TS↓

Chocolate

DS↓

Chocolate was a later entry into the world of sweets. The ruling Aztec families in Mexico enjoyed a cocoa bean drink called

Decision Point
■ Should the side heading be at the bottom of page one or at the top of page two?

Any paragraph at the bottom of the page should have at least two lines.

Analytical Practice

Format
50-character line
Single spacing

Practise each line twice.
Practise as quickly as you can.

Analyze Your Practice

Take two 1-min timings on
each sentence.
Each sentence contains the
alphabet.
Circle all errors.

Alternate-Hand Words

1 am if nap fur may jam bud lane male duck clap hair

2 it do wig oak dog cub box lens duck rush turn down

Alphabetic Sentences

3 The zebra quickly jumped over the west gate to the
farm and made his exit.

4 Exactly what is it he had in mind for the big pay,
or is my keen inquiry just a bit overzealous?

Selected Letter Practice

1. Circle all errors in the Alphabetic Sentences.
2. From your errors, choose the letter or letters which gave you difficulty.
3. Select the appropriate drill lines in the Selected Letter Practice.
4. Practise each line twice concentrating on accuracy.
5. If you had no errors in the Alphabetic Sentences, or if you complete the accuracy lines before
your teacher calls **time**, start at line A and **push** for speed. Practise each line once.

After Selected Letter Practice,
take two 1-min timings on each
Alphabetic Sentence and
determine if you have
improved.

A 5 as at and are was has any that have also data made
6 Ask about all albums again as many may be on sale.

B 7 be by but buy boy bun bug been both baby break bag
8 The baby smiles and blows big bubbles in her bath.

C 9 can cat car copy coke cold could check cover claim
10 We can go to the concert if classes are cancelled.

D 11 did due add done deeds data dress dull order denim
12 The deed was done before Dora could do the damage.

E 13 we be the ear end been ever were piece erect enter
14 The five entrances and exits were heavily guarded.

F 15 if of for off fad fluff foul offer found first fad
16 Fifteen people fainted at the fall fair on Friday.

· · · · 1 · · · · 2 · · · · 3 · · · · 4 · · · · 5 · · · · 6 · · · · 7 · · · · 8 · · · · 9 · · · · 10

Practise each line once.
Practise each line again.

Production Practice

Each line will end evenly at the
right margin when the rules are
applied correctly.

Number Practice

12 All 162 planes will leave from gate 673 at 17:35 on Tuesday.

13 Their team got 4 runs in 2 innings to win the game 16 to 10.
  · · · · 1 · · · · 2 · · · 3 · · · · 4 · · · · 5 · · · 6 · · · · 7 · · · · 8 · · · · 9 · · · · 10 · · · · 11 · · · · 12

Production 1

Set a 60-character line and double spacing. Input each line once, hyphenating the words according to the Hyphenation Rules.

1 slender tactics snobbish crammed tournaments dribbling

2 unlikely sandwich curbed scaffold sulphur thirteen tanks

3 demolition calcium camping positions washable Kathleen

4 whiter ourselves don't S.P.C.A. effortless eggs enrolling

5 follow-up contend passed rowboats craftsman darker looked

6 memorandum mix-up Richard mischief flights certainly yet

7 bombardment breath-taking happened translucent tearing

8 sponsor soothing solid sportsmanship stairwell sawdust

9 paid padding longshoremen mammoth argued appliance area

10 ensure forsake New Brunswick mutual nightmare private via

Formatting Guide for Subheadings in Reports

Subheadings	• Centre and underscore the subheadings. Capitalize the first letter of each main word in the subheading.
Spacing	• Triple space before a subheading. • Double space after a subheading. *Note:* If a subheading is directly followed by a side heading, double space between the two headings.

G17 go gag gate grip give germ grade being going guess
18 Give the girl the gold gloves and the green gowns.

H19 he the has she why this here have high heavy hotel
20 The hot hired hands held their hurting heads high.

I21 it is oil air via into iris item their which civil
22 His sister insists on licking the pink icing dish.

J23 job jet jug join joke jail jewel jeans juicy juror
24 Joe judges he left his jacket at the jazz concert.

K25 kind keg key duck link knew knife asks knock wreck
26 Kevin likes to eat all kinds of cakes and cookies.

L27 old log leg oil all able like well lily link lilac
28 Local hillbillies like to sell coleslaw and chili.

M29 me my am may him man mast made some make madam mat
30 Many mechanics moved more machines into the rooms.

N31 on an no and not can new when only than find thank
32 Nine men and one woman have not been to the canal.

O33 to of on or do no you for your onto from into copy
34 Go to one audio shop and one radio shop for forms.

P35 up per pop put pay pair hope plum open pipe proper
36 Please put paper, apples, and popcorn in packages.

Q37 quit quiz aqua quack equal quart quiet quote quick
38 Quentin questioned if these quantities were equal.

· · · · 1 · · · · 2 · · · · 3 · · · · 4 · · · · 5 · · · · 6 · · · · 7 · · · · 8 · · · · 9 · · · · 10

Reports with Side Headings and Subheadings

Format
60-character line
Single spacing

Practise each line twice.
Practise as quickly as you can.

Skill Building

Practise at a controlled rate.
Circle your errors. Do Speed
Improvement if you had three
errors or less. Do Accuracy
Improvement if you had four
errors or more.

Think **accuracy**. Take two 15-s
timings on each line. Take two
30-s timings on the complete
set of lines.

Try to do each timing faster.
Take two 15-s timings on each
set of two lines. Take two 30-s
timings on the complete set of
lines.
■ Do Evaluate Your Progress
and determine if you have
improved.

Left-Hand Words

1 raw test wear trades Barbara wax sewer barber draft fast sad

2 Ada regret secret addresses zest crew reads great tea tastes

Evaluate Your Progress

3   Taking dictation requires that one have patience, tact,

and the necessary skills. Dictation can be as difficult for

the secretary as it is for the originator. Any distractions

may cause the loss of the train of thought. Important ideas

that are interrupted may be difficult to recapture. Both of

the individuals must realize that it is necessary to work as

a team for successful and efficient dictation.

. . . .1. . . .2. . . .3. . . .4. . . .5. . . .6. . . .7. . . .8. . . .9. . . .10. . . .11. . . .12

Accuracy Improvement

4 so throw island turkey maid but bicycle body bus rifle burnt

5 wed react drawer freeze added agreed debate stew after swear

6 odd kneel pepper classic approval worried attitude carry see

7 on milk Jimmy lion kimono mop my you in opinion join Joy him

Speed Improvement

8 It is necessary to keep a summary of all our annual charges.

9 As we had not heard from them for months, we became worried.

10 If it is not possible for you to return the books, call him.

11 The charges made by your company must be dropped by Tuesday.

. . . .1. . . .2. . . .3. . . .4. . . .5. . . .6. . . .7. . . .8. . . .9. . . .10. . . .11. . . .12

R 39 or red for our are car her rare very road ran rear

40 I tried to rewrite part of my first four chapters.

S 41 is as so was his set ask this some soap surf sense

42 Asking his sisters to sing these songs is foolish.

T 43 to it at the but two tot that text this they tents

44 I start the day with coffee and whole-wheat toast.

U 45 us up our out you run cut your such unit user upon

46 Your sudden outburst of anger was quite upsetting.

V 47 van ever evil very vein five view have even heaven

48 The heavy moving vans drove over her ivory gloves.

W 49 we was who few way will with were know would which

50 We saw two wood wigwams as we walked by the woods.

X 51 ox axe box six wax next taxi axis text index extra

52 It will be an extra expense if we fix the boxcars.

Y 53 my any may yes why your very only type reply years

54 Many young boys and girls play in the playgrounds.

Z 55 size quiz zero pizza plaza amaze crazy zebra zones

56 What size of pizza should we order from the plaza?

· · · · 1 · · · · 2 · · · · 3 · · · · 4 · · · · 5 · · · · 6 · · · · 7 · · · · 8 · · · · 9 · · · · 10

Sentences with Numbers

Take two 1-min timings on
each sentence.
Circle all errors.

57 The concert begins at 16:30 and we sit in Row B49.

58 Put the 25 books, 38 cards, and 7 hats in the box.

· · · · 1 · · · · 2 · · · · 3 · · · · 4 · · · · 5 · · · · 6 · · · · 7 · · · · 8 · · · · 9 · · · · 10

Assess Your Progress

Set for double spacing. Take
two 3-min or two 5-min timings.
Circle all errors. Calculate
Gross Words Per Minute
(GWPM).
Record your best timing on
your personal progress chart.

Three- or Five-Minute Timing

		1	CW	3
Humans are not the only species given to getting drunk.		12	12	4
It occurs among the paw-and-wing set also. Robins are known		24	24	8
to become intoxicated on the bright red berries of the happy		36	36	12
Florida holly. A flock of robins will strip any handy trees		48	48	16
bare in a couple of hours, after which they do a lot of low-		60	60	20
altitude flying in wobbly circles. The robins can be easily		72	72	24
grounded and tend to fall off telephone wires.		81	81	27
Bears regularly become intoxicated when apple trees are		12	93	31
handy. They gorge themselves on the fruit until they become		24	105	35
uncomfortably stuffed. Their great body heat then turns the		36	117	39
swelled stomachs into active stills which ferment the apples		48	129	43
into potent applejack. Afterward, the puzzled bears stagger		60	141	47
into the woods and loll around for hours. The bears attempt		72	153	51
to sleep off the benders and may wake up with a hangover.		83	164	55
The most interesting drinkers in the animal kingdom are		12	176	59
found among the ants. Some ants get drunk on a nectar which		24	188	63
they extract from the bodies of certain beetles. Since ants		36	200	67
are always hurrying about on their household errands and are		48	212	71
very community-minded, the entire hill becomes involved. It		60	224	75
is difficult for the drunk ant to rest as the others attempt		72	236	79
to rouse him/her. They may even dump the boozer into water.		84	248	83

```
• • • • 1 • • • • 2 • • • 3 • • • • 4 • • • • 5 • • • 6 • • • • 7 • • • • 8 • • • • 9 • • • • 10 • • • • 11 • • • • 12      1 min
            1                    2                    3                    4                  3 min
```

SI 1.47

Composition

Compose a short advertisement for a new product which is to be introduced on television, radio, or in magazines and newspapers in the near future. Supply a suitable title for the product you choose.

Prepare a rough copy of your advertisement. Print a copy if you are using a computer. Edit and make any necessary corrections in pen or pencil. Then, make a good copy of the advertisement.

Selected Number Practice

1. Circle all errors in the Sentences with Numbers.
2. From your errors, choose the number or numbers which gave you difficulty.
3. Select the appropriate drill lines in the Selected Number Practice.
4. Practise each line twice concentrating on accuracy.
5. If you had no errors in the Sentences with Numbers, or if you complete the accuracy lines before your teacher calls **time**, start at line 0 and **push** for speed. Practise each line once.

Practise each line twice.
Practise as quickly as you can.

1 59 1 not 11 in 121 as 1 for 111 like 11 and 1 gets 11

2 60 2 for 21 so 22 do 2 at 222 but 12 of 2 122 not 221

3 61 3 in 333 for 31 and 3 313 so 3 is 33 to 323 as 333

4 62 4 by 44 like 44 is 4 144 as 4 for 414 but 43 as 44

5 63 5 and 5 as 55 in 5 155 not 55 to 53 for 5 like 555

6 64 6 were 626 the 66 for 62 but 6 166 are 66 to 6 626

7 65 7 in 7 717 not 77 are 72 is 7 yet 76 for 77 and 71

8 66 8 are 838 and 8 is 88 to 8 288 in 8 for 881 and 88

9 67 9 but 969 yet 99 for 9 929 by 9 like 9 to 9 not 99

0 68 0 is 10 for 900 as 8 020 and 100 now 200 for 9 030

• • • • 1 • • • • 2 • • • • 3 • • • • 4 • • • • 5 • • • • 6 • • • • 7 • • • • 8 • • • • 9 • • • • 10 are calling a close friend. Ask at the beginning of the conversation if you've called at a convenient time. If someone calls you at an inconvenient time, say so, and offer to call back later.

Make a Good Impression

Be pleasant and considerate. Pronounce your words carefully. Don't speak too loudly. Avoid chewing gum or eating while talking, and don't carry on a three-way conversation with someone on the phone and with someone in the room. If necessary, excuse yourself for a moment, and when you return to the phone, give your full attention to the caller.

Explain When You Leave

If you must leave the line, explain the reason. If you know it will be some time before you can return to the phone, offer to call the person back.

Take a Message

If a phone call is for someone else and that person isn't available, take a message. Get all the details -- the caller's name and number. Jot down the time of the call -- and be sure the person being called gets the message!

■ Did you include the page number at the top of page two?

Production

Using the Backspace Method, centre the following table attractively on a full sheet of paper.

Canadian Colleges and Universities

University of British Columbia	Vancouver
University of Calgary	Calgary
Carleton University	Ottawa
Laurentian University	Sudbury
Laval University	Quebec
McMaster University	Hamilton
Nipissing University College	North Bay
Ontario Veterinary College	Guelph
Osgoode Hall Law School	Toronto
University of Saskatchewan	Saskatoon
University of Western Ontario	London

■ The **c** in the word McMaster is on the line. In handwritten copy it is written above the line.

■ Did you centre the title in caps?

Timing

Set for double spacing. Take two 2-min timings. Circle all errors. Calculate Gross Words Per Minute (GWPM). Record your best timing on your personal progress chart.

SI 1.38

Two-Minute Timing

	1	2
A glider is a motorless aircraft. It was the	10	5
first type of flying machine to remain in the air.	20	10
Many attempts were made to fly with crude gliders.	30	15
Today people run down a huge hill against the wind	40	20
and leap into the air. The legs and body are used	50	25
to maintain balance. The intent is to soar like a	60	30
graceful bird. Gliding is a popular activity.	69	35

```
· · · 1 · · · · 2 · · · 3 · · · · 4 · · · · 5 · · · 6 · · · 7 · · · · 8 · · · 9 · · · · 10     1 min
        1           2           3           4           5              2 min
```

Production 2

Input the following report which uses side headings. Use correct format. Remember to listen for the right margin signal if you are using a typewriter as the production does not use the standard report line length. You will have to decide where to end page one so that you will have a bottom margin of 6-10 lines. If you are using a computer, is there a top/bottom margin default?

13

DEVELOPING GOOD TELEPHONE MANNERS

TS

The telephone is the most frequently used method of distance communication. Most companies conduct a major portion of their transactions over the telephone.

Telephone manners are important in a business setting, as well as in the home. During a telephone call, both parties are unable to see each other. The impression given (and received) over the telephone must come from the voice, speech, vocabulary, and manners.

Here are some tips for developing good telephone manners.

TS

Be Reasonable

DS

Make your calls at a reasonable hour. Never call late at night or early in the morning. When you do call, let the phone ring from seven to ten times to allow the person called enough time to answer. When your phone rings, answer as promptly as possible.

TS

Check the Number

DS

If you are in any doubt, check the number you are calling before you dial. If you do dial a wrong number, always apologize for the error. Be sure you have the correct number before you dial again.

TS

Identify Yourself

DS

Whenever you phone someone, identify yourself. Guessing games drive people crazy. Give your full name, unless you

Open Tables with Blocked Column Headings

Format
50-character line
Single spacing

Practise each line twice.
Practise as quickly as you can.

Format
50-character line
Single spacing

Practise each line twice.
Practise as quickly as you can.

Skill Building

Practise each line once.
Repeat *or* take two
15-s timings on each line.

Practise each line once.
Practise each line again.

Edit each line by correcting
two errors.
Practise each line once with
the corrections.

Hyphenation Rule

Read the Hyphenation Rule.
Practise each line once,
hyphenating the words
according to the Hyphenation
Rules.
Each line will end evenly at the
right margin when the rules
are applied correctly.

One-Hand Words

1 no as dare pin fat hop saw scar pull lily fed cast

2 at on joy axe add lip you card deaf test edge pump

Common-Word Sentences

3 John wants to go to the docks to watch four ships.

4 The cars raced around the curves and up the hills.

5 The child played with his toy boat and three cars.

Sentences with Numbers

6 The terms of the January 9 invoice are 2/10, n/30.

7 The metric date for August 31, 1989 is 1989 08 31.

Editing Practice

8 Every one loves to read stories with happy ending.

9 my favourite ice cream flavour is buttered almond.

10 The interior fo campers are often lined with wood

· · · · 1 · · · · 2 · · · · 3 · · · · 4 · · · · 5 · · · · 6 · · · · 7 · · · · 8 · · · · 9 · · · · 10

Hyphenation

Rule 4: Do not hyphenate words of one syllable.

Examples:

washed baked blonde burnt could danced dealt house milked

11 cooked play tacked large light cramped toast right

12 tipped schemes sharp searched versed youth through

13 ruthless wide-awake route loose-leaf should fight

14 feared face-off household yearn co-workers stream

15 playpen pilgrimage marriages shrink shrinkage

· · · · 1 · · · · 2 · · · · 3 · · · · 4 · · · · 5 · · · · 6 · · · · 7 · · · · 8 · · · · 9 · · · · 10

Production Practice

■ Do you have preset tabs?
■ Do you have a top/bottom margin default?

Hyphenation Review

■ Do you have an indent option?

Production 1

Review the correct format for enumerated material in Lesson 61. Input the Review of Hyphenation Rules on a full sheet of paper. Set a 60-character-line (pica — 10 pitch) or a 70-character line (elite — 12 pitch). Use correct format for this enumerated material. The title is on line 13. *Note:* This will not be vertically centred.

Review of Hyphenation Rules

1. Hyphenate words between speech syllables (pic-ture).

2. Hyphenate words between double letters of speech syllables (gram-mar).

3. Divide only after the hyphen in a compound word (twenty-one).

4. Do not hyphenate words of one syllable (washed).

5. Do not leave a one-letter syllable at the beginning or end of a line (agree).

6. Avoid leaving a two-letter syllable at the beginning or end of a line (reply).

7. A one-letter syllable in the middle of a word should not be carried over to the new line. When two separately sounded vowels come together in a word, divide between them (dedi-cate).

8. Do not hyphenate proper names (Canada).

9. Do not hyphenate abbreviations, numbers, or contractions (couldn't).

Formatting Guide for Side Headings in Reports

Side Headings	• Underscore at the left margin. Capitalize the first letter of each main word in the side heading.
Spacing	• Triple space before a side heading.
	• Double space after a side heading.

Production 1

Centre the following table on a half sheet of paper. Use block centring for the column headings.

```
      THE FIRST MCDONALD'S MENU IN CANADA
    DS↓
        Richmond, British Columbia
   TS|        June 1, 1967
     ↓
          Item              Price
    DS↓
       ↓Hamburger           20 cents
        Cheeseburger        25
        French Fries        20
        Hot Apple Pie       25
        Shakes              20
        Milk                15
        Coca-Cola           10
        Orangeade           10
        Coffee              10
        Hot Chocolate       10
```

Production 2

Centre the following table attractively on a half sheet of paper. Use variable spacing in the body of the table.

```
        METRIC RANGE OF MASSES
      TS|
        Item↓               Mass
    DS↓
       ↓Jumbo jet Boeing 747   340 t
        Elephant                 7 t
        Volkswagen               1 t

        Large motorcycle       250 kg
        Good-sized turkey       10 kg
        Desk telephone           2 kg
```

Flashlight D cell   100 g
A slice of bread   25 g
A nickel   5 g

Small blueberry   500 mg
Cherry stem   100 mg
Postage stamp   20 mg

↑
Align
numbers.

Reports with Side Headings

Format

60-character line
Single spacing

Practise each line twice.
Practise as quickly as you can.

Skill Building

Practise at a controlled rate.
Circle your errors. Do Speed
Improvement if you had three
errors or less. Do Accuracy
Improvement if you had four
errors or more.

Think **accuracy**. Take two 15-s
timings on each line. Take two
30-s timings on the complete
set of lines.

Try to do each timing faster.
Take two 15-s timings on each
set of two lines. Take two 30-s
timings on the complete set of
lines.
■ Do Evaluate Your Progress
and determine if you have
improved.

Practise each line once.
Practise each line again.

Alternate-Hand Words

1 if Diane icicle visible chairman flap socks formal hand burn

2 am hair penalty flame snake problem pant eye ornament handle

Evaluate Your Progress

3 The rented blue van was waiting for the students at the
school. Students were arriving with their luggage, sleeping
bags, and whatever would be used in the play. They would be
leaving for the drama festival which was being held in Trail
this year. This was the first time their school had won the
zone competition; they were going to the provincials. Other
students, parents, and teachers were there to see them off.

· · · · 1 · · · · 2 · · · · 3 · · · · 4 · · · · 5 · · · 6 · · · · 7 · · · · 8 · · · · 9 · · · 10 · · · · 11 · · · · 12

Accuracy Improvement

4 fill meet follow appear final spilled cannot guess immediate

5 my link pull holy minimum jolly join plum hill lip upon yolk

6 pa cow virus quantity right also aid man then kept corn clay

7 dear area extra reads safest garages attract baggage address

Speed Improvement

8 After we have checked the oil, drive your car to the garage.

9 It appears that the enclosed paper was done by someone else.

10 The pretty kitten in the corridor got my attention all week.

11 It is difficult to offer good food and coffee in our school.

Number Practice

12 Bus 490 left at 16:28 and will take 32 h to travel 2 956 km.

13 She had a 350 mL vanilla milkshake and 125 g of fudge today.

· · · · 1 · · · · 2 · · · · 3 · · · · 4 · · · · 5 · · · · 6 · · · · 7 · · · · 8 · · · · 9 · · · 10 · · · · 11 · · · · 12

Set for double spacing. Take two 2-min timings. Circle all errors. Calculate Gross Words Per Minute (GWPM). Record your best timing on your personal progress chart.

SI 1.16

Two-Minute Timing

1 2

```
        She sadly placed the little brown dish out by     10  5

the door.  It had once again been filled with more        20  10

fresh clean water.  The other little dish was blue        30  15

and it was ready to be used.  Her eyes filled with        40  20

tears as she looked at the dishes.  Berty had been        50  25

their family dog for five years.  He had been gone        60  30

for three days now.  As she looked up, she saw the        70  35

man from city hall.  Berty was under his arm.             79  39
```

```
· · · 1 · · · · 2 · · · · 3 · · · · 4 · · · · 5 · · · 6 · · · · 7 · · · · 8 · · · · 9 · · · · 10     1 min
         1              2              3              4              5                 2 min
```

Composing Practice

Think and answer as quickly as you can without hesitating.

Composition

Revise the following sentences, replacing the wrong word in each sentence with the correct word from the list below.

delegates	cosmic	distinguished
fragrant	corps	junction
launch	aspires	entertain

```
1. Tomorrow the captain will lance the ship.

2. Alan joined the officers' training corpse.

3. All delicates to the conference arrived early.

4. Astronauts must guard against cosmetic rays.

5. Our principal is a very extinguished person.
```

The snake lifted its small head, hissed and then struck	12	12	4
quickly. Its fangs sunk deep into the foot of the woman who	24	24	8
had unwittingly disturbed it. The woman froze in the grass,	36	36	12
her eyes glazed with terror. She screamed, ran a few steps,	48	48	16
and dropped dead. Instant death by snakebite? People don't	60	60	20
die that suddenly from a bite. That woman died from fright.	72	72	24
The snake was harmless and not poisonous.	80	80	27
There are many documented cases of such deaths, and all	12	92	31
testify to the terrible power which the venomous snakes have	24	104	35
upon the imaginations of people. Each year more than 30 000	36	116	39
people die from snakebites. With the spread of civilization	48	128	43
into all parts of the world, there is great demand for anti-	60	140	47
venin. This demand has also caused the price to rise.	70	150	50
Not all snakebites are accidental; some are suicides or	12	162	54
homicides. The snake has been used as a murder weapon since	24	174	58
time began, especially in Asia. Cleopatra's death is one of	36	186	62
the most famous suicide cases.	42	192	64

```
· · · · 1 · · · · 2 · · · · 3 · · · · 4 · · · · 5 · · · 6 · · · · 7 · · · · 8 · · · · 9 · · · · 10 · · · · 11 · · · · 12
              1                    2                   3                   4
```

1 min

3 min

Assess Your Progress

Set for double spacing. Take two 3-min *or* two 5-min timings. Circle all errors. Calculate Gross Words Per Minute (GWPM).
Record your best timing on your personal progress chart.

For a 5-min timing, divide the total words as indicated in the CW column by five to calculate Gross Words Per Minute (GWPM).

SI 1.44

(/)/ Open Tables with Blocked Column Headings

Format
50-character line
Single spacing

Practise each line twice.
Practise as quickly as you can.

Skill Building

Practise each line once.
Repeat *or* take two
15-s timings on each line.

Hyphenation Rule

Read the Hyphenation Rule.
Practise each line once,
hyphenating the words
according to the Hyphenation
Rules.
Each line will end evenly at the
right margin when the rules
are applied correctly.

Practise each line once.
Practise each line again.

Practise each underlined word
four times. Practise each line
once concentrating on the
underlined words.

One-Hand Words

1 we ink bad pop gas hill were dead junk exact bread

2 in are oil you hum debt join fade link refer straw

Common-Word Sentences

3 Henry crossed the street and entered the building.

4 Give your card to the lady in the pale blue dress.

5 The lights were out for five days after the storm.
· · · · 1 · · · · 2 · · · · 3 · · · · 4 · · · · 5 · · · · 6 · · · · 7 · · · · 8 · · · · 9 · · · ·10

Hyphenation

Rule 5: Do not leave a one-letter syllable at the beginning or end of a line.

Examples:

agree along equal item open odour silky taxi

6 handy party about above hairy ozone many acute era

7 wavy aboard ready stuffy avail aware avoid healthy

8 skinned well—spoken hairless copy canning locked

9 dropped chairman leaflet climbed five—star jumps

10 hurtful hard—hearted such thrilled tanned kitten

Sentences with Numbers

14 The store at 101 St. and 107 Ave. has 62 red rugs.

15 Call Sue at 242-9751 by 18:30 so she can bring 64.

Spelling Practice

16 Who will be your opponents in the golf tournament?

17 Their analysis of the situation was very accurate.
· · · · 1 · · · · 2 · · · · 3 · · · · 4 · · · · 5 · · · · 6 · · · · 7 · · · · 8 · · · · 9 · · · ·10

7

Page 2

TS

In the COMPANY PROGRAM, high school students meet one evening a week, from October to May. They start, operate, and finally, liquidate their own small companies. Along with adult advisers from business and industry, they decide on a product to produce and sell, or a service to offer. Each JA company is composed of 12 to 20 teenage members. Volunteers give advice, but the teenagers make the decisions and do the work. They open bank accounts, pay wages, keep records, etc.

Business firms find that JA graduates become more knowledgeable employees and consumers. They have been exposed to business operations and have an understanding of working with people. JA benefits young people by building self-confidence and leadership ability. JA provides excellent human relations training and realistic work experience.

Basic English

it's: contraction of **it is**
its: the possessive form of **it**, belonging to

Read the definition of each word.
Practise each sentence once using the correct word in parentheses.

18 The cat licked (it's, its) paws.

19 (It's, its) best to check the phone number before dialing.

20 I think (it's, its) supposed to be a surprise party.

Reach to the (and) Keys

Use the left shift key and the **L** finger.

Use the left shift key and the **;** finger.

Practise each line twice.

21 lll l9l l(l l(l lll (((l(l(l((l(9 l(9 (l (l ((

22 ;;; ;0; ;); ;); ;;;))) ;) ;) ;)) ;)0 ;)0););))

23 Lance (the goalie) passed the puck to Grant first.

24 Elsa likes: (1) computing, (2) math, and (3) art.

Production Practice

■ *program* or *programme*

Know the preference in your area of Canada.

Production 1

Centre the following three-column table on a half sheet of paper. Use block centring for the column headings.

		ONTARIO PLACE
DS ↓		
	Program Events	
	(July 1–July 31)	
DS ↓		
	THE FORUM	
TS ↓		

Date	Time	Event
July 1	20:00	Hagood Hardy
July 5	20:30	Dr. Hook
July 7	20:30	The Toronto Symphony
July 12	(events all day)	UKRANIAN HERITAGE DAY
July 24	20:30	Preservation Hall Jazz Band
July 27	(events all day)	ITALIAN DAY

⌐6⌐   ⌐6⌐

Production 2

Input the following two-page report. It will be necessary to determine when to stop at the bottom of page one. If you are using a typewriter, a backing sheet will help you determine the bottom margin for page one. If you are using a computer, determine if there is a top/bottom margin default.

This report uses a 60-character line (pica—10 pitch).

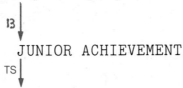

13

JUNIOR ACHIEVEMENT

TS

Junior Achievement (JA) is a non-profit organization which teaches young people how free enterprise works. Over the past 68 years, more than nine million young people in 17 countries have participated in JA activities.

Support for JA programs comes mainly from the business community which contributes money, equipment, and volunteers.

JA began in Canada in the 1950s. Presently, there are 40 JA areas in Canada, offering "hands-on" business experience to students through three major educational programs.

BUSINESS BASICS is a program for fifth and sixth grade students. It gives these young people their first look at the business world. This program is conducted weekly in-class, often by trained Achievers, as well as by adult consultants from the business community. The four-week program covers business organization, management, production, and marketing.

In PROJECT BUSINESS, eighth and ninth grade students learn about basic economic principles, the stock market, consumerism, and career planning from business executives. They also participate in field trips to local businesses.

Title:

Body:

■ Do you know how to triple space after the title when the line spacing for the body is double spacing?

■ If you are using a computer,
• Is word wrap *on*?
• Did you read the software and printer manuals to determine the top and bottom margin defaults?

■ Are you near the end of page one?

Production 2

Arrange the following as an attractive three-column table.

Handwriting Traits
(and their interpretations)

Trait	Degree	Characteristic
Slant	moderate forward	healthy extrovert
	extreme forward	emotional
	mild backward	reserved
Size	small	modest
	medium	private but social
	large	confident
Thickness	bold	adventurous
	average	balanced
	light	sensitive

The symbol ∿ means transpose.

■ Did you centre the title in caps?

Two-Minute Timing

	1	CW	2

They walked quickly down the lane. The faint
sound seemed far behind them. Not one of them was
able to look back. There was an eerie hoot from a
big owl. All of a sudden, the low moon was hidden
by a huge, black cloud.

The trees in the lane cast strange shadows on
the path. The sound behind them grew louder. Was
it their imagination or was it really close behind
them?

	1	CW	2
	10	10	5
	20	20	10
	30	30	15
	40	40	20
	44	44	22
	10	54	27
	20	64	32
	30	74	37
	1	75	38

· · · 1 · · · 2 · · · 3 · · · 4 · · · 5 · · · 6 · · · 7 · · · 8 · · · 9 · · · 10   1 min
1   2   3   4   5   2 min

Timing

Set for double spacing. Take two 2-min timings. Circle all errors. Calculate Gross Words Per Minute (GWPM). Record your best timing on your personal progress chart.

SI 1.19

In the COMPANY PROGRAM, high school students meet one evening a week, from October to May. They start, operate, and finally, liquidate their own small companies. Along with adult advisers from business and industry, they decide on a product to produce and sell, or a service to offer. Each JA company is composed of 12 to 20 teenage members. Volunteers give advice, but the teenagers make the decisions and do the work. They open bank accounts, pay wages, keep records, etc.

Business firms find that JA graduates become more knowledgeable employees and consumers. They have been exposed to business operations and have an understanding of working with people. JA benefits young people by building self-confidence and leadership ability. JA provides excellent human relations training and realistic work experience.

■ Are you near the end of page one?

■ Did your teacher show you how to use a backing sheet if you are using a typewriter?

36

$ / Open Tables with Blocked Column Headings

Format
50-character line
Single spacing

Practise each line twice.
Practise as quickly as you can.

Skill Building

Practise each line once.
Repeat *or* take two
15-s timings on each line.

Hyphenation Rule

Read the Hyphenation Rule.
Practise each line once,
hyphenating the words
according to the Hyphenation
Rules.
Each line will end evenly at the
right margin when the rules
are applied correctly.

Use the right shift key and the
F finger.
Practise each line twice.

Do not space after the $.

Practise each line once.
Practise each line again.

Alternate-Hand Words

1 it by wit cut fog map sob held worn heir fork corn

2 he is rug lap bow sir bug malt name flap work hand

Common-Word Sentences

3 Most of what you need is in the third storage bin.

4 His dark coat is wet from being outside all night.

5 The door would not close so the puppy ran past me.

Hyphenation

Rule 6: Avoid leaving a two-letter syllable at the beginning or end of a line.
Examples:

reply enjoy former medium oiler object poorly ulcers

6 ordeal order widely absent ago logic maybe repairs

7 resort quicker locker machines direct older duplex

8 condemned perfect option defrost daylight depot

9 one-time passing perjury owing opposition pair

10 indoors displacements painter paper also smaller

Reach to the $ Key

11 fff f4f f$f fff $$$ f$ f$ f$$ f$4 f$4 $f $f f$$ f$

12 Albums cost $7.98 or $8.29, but some may be $6.45.

13 The bills for $2.95, $13.64, and $85.72 were lost.

Sentences with Numbers

14 Prices went from $96.87 to $137.50 after 15 weeks.

15 A 3-wood costs $24.95 and a 9-iron will be $36.85.

· · · · 1 · · · · 2 · · · · 3 · · · · 4 · · · · 5 · · · · 6 · · · 7 · · · · 8 · · · · 9 · · · · 10

Production

Input the following report. This report is two pages long. It will be necessary to determine when to stop at the bottom of page one. If you are using a typewriter, a backing sheet will help you determine the bottom margin for page 1. If you are using a computer, determine if there is a top/bottom margin default.

This report uses a 70-character line (elite--12 pitch)

13 ↓

JUNIOR ACHIEVEMENT

TS ↓

5 Junior Achievement (JA) is a non-profit organization which teaches young people how free enterprise works. Over the past 68 years, more than nine million young people in 17 countries have participated in JA activities.

Support for JA programs comes mainly from the business community which contributes money, equipment, and volunteers.

JA began in Canada in the 1950s. Presently, there are 40 JA areas in Canada, offering ''hands-on'' business experience to students through three major educational programs.

BUSINESS BASICS is a program for fifth and sixth grade students. It gives these young people their first look at the business world. This program is conducted weekly in-class, often by trained Achievers, as well as by adult consultants from the business community. The four-week program covers business organization, management, production, and marketing.

In PROJECT BUSINESS, eighth and ninth grade students learn about basic economic principles, the stock market, consumerism, and career planning from business executives. They also participate in field trips to local businesses.

■ Do you know how to triple space after the title when the line spacing for the body is double spacing?

■ If you are using a computer,
• Is word wrap *on*?
• Did you read the software and printer manuals to determine the top and bottom margin defaults?

■ Did you place your balance line 12 lines from the bottom of the page?

16 When does michael expect to by his new motorbike?

17 People need 60minutes a day of physical actiśty.

18 Never enter competitition when you are out   of shape.

· · · · 1 · · · · 2 · · · · 3 · · · · 4 · · · · 5 · · · · 6 · · · · 7 · · · · 8 · · · · 9 · · · · 10

Production

Centre the following table on a full sheet of paper. Arrange it attractively.

Production Practice

■ Use capital letters for Roman Numerals.

```
Title:  MEDAL STANDINGS

Subtitles:  XV Olympic Winter Games
            Calgary, 1988

Column Headings:  Country / G / S / B / T
```

■ G stands for Gold
S stands for Silver
B stands for Bronze
T stands for Total

Country	G	S	B	T
Soviet Union	11	9	9	29
East Germany	9	10	6	25
Switzerland	5	5	5	15
Austria	3	5	2	10
West Germany	2	4	2	
Finland	4	1	2	
Netherlands	3	2	2	
Sweden	4	0	2	
United States	2	1	3	
Italy	2	1	2	
Norway	0	3	2	
CANADA	0	2	3	
Yugoslavia	0	2	1	
Czechoslovakia	0	1	2	
France	1	0	1	
Japan	0	0	1	
Liechtenstein	0	0	1	

complete the final column

8   4   4   4

■ Did you centre the key line?

Reports

Informal reports are written to give information about routine facts or information.
Formal reports are written to give information about a study of a particular problem or topic.

Reports may be either one-page or multi-page.

A one-page report may or may not require a title page. If a title page is not required, the author's name should appear on the report page, after the title, at the bottom of the page, or in a designated area.

A multi-page report usually consists of a title page (see Lesson 85), a table of contents (if the report is long), the body of the report, and then the bibliography (see Lesson 87).

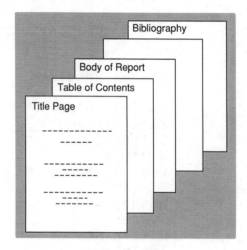

Formatting Guide for Reports

Line Length	• Set a 70-character line (elite — 12 pitch) or a 60-character line (pica — 10 pitch).
Spacing	• The body is usually double spaced. • For particularly long reports, use single spacing or one and one-half spacing.
Top Margin	• Page one The title is on line 13. • Page two The page number is on line 7.
Bottom Margin	• Leave 6-10 blank lines (usually 6 lines).
Page Numbering	• Page one No page number. • Page two Place the page number on line 7, pivoting from the right margin followed by a triple space.
Title	• Capitalize and centre the title on line 13. Then, triple space to the body of the report.
Subtitle (when used)	• Capitalize the first letter of each main word in the subtitle and centre it double spaced below the title. Then, triple space to the body of the report.
Paragraphs	• Indent paragraphs five spaces.

Set for double spacing. Take
two 2-min timings. Circle all
errors. Calculate Gross Words
Per Minute (GWPM). Record
your best timing on your
personal progress chart.

SI 1.19

Composing Practice

Think and answer as quickly
as you can without hesitating.

Two-Minute Timing

		1	CW	2

When you were young, going to visit family or
friends was not always a good time. You know what
it was like to have to sit quietly with nothing at
all to do. The time went by so slowly.

Some people did have so many books to look at
and lots of special toys to play with. A glass of
milk and a plate of cookies made the day. All the
visits should have been like that.

	CW 1	CW	CW 2
	10	10	5
	20	20	10
	30	30	15
	38	38	19
	10	48	24
	20	58	29
	30	68	34
	37	75	38

· · · · 1 · · · · 2 · · · · 3 · · · · 4 · · · · 5 · · · · 6 · · · · 7 · · · · 8 · · · · 9 · · · · 10   1 min

     1   2   3   4   5   2 min

Composition

Antonyms are words of opposite meaning. (For example, an antonym for *hot* would
be *cold*.) Set the left margin at 25. Set a tab at 50. Input the following words at your
left margin, and input the antonyms (or opposites) at the tab.

dry   wet

success

false

noise

rare

heavy

friend

Spacing Reminder: Dollar Sign $

No space after a dollar sign.

Summary of Editors' Marks (Proofreaders' Marks)

⁊ new paragraph	⁊Begin a new paragraph	Begin a new paragraph
⌒ close up space	put to‿gether	put together
∧ insert space	space once�˰here	space once here
∧ insert words	this⟍is omitted *word*	this word is omitted
⌐ move left	⌐ move to left margin	move to left margin
⌐ move right	⑤Indent five spaces	Indent five spaces
∿ transpose	out ⟋of⟍order	out of order
ℛ delete	omit this ~~extra~~ word	omit this word
≡ put in capitals	use the shift lock	use the SHIFT lock
/ lower case	do not ¢apitalize	do not capitalize
STET leave in	do not ~~delete~~ this word *STET*	do not delete this word
⋏ insert period	end of this line˄	end of this line.
# extra space	#⟩this should be double spaced	this should be
		double spaced

37

Programs

Format
50-character line
Single spacing

Practise each line twice.
Practise as quickly as you can.

One-Hand Words

1 up as ink act link sad we brew dart cast brag limp

2 on at wet lip dare him oil hoop steer beet far mop

Skill Building

Practise each line once.
Repeat *or* take two
15-s timings on each line.

Common-Word Sentences

3 I am sure the manager will be at the next meeting.

4 The new cook put an extra cup of milk in the cake.

5 The dog lay on the floor until the baby came home.

Practise each line once.
Practise each line again.

Sentences with Numbers

6 One 23 cm pizza costs $4.75 and a 60 cm is $16.25.

7 At 18:30 turn to channel 3 for lap 9 and round 15.

. . . . 1 . . . . 2 . . . . 3 . . . . 4 . . . . 5 . . . . 6 . . . . 7 . . . . 8 . . . . 9 10

Hyphenation Rule

Hyphenation

Rule 7: A one-letter syllable in the middle of a word should not be carried over to the new line.
When two separately sounded vowels come together in a word, divide between them.

Examples:

dedi-cate gradu-ation maga-zine jani-tor mini-mum
valu-able

Read the Hyphenation Rule.
Practise each line once,
hyphenating the words
according to the Hyphenation
Rules.
Each line will end evenly at the
right margin when the rules
are applied correctly.

8 graduate president radiator maximum residents

9 gasoline regulates fixation positive sanitary

10 bruised quick-witted occurring dwelling windows

11 legalize air-conditioned clearly parenthood cool

12 congratulations ideas productive recommends

Spelling Practice

Practise each underlined word
four times. Practise each line
once concentrating on the
underlined words.

13 Richard's <u>experience</u> with <u>foreign</u> cars is limited.

14 The key <u>personnel</u> had <u>similar</u> offices in the area.

. . . . 1 . . . . 2 . . . . 3 . . . . 4 . . . . 5 . . . . 6 . . . . 7 . . . . 8 . . . . 9 10

Reports

Format

60-character line
Single spacing

Practise each line twice.
Practise as quickly as you can.

Skill Building

Practise at a controlled rate. Circle your errors. Do Speed Improvement if you had three errors or less. Do Accuracy Improvement if you had four errors or more.

Right-Hand Words

1 him kilo pupil opinion monopoly pull oily union pin ink only

2 ill you John lip moon hoop jump limp Jim pulp hill nylon Kim

Evaluate Your Progress

3   The car started to stall as he drove up the hill. When

he stopped at the traffic light, the engine quit. The truck

behind pushed him through the intersection and into the next

street. He got out, opened the hood and looked at the sleek

engine. Whatever was causing the problem was not obvious to

him. A driver who was across the street offered to help him

get the car running again.

· · · ·1· · · ·2· · · ·3· · · ·4· · · ·5· · · ·6· · · ·7· · · ·8· · · ·9· · · ·10· · · ·11· · · ·12

Think **accuracy**. Take two 15-s timings on each line. Take two 30-s timings on the complete set of lines.

Accuracy Improvement

4 see mood queer huddle chilly scatter nutshell different week

5 up only hymn look milk pumpkin noun oil pool plump puppy mop

6 me girl lake surname rock tight born fix risk height visible

7 better address pass filling agrees doll steel floor meetings

Speed Improvement

8 Perhaps it would be best if they did not work together here.

9 If we are properly told what to do, we will finish the jobs.

10 Rules and regulations are required for these four new games.

11 It is impossible to discuss staff needs with this committee.

Try to do each timing faster. Take two 15-s timings on each set of two lines. Take two 30-s timings on the complete set of lines.

■ Do Evaluate Your Progress and determine if you have improved.

Practise each line once.
Practise each line again.

Number Practice

12 She bought 19 oranges, 36 apricots, 42 apples, and 8 lemons.

13 The number was 717-806, but the 27 boys said it was 717-904.

· · · ·1· · · ·2· · · ·3· · · ·4· · · ·5· · · ·6· · · ·7· · · ·8· · · ·9· · · ·10· · · ·11· · · ·12

Basic English

personnel: staff
personal: belonging to a particular person

15 All his (personnel, personal) belongings were in the trunk.

16 We are proud of the achievements of our (personnel, personal).

17 Tell us your (personnel, personal) opinion of this new product.

Leaders

A leader is a period. A line of leaders is preceded and followed by a blank space.

Displays with Leader Lines

1. From the left margin, input the beginning of the line, the space, and a period.

2. From the right margin, backspace from the end of the line plus one space and one period. Input period, space, and the end of the line information.

Adult .   . $3.50
      ^   ^

3. Fill in the space between the two periods with a line of leaders.

Adult $3.50

4. Repeat these steps for each line.

Unit IV

Objectives

By completing this unit *you* will:

1 Improve keyboard control.

2 Review the hyphenation, capitalization, and metric rules.

3 Learn to format reports.

4 Learn to format reports with side headings, subheadings, and enumerations.

5 Learn to recognize and review commonly used editors' marks.

6 Learn to format title pages.

7 Learn to format footnotes.

8 Learn to format bibliographies.

9 Learn to format résumés and application letters.

10 Work toward developing a minimum speed of 30 words per minute with five or fewer errors on a five-minute timing; or 30 words per minute with three or fewer errors on a three-minute timing.

Note: Additional production practice for this unit may be found on page 343.

This includes four reports and one bibliography.

Production 1

Using a 40-character line, centre the following program attractively on a half sheet of paper.

THE DRAMA CLUB

presents

Sandy Wilson's

T H E   B O Y   F R I E N D

January 29, 30, 31

8:15 p.m.

TS↓

Admission Prices

```
Adult ............................ $3.50
With student card ................  3.00
Age 12 and under .................  2.50
```

Production 2

Centre the following program on a half sheet of paper. Read the changes before starting.

REGISTER NOW

for

THE COMMUNITY SCHOOL WINTER PROGRAMS

fees range
from
$10 to $25
for
9 sessions

TS↓

Registration Dates

change to metric time

```
Monday, January 5 ....[ 7:00 to 9:00 ] p.m.
Tuesday, January 6 ...[ 6:00 to 8:00 ] p.m.
Monday, January 12 ...[ 7:00 to 9:00 ] p.m.
```

TS↓

Use a 50-character line

Call 233-4181
for
further details

Production 3

Input the following business letter on 3M letterhead. Use full block letter style with mixed punctuation. Input an appropriate envelope or an envelope label. Remember to include all the missing letter parts.

To: *Village Supplies Ltd. 26-27 Street North Brandon, Manitoba R7B 1J4*

From: *A. R. Jenkins, Energy Control Department*

Gentlemen / Thank you for your letter requesting more information about Scotchtint Insulation Film.

We have enclosed some literature which will explain more fully the advantages of this energy-saving product. Not only does it reduce energy loss during the winter heating season, but it also deflects up to 75 per cent of the sun's heat and reduces glare by 82 per cent. This cuts summer air conditioning costs.

Scotchtint is just one of our energy control products. We would be pleased to have a district representative visit you to answer any other questions you may have. /

Set for double spacing. Take two 2-min timings. Circle all errors. Calculate Gross Words Per Minute (GWPM). Record your best timing on your personal progress chart.

SI 1.13

Two-Minute Timing

       The sound of the siren grew louder. They saw
the police car race past. They drove three blocks
and then saw the mess. A small red sports car had
made a left turn in front of a city bus. One girl
had been thrown from the car. The driver was down
on the seat. There was not much left of the small
car. None of the people on the bus had been hurt.
They drove very slowly from then on.

	1	2
	10	5
	20	10
	30	15
	40	20
	50	25
	60	30
	70	35
	77	39

• • • 1 • • • 2 • • • • 3 • • • 4 • • • 5 • • • 6 • • • 7 • • • 8 • • • 9 • • • 10   1 min

         1   2   3   4   5   2 min

Production 1

Input a rough draft in order to determine the number of lines. Vertically centre a second copy on a half sheet of paper. Use correct format for enumerated material.

Title: Some Seat Belt Facts

Enumerations: 1. Seat belts can help prevent serious collisions by keeping the driver behind the wheel and in control of the car.

2. Unbelted passengers can seriously injure others by striking or crushing them against the car in a collision.

3. A child should never be held in an adult's lap.

4. Seat belts keep people conscious and uninjured enabling them to get free of the car.

Production 2

You wish to enrol in a driver education course. Complete the Driver Education Application Form.

■ If you are using a computer, ask your teacher if you should do this or a different production exercise?

DRIVER EDUCATION APPLICATION FORM

Time	Sessions		Fee
Tuesdays	1. September 15	--October 30	$83
16:00 to	2. November 3	--December 12	
18:00	3. January 10	--February 24	
	4. March 2	--April 18	
	5. May 1	--June 13	

SCHOOL _____

Name _____

Address _____
(including postal code)

_____

_____

Telephone Number _____ Parent/Guardian _____

Business Phone No. _____

Birth Date _____

Cheque Enclosed $ _____ Money Order Enclosed $ _____

Cheque or Money Order Signed by _____

Session No. _____ Date of Session _____

Programs

Format
50-character line
Single spacing

Practise each line twice.
Practise as quickly as you can.

Skill Building

Practise each line once.
Repeat *or* take two
15-s timings on each line.

Hyphenation Rule

Read the Hyphenation Rule.
Practise each line once,
hyphenating the words
according to the Hyphenation
Rules.
Each line will end evenly at the
right margin when the rules
are applied correctly.

Practise each line once.
Practise each line again.

Edit each line by correcting
two errors.
Practice each line once with
the corrections.

Alternate-Hand Words

1 an to dot rib own did city body worn dock pay torn

2 if or six own bus tie got auto they risk both dial

Common-Word Sentences

3 When will you be able to visit your three cousins?

4 Ask him to make a list of all the supplies needed.

5 The radio was on all day and Marco listened to it.

· · · · 1 · · · · 2 · · · · 3 · · · · 4 · · · · 5 · · · · 6 · · · · 7 · · · · 8 · · · · 9 · · · ·10

Hyphenation

Rule 8: Do not hyphenate proper names.

Examples:

Canada Inuit English French Hudson Bay Kawasaki

6 Charlie Brown Teresa Gregory January Olympics Ford

7 Wimbledon August Klondike Days Pitman Honda Fonzie

8 relocate regiment Coca-Cola keenness labelling

9 Air Canada hollow immortal pavement jacket lamb

10 knuckle punishment prompt repetition gruesome

Sentences with Numbers

11 Those bills for $5.10 and $7.49 must be paid soon.

12 The store has items 37-659 and 48-1527 for $23.81.

Editing Practice

13 Please call Mr. Foster orf an appointment with us.

14 You have 30 minutes to complet the test question

15 Use a dictionaryto find the spellling of the word.

· · · · 1 · · · · 2 · · · · 3 · · · · 4 · · · · 5 · · · · 6 · · · · 7 · · · · 8 · · · · 9 · · · ·10

Evaluate Your Progress

Format
60-character line
Single spacing

Take two 30-s timings on each line. Practise each phrase as quickly as you can.

Common Phrases

1 please return/please arrange/please reply/please consider it/

2 when they/when will/when we/when may/when possible/when your/

Practise each line twice.

Common-Word Sentences

3 Always keep a pen or pencil and notepad near your telephone.

4 In all the excitement, they forgot to give us the addresses.

5 Please pick up your reservations four days before your trip.

· · · · 1 · · · · 2 · · · · 3 · · · · 4 · · · · 5 · · · · 6 · · · · 7 · · · · 8 · · · · 9 · · · ·10· · · ·11· · · ·12

Timing

Set for double spacing. Take two 3-min timings. Circle all errors. Calculate Gross Words Per Minute (GWPM). Record your best timing on your personal progress chart.

Three-Minute Timing

	1	CW	3
Baby elephants are cared for not only by their mothers,	12	12	4
but by several female elephants. These aunts will take over	24	24	8
the care of the little ones when a mother is ill, absent, or	36	36	12
dead. A game warden saw two adult females rescue a male who	48	48	16
had slipped into a river and was drowning. The aunts rushed	60	60	20
down the bank, dropped into the water, retrieved the excited	72	72	24
baby, and carried him to shore with their mighty tusks.	83	83	28
This protective instinct within the herd is not limited	12	95	32
only to helping the young. The same observer saw a sick old	24	107	36
elephant who was slowly dying. As the elephant grew weaker,	36	119	40
his companions grew more attentive. All of them showed some	48	131	44
signs of anxiety. When the old fellow collapsed, others ran	60	143	48
to him. One of them quickly began to blow air into his open	72	155	52
mouth. He was saved by artificial respiration.	81	166	55

· · · · 1 · · · · 2 · · · · 3 · · · · 4 · · · · 5 · · · · 6 · · · · 7 · · · · 8 · · · · 9 · · · ·10· · · ·11· · · ·12   1 min

      1   2   3   4   3 min

SI 1.44

Production Practice

■ *program* or *programme*

Know the preference in your area of Canada.

Production

Arrange the following program attractively on a full sheet of paper.

FIFTY–SIXTH ANNUAL GRADUATION

Friday, October Twenty–Fourth

TS ↓

P R O G R A M M E

TS ↓

O Canada

Invocation .... Reverend J. Mould

Chairman's Remarks .... Mr. D. B. Thorburn

Regional Superintendent .... Mr. J. Masewich

Student Council President .... Shirley Phillips

****

Presentation
of
Honour Graduation Diplomas
Secondary School Graduation Diplomas
Honour Certificates
Scholarships, Awards, and Prizes

****

Musical Selection .... School Band

Valedictorian .... Brian Marling

Production 2

Input the following business letter on Spruce Grove Composite High School letterhead. Use full block letter style with mixed punctuation. Input an appropriate envelope or an envelope label.

Remember to include all the missing letter parts.

spruce grove composite high school

1000 Calahoo Road, Spruce Grove, Alberta T7X 2T7   962-0800

County of Parkland No. 31

Ms. Barbara Allen
Public Relations Officer
Scotiabank
44 King Street West
Toronto, Ontario
M5H 1H1

Thank you for sending copies of your Monthly Review and of your Scotiabank Budget Book. A number of our teachers have expressed an interest in using both publications in their classes.

Please place our name on your mailing list to receive a class set of 40 copies of the Monthly Review. These copies will be shared by several teachers in our business department. May we also receive 120 copies of the Scotiabank Budget Book for use in our Introduction to Business courses.

Thank you for your cooperation in supplying us with this material.

Cheryl Willoughby
Business Education Department

SI 1.40

Composing Practice

Think and answer as quickly as you can without hesitating.

Two-Minute Timing

		1	CW	2

Many students like to have part—time jobs.   A · 10 | 10 | 5

little extra money can be very helpful.   You might · · · · 20 | 20 | 10

find that it helps pay for your clothes and little · · · · 30 | 30 | 15

expenses, such as shows or dances.   If you plan to · · · · 40 | 40 | 20

go to college or university, it would be very wise · · · · 50 | 50 | 25

to set aside a small amount each week towards your · · · · 60 | 60 | 30

future education. · · · · 63 | 63 | 31

A part—time job can help you to decide on the · · · · 10 | 73 | 36

nature of your future career.   Look for a job with · · · · 20 | 83 | 41

a company that interests you. · · · · 26 | 89 | 45

· · · · 1 · · · · 2 · · · · 3 · · · · 4 · · · · 5 · · · · 6 · · · · 7 · · · · 8 · · · · 9 · · · · 10   1 min

1   2   3   4   5   2 min

Composition

Creepy Crawlers: How many insects, reptiles, or animals can you name that crawl close to the earth and cannot fly? Centre each one on a separate line. Begin your list with the following:

snake

centipede

Production 1

Input a rough draft in order to determine the number of lines. Vertically centre a second copy on a full sheet of paper. Use correct format for enumerated material.

■ Did you listen for the right margin signal? OR Did you use word wrap?

Motorcycling – Safe Driving Tips

1. Drive defensively. Be ready to allow for any action other drivers may take.

2. Look out for intersections. Always be ready to stop quickly if necessary.

3. Road conditions and surfaces affect the stability of a motorcycle much more than that of a car. Always be aware of the conditions and road surface ahead of you.

4. Know the law. The rules of the road apply to motorcyclists as well as to other motorists.

5. Give the required hand signals (or signal with a signalling device).

6. Keep a safe distance according to the speed you are travelling.

7. Maintain a safe motorcycle. Have it checked regularly by a competent mechanic or set up your own inspection schedule to ensure that your motorcycle is in top condition.

8. Develop proper riding habits and operating techniques.

9. Know how to brake properly – this is one of the most important skills of motorcycling.

10. An approved helmet should be worn at all times when riding a motorcycle.

■ Align the units in two-digit numbers. e.g.　9.
　　　　　　10.

Skill Building / Programs

Format
50-character line
Single spacing

Practise each line twice.
Practise as quickly as you can.

Skill Building

Practise each line once.
Repeat or take two
15-s timings on each line.

Practise each line once.
Repeat or take two
15-s timings on each line.

Hyphenation Rule

Read the Hyphenation Rule.
Practise each line once,
hyphenating the words
according to the Hyphenation
Rules.
Each line will end evenly at the
right margin when the rules
are applied correctly.

■ Use periods without
spaces in geographical
abbreviations.

■ Do not use periods or
spaces with acronyms (well-
known abbreviations).

Take two 30-s timings on each
line. Do each phrase as
quickly as you can.

One-Hand Words

1 as raw hop tag are hulk read loon wart union aware

2 my stare him date mop lion street up were hop fast

Alternate-Hand Words

3 or and bud fig oak busy dock foam they digit shape

4 he rod fix doe eye worn pant lamb corn elbow tight

Common-Word Sentences

5 When will they be able to visit us at the cottage?

6 When her work was finished, she played the guitar.
· · · ·1· · · ·2· · · ·3· · · ·4· · · ·5· · · ·6· · · ·7· · · ·8· · · ·9· · · ·10

Hyphenation

Rule 9: Do not hyphenate abbreviations, numbers, or contractions.

Examples:

couldn't $11.50 #115734 RCMP won't doesn't 20/20 UNESCO

7 shouldn't etc. No. 8256 that's they're $363 000.00

8 VISA 262-1157 U.S.A. wouldn't $82 Policy No. 33221

9 demanding keyboard outer outbidding YMCA royal

10 vagueness tongue play-by-play pneumonia whether

11 listings isn't sardine shrink inbound caretaker

Common Phrases

12 on the/on them/on our/on it/on her/on each/on your/

13 in fact/in it/in our/in all/in your/in time/in few/

14 for your/for me/for this/for you/for the/for these/
· · · ·1· · · ·2· · · ·3· · · ·4· · · ·5· · · ·6· · · ·7· · · ·8· · · ·9· · · ·10

Graduated Speed Practice
1. Turn to Lesson 30, page 84.
2. Drill on the appropriate Graduated Speed Practice.

Unit Review

Format

60-character line
Single spacing

Practise each line twice.
Practise as quickly as you can.

Common Words

1 copy class require useful public enclosure month all request

2 information explain away control pleased business won trusts

Number and Character Practice

3 The manual read, "Quality is more important than quantity".

4 We are missing the following invoices: #2163, #4957, #9788.

5 Ben works for the A & W on Saturdays from 08:00 until 17:00.

6 We understood you would ship 130 cases @ $7.95/case at once.

7 Rearrange the price tags in this order: 99¢, 73¢, 67¢, 26¢.

· · · · 1 · · · · 2 · · · · 3 · · · · 4 · · · · 5 · · · · 6 · · · · 7 · · · · 8 · · · · 9 · · · · 10 · · · · 11 · · · · 12

Speed Drills

Take two 15-s timings on each
line. Take one 30-s timing on
the set of lines.
■ Did you do each timing
faster?

Timing

Set for double spacing. Take
two 3-min timings. Circle all
errors. Calculate Gross Words
Per Minute (GWPM). Record
your best timing on your
personal progress chart.

Three-Minute Timing

	1	CW	3
Moving from one place to another is a common experience	12	12	4
for many families. The move may be to another neighbourhood	24	24	8
in the same town or to a new location in another province in	36	36	12
Canada or in a foreign country. The family may cut its ties	48	48	16
and be uprooted to a very different environment. All of the	60	60	20
family members will learn how to handle situations which are	72	72	24
very new. Many changes will have to be made.	81	81	27
There are always regrets when leaving good friends. It	12	93	31
is natural to feel this way. On the bright side, a new area	24	105	35
will provide a chance to meet more friends. A move can be a	36	117	39
growing experience for the whole family. New grocery stores	48	129	43
must be found, a doctor has to be located, and school has to	60	141	47
be attended. These aspects of moving ought to be challenges	72	153	51
that everyone meets with eagerness and hope for the future.	83	164	55

· · · · 1 · · · · 2 · · · · 3 · · · · 4 · · · · 5 · · · · 6 · · · · 7 · · · · 8 · · · · 9 · · · · 10 · · · · 11 · · · · 12

1 min

    1   2   3   4

3 min

SI 1.47

Basic English

compliment: praise
complement: to complete

15 Mr. West (complimented, complemented) the student on his project.

16 Accessories often (compliment, complement) an outfit.

17 A (compliment, complement) is appreciated when it is sincere.

Alphabetic Sentences

18 Jacklyn cooked some zucchini squash for supper and served Max a big portion with milk and crackers.

19 The female lynx quickly attacked the grizzly bears when they approached the jagged entry to the cave.

. . . . 1 . . . . 2 . . . . 3 . . . . 4 . . . . 5 . . . . 6 . . . . 7 . . . . 8 . . . . 9 10

Selected Letter Practice
1. Turn to Lesson 33, page 94.
2. Select the appropriate letters.

Two-Minute Timing

	1	CW	2
Bike riding is a fun way to stretch your legs	10	10	5
and lungs. The fresh air will make you feel good,	20	20	10
and cycling might help you to work off those extra	30	30	15
pounds.	32	32	16
Take good care of your bike. It takes only a	10	42	21
few minutes each month to clean and oil the moving	20	52	26
parts of your bike. Be sure to pump air into your	30	62	31
tires when they become soft. Keeping your bike in	40	72	36
good running order is a matter of common sense.	49	81	41

. . . . 1 . . . . 2 . . . . 3 . . . . 4 . . . . 5 . . . . 6 . . . . 7 . . . . 8 . . . . 9 10   1 min

    1   2   3   4   5   2 min

SI 1.20

Timing

Set for double spacing. Take two 3-min timings. Circle all errors. Calculate Gross Words Per Minute (GWPM). Record your best timing on your personal progress chart.

SI 1.54

Three-Minute Timing

	1	CW	3
Grandma Moses was an American primitive painter who was	12	12	4
born in 1860 and died in 1961. She began painting at 76 and	24	24	8
never attended art classes. In the year following her 100th	36	36	12
birthday she painted 25 pictures. Before she began to paint	48	48	16
her specialty was canvas embroidery. When arthritis made it	60	60	20
difficult to grasp the needles used for the delicate stitch-	72	72	24
ing, she became a painter.	77	77	26
Critics have praised her work for its freshness, as she	12	89	30
painted with an innocent view of humans. She did simple but	24	101	34
realistic scenes of rural life. Colourful and lively scenes	36	113	37
from her childhood have been viewed by many people. Her art	48	125	41
was displayed in the first one-woman art show.	57	134	47

```
• • • •1• • • •2• • • •3• • • •4• • • •5• • • •6• • • •7• • • •8• • • •9• • • •10• • • •11• • • •12        1 min
       1                    2                    3              4                  3 min
```

Composing Practice

Think and answer as quickly as you can without hesitating.

Composition

Many animals have defence mechanisms that they utilize when threatened or alarmed. Explain using sentence format what the defence mechanism is for each of the following animals. Use a separate sentence for each one.

beaver, porcupine, rattlesnake, skunk, chameleon

Production

Arrange the following program attractively on a full sheet of paper. Indent three spaces for the second line of a continuation line. Insert leaders between the two columns.

PRESENTATION
of
Proficiency Scholarships and Awards

GENERAL PROFICIENCY

Gold Medallist .... Despina Massis

Grade 12 .... Jeannette Goguen

Grade 11 .... Elena Bellino

Grade 10 .... Gail Inouye

Grade 9 .... Mary Ficco

TS

SPECIAL AWARDS AND SCHOLARSHIPS

DS

Steel Company of Canada .... Karen Recchia

Canadian Institute of Food
3 Science and Technology .... Byung Wook Chun

Kiwanis Club Award .... Howard Chou

Lions Club Award .... Joan Apap

Rotary Club .... Maureen Bynoe

I. O. D. E. .... Barbara Wardle

University of Toronto
3 Open Admission Scholarship .... Despina Massis

St. Michael's College
3 Scholarship .... Marie Louise Savella

■ Indent three spaces for continuation line.

The symbol 3 means indent 3 spaces.

Production 2

Input the following business letter on Scotiabank letterhead using full block letter style with mixed punctuation. Input an appropriate envelope or an envelope label. Remember to include all missing letter parts.

Scotiabank Ⓢ
THE BANK OF NOVA SCOTIA

General Office, 44 King Street West, Toronto, Ontario, Canada M5H 1H1

To: Ms. Cheryl Willoughby / Business Education Department / Spruce Grove Composite High School / 1000 Calahoo Road / Spruce Grove, Alberta / T7X 2T7
From: Barbara Allen / Public Relations Officer /

Thank you for your recent letter requesting copies of our publications.

We have sent you several copies of our Monthly Review, an economic publication. If you find these of use in your classes, please advise us and we will put your name on our mailing list.

Also enclosed is our Scotiabank Budget Book. These are also available in quantities, should you require them.

We hope that these items will be useful to you. Thank you for thinking of Scotiabank.

Yours truly,

Reproduced with the permission of The Bank of Nova Scotia.

40

Open Tables with Shorter Column Headings

One-Hand Words

1 at we kill desert kin west aged rest pull tree fee

2 my as pink rag pin him nook face case draw mop few

Common-Word Sentences

3 Make a list of six books and albums that you like.

4 Their new office is down that hallway on the left.

5 The theme and title kept them both busy for hours.

Sentences with Numbers

6 The 186 hay fields were 350 m long and 274 m wide.

7 There are 3 kittens and 17 puppies in the 9 boxes.

Editing Practice

8 Knee prob lems are common to jogger and sprinters.

9 See Castle Dracula for the night mare of yuur life!

10 The ICON andthe Apple IIE are personel computers.

· · · · 1 · · · · 2 · · · · 3 · · · · 4 · · · · 5 · · · · 6 · · · · 7 · · · · 8 · · · · 9 · · · · 10

Two-Minute Timing

You must be aware of what you eat. Our diets
play a large part in how we feel. Everyone should
take special care to develop good eating habits.

Try to start each day with a proper meal. So
often people are in a hurry and skip breakfast. A
balanced breakfast will provide you with a lasting
energy. It is probably the most important meal of
the day.

1	CW	2
10	10	5
20	20	10
30	30	15
10	40	20
20	50	25
30	60	30
40	70	35
41	71	35

· · · · 1 · · · · 2 · · · · 3 · · · · 4 · · · · 5 · · · · 6 · · · · 7 · · · · 8 · · · · 9 · · · 10   1 min

    1   2   3   4   5   2 min

Production Practice

■ If you are using a computer, did you ask your teacher for another exercise?

Production 1

Complete the Application Form for Part-Time Employment.

Last Name

First Name and Initials

Social Insurance Number ▲

Address (Residence)

Postal Code

Telephone No.

Second Contact No.

A. ☐ Male ☐ Female Date of Birth D M Y

B. Status Indian, Inuit Metis or Non-status Indian ☐ Yes ☐ No

C. Disabled/Handicap You Wish Considered ☐ Yes ☐ No

D. Visible Minority ☐ Yes ☐ No

Are You Legally Entitled to Work in Canada ☐ Yes ☐ No

Are You Presently Attending School or an Academic Institution this Year ☐ Yes ☐ No

If Yes, Where?

Major or Course of Study

Will You be Attending School or an Academic Institution in the Upcoming Academic Year? ☐ Yes ☐ No

What Year or Grade

Availability for Work (Summer) Date Available From D M D To

Times Available ☐ Day ☐ Evening ☐ Night ☐ Weekend

Hours Available

Types of Summer Jobs Preferred 1 2 3

☐ Full Time ☐ Part Time ☐ Shift Work Odd Jobs ☐ Yes ☐ No

Part Time After School ☐ Yes ☐ No Hours Available

Drivers Licence ☐ Yes ☐ No Class

Words Per Minute Typing Dictaphone Shorthand Word Processing

Are You a National Lifeguard ☐ Yes ☐ No

Transportation ☐ Use of Car ☐ Local Transit ☐ Bicycle ☐ Truck ☐ Other

Skills — Computer Languages, Hardware, Software, Experience, Mechanical Ability Photography, Scuba Diving Certificates, Hobbies, First Aid Course etc.

Languages Spoken: French ☐ Good ☐ Fair English ☐ Good ☐ Fair Written: ☐ Good ☐ Fair ☐ Good ☐ Fair

Describe Previous Work (Duties or Occupation/Volunteer Experience) How Long What Year

Name of Business or Organisation

Date Signature

Your voluntary response to questions A, B and C will assist us to make statistical analysis of service needs and support for various segments of the population and designed target group clients. In addition question (B) is to identify native students who may wish to be considered for special programs and services designed for natives; question (C) is to identify students who may wish to be considered for programs which have special measures for the disabled or handicapped.

Employment and Immigration Canada Emploi et Immigration Canada

STUDENT REGISTRATION

EMP-2837E (12-86)

Open Tables with Column Headings Shorter than Columns

```
              City              Province

        Drumheller        Alberta
        Flin Flon         Manitoba
       *Shawinigan Falls  Quebec
        Truro             Nova Scotia*
```

*The key line is: Shawinigan Falls _____ Nova Scotia.
                                   │ 6 spaces │

Backspace Method

To Set a Left Margin and a Tab for Column 2

1. To set a left margin using the Backspace Method, backspace **once** for every two letters in the longest item (the key words) in each column and for the six spaces between the two columns. You have now centred the key line.

   - Note the character or cursor position.
   - Set the left margin at this point.

2. Clear all tabs. To set a tab for the second column, forward space from the left margin the key words in column one, plus the six spaces between columns.

   - Note the character or cursor position.
   - Set a tab at this point.

To Centre Headings Over Columns

3. • Go to the centre point of the first column by starting at the left margin and forward spacing **once** for every two letters and spaces in the key words of the column.

   ```
   Shawinigan Falls
   ﹀ ﹀ ﹀ ﹀ ﹀ ﹀ ﹀ ﹀
   ```

   • Next, backspace **once** for every two letters and spaces in the column heading.

   ```
   City
   ﹀ ﹀
   ```

   • Input the column heading.

4. • Go to the centre point of the second column by starting at the beginning of the second column (at the tab) and follow the same procedure. Forward space **once** for every two letters and spaces in the key words of the column.

   ```
   Nova Scotia*
   ﹀ ﹀ ﹀ ﹀ ﹀ *
   ```

   • Then, backspace **once** for every two letters and spaces in the column heading.

   ```
   Province
   ﹀ ﹀ ﹀ ﹀
   ```

   • Input the column heading.

   *Ignore odd letters or spaces.

Note: Master the Backspace Method.

Unit Review

Format

60-character line
Single spacing

Practise each line twice.
Practise as quickly as you can.

Speed Drills

■ Try to practise each timing faster.
Take two 15-s timings on each line. Take one 30-s timing on the set of lines.

Take two 15-s timings on each line. Take one 30-s timing on the set of lines.
■ Did you do each timing faster?

Practise each line once.
Practise each line again.

Read the definition of each word.
Practise each sentence once using the correct word in parentheses.

Alternate-Hand Words

1 is nap with lens gland title signal element surname chairman

2 or dog when rock flame their formal flap fit pens whale land

Sentences with Double-Letter Words

3 An abscess in a tooth can affect tissue and cause suffering.

4 The yellow daffodils looked pretty in the green bamboo vase.

5 Pioneers supply moccasins made of deer hide and rabbit skin.

Common-Word Sentences

6 They stopped to get the presents as he decided to stay home.

7 They stopped at the plaza to buy the presents for the party.

8 The slow easy beat of the drum helped to relax the audience.
· · · ·1· · · ·2· · · ·3· · · ·4· · · ·5· · · ·6· · · ·7· · · ·8· · · ·9· · · ·10· · · ·11· · · ·12

Number Practice

9 She has 18 skirts, 29 dresses, 33 tops, and 41 hats for you.

10 The 729 groups took 586 days to complete the 29 730 km trip.
· · · ·1· · · ·2· · · ·3· · · ·4· · · ·5· · · ·6· · · ·7· · · ·8· · · ·9· · · ·10· · · ·11· · · ·12

Basic English

lend: grant the use of something (verb)
loan: the temporary use of something (noun)

11 I will (lend, loan) you the money until the beginning of December.

12 Sumio found it necessary to take out a (lend, loan) for his car.

13 Will you (lend, loan) me that record? I will return it tomorrow.

Production 1

Using the Backspace Method, centre the following two-column table on a half sheet of paper. Centre the column heading horizontally over each column.

ELECTRONIC GAMES

Company	Game
Nintendo	The Legend of Zelda
Atari	Flight Simulator II
Sega	Grand Prix
Fidelity	Chess Computer
Tech	Electronic Baseball
Broderbund	Spelunker
Nintendo	Metroid
Konami	The Goonies II

Production 2

Using the Backspace Method, centre the following table attractively on a half sheet of paper.

Expressing Time

12 - Hour Clock	24 - Hour Clock
5:30 a.m.	05:30
11:25 a.m.	11:25
12:00 a.m. (noon)	12:00
2:15 p.m.	14:15
6:00 p.m.	18:00
10:45 p.m.	22:45
12:00 p.m. (midnight)	24:00 or 00:00

Composition

Answer the following sports questions.
1. Name four sports in which nets are used.
2. Name three sports in which players can score goals.
3. Name five sports in which a type of ball is used.
4. Name three sports in which the players must use racquets.
5. Name five sports which have not been covered in the above questions.

Production 3

Input the following letter on Spruce Grove Composite High School letterhead. Use full block letter style with mixed punctuation. Input an appropriate envelope or an envelope label.

Mr. O. Toshiaki, Principal/s
Sendai Ikuei Gakuen High School / 4-1, Miyagino 2-chome / Sendai/
Miyagi / 983 JAPAN.

Thank you for your letter of April 2, 19-- in which you agreed to have Alison Daley participate in your Student Exchange Program as of August 31, 19--.

As requested, I am returning the completed Form 2400 for Tanaka-san. All of us are looking forward to her visit. at Spruce Grove I will meet her at Vancouver International

Alison will be arriving in Tokyo on Canadian Airlines flight CP3 from Vancouver at 16:55 on September 1, 19--.

Airport and accompany her to Alberta. Thank you for ~~agreeing~~ participating in the Student Exchange Program again. Sincerely Cheryl Willoughby, Bus Ed Dept.

Set for double spacing. Take two 2-min timings. Circle all errors. Calculate Gross Words Per Minute (GWPM). Record your best timing on your personal progress chart.

SI 1.78

Two-Minute Timing

			1	2
Their note of 1989 06 28 invited us to the 125th annual			12	6
party. A two-course dinner will be served at 19:00, and the			24	12
dance will begin at 21:45. The cost is $19.50 per guest; no			36	18
money refunded after 1989 07 15. Bus tickets cost $6.50 for			48	24
the return trip. Tickets are available at 1872 - 82 Avenue,			60	30
or 1793 - 71 Street until 1989 07 26.			67	33

• • • • 1 • • • • 2 • • • • 3 • • • • 4 • • • • 5 • • • • 6 • • • • 7 • • • • 8 • • • • 9 • • • • 10 • • • 11 • • • • 12   1 min

1   2   3   4   5   6   2 min

Open Tables with Shorter Column Headings

Format
50-character line
Single spacing
Practise each line twice.
Practise as quickly as you can.

Skill Building

Practise each line once.
Repeat *or* take two
15-s timings on each line.

Alternate-Hand Words

1 to pay of jam pen lap ant snap girl bow chapel rot

2 he so jay tow ape fig key lake pant bush span lamb

Common-Word Sentences

3 The terms state that the work must be done neatly.

4 The card games lasted until noon so she left late.

5 The girls may go by bus to the chapel in the city.

Practise each line once.
Practise each line again.

Sentences with Numbers

6 Bus 526 made 18 stops in 76 km on the return trip.

7 The scores were 46 to 27 and 38 to 15 for 2 games.

Practise each underlined word
four times. Practise each line
once concentrating on the
underlined words.

Spelling Practice

8 Check the library bulletin board for your notices.

9 A calendar of events was recorded in the brochure.

Read the definition of each
word.
Practise each sentence once
using the correct word in
parentheses.

Basic English

dessert: part of a meal
desert: desolate and barren region
  to abandon

10 What were you planning to have for (dessert, desert)?

11 Tropical fruit can be grown in (dessert, desert) oases.

12 Ann—Marie would not (dessert, desert) a friend in need.

· · · · 1 · · · · 2 · · · · 3 · · · · 4 · · · · 5 · · · · 6 · · · · 7 · · · · 8 · · · · 9 · · · · 10

Production 2

Input the following business letter on Royal York Minor Hockey League letterhead. Use full block letter style with mixed punctuation. Input an appropriate envelope or an envelope label. Remember to include all missing letter parts.

ROYAL YORK MINOR HOCKEY LEAGUE

"TO KEEP A BOY OUT OF HOT WATER ... PUT HIM ON ICE"

To: Mr. Eric Fitzgibbon
9 Tollington Road
Weston, Ontario
M9R 2C7

Enclosed is your registration form for this year's Royal York House League hockey. The upcoming season's activities have been carefully planned, and we look forward to having you participate again.

Please fill out the enclosed form in the places indicated and return the entire form to me in the enclosed self-addressed envelope, together with a cheque covering the registration fee.

We plan to commence hockey at the end of September, and you will be contacted prior to that time by your series convenor.

Be sure to send in your registration form as soon as possible.

Bob Yuzwin

President

ROYAL YORK HOUSE LEAGUE & SELECTS
ETOBICOKE HOCKEY ASSOCIATION
METROPOLITAN TORONTO HOCKEY LEAGUE
ONTARIO HOCKEY ASSOCIATION

Production 1

Using the Backspace Method, centre the following three-column table attractively. Centre the column headings horizontally over each column.

Remember: The title should be in all capital letters and the column headings should be underscored.

Title: Sport Shoes

Column Headings: Make / Name of shoes / Category

```
Reebok / Phase 1 / Men's/Women's Court
New Balance / 830 / Men's Training
Romika / Finesse / Women's Court
Adidas / Lendl Supreme / Junior Court
Reebok / Freestyle Brites / Women's Aerobic
Nike / Cross Trainer / Men's Training
Avia / 460 / Women's Fitness
Puma / Attack / Men's Tennis
```

- Did you capitalize the title?

- Did you underscore the column headings?

Production 2

Using the Backspace Method, centre the following three-column table attractively on a half sheet of paper.

Title: Sidewalk Sale Specials

Column Headings: Store / Special / Price

Woodwards	Braun Silencio Dryer	$ 25.99
The Bay	Sony Walkman WM-F46	129.88
Shoppers Drug Mart	Magnetic Photo Album	4.77
Pet Fair	Cockatiels	59.80
Hakim Optical	Foster Grant Sunglasses	12.00
Sears	Canon SolarCalc	24.66

- Did you centre the key line?

Two-Minute Timing

	1	2

There were two unique visitors at the Calgary | 10 | 5

Zoo. Giant pandas from China were on loan for six | 20 | 10

months. Pandas are bearlike mammals, mostly white | 30 | 15

with black legs and shoulders. Pandas are related | 40 | 20

to racoons. They do not eat meat. They thrive on | 50 | 25

bamboo shoots. Pandas are gentle and they are not | 60 | 30

often in a hurry. They love to play and have fun. | 70 | 35

About one million people will see the pandas. | 79 | 39

```
· · · · 1 · · · · 2 · · · · 3 · · · · 4 · · · · 5 · · · · 6 · · · · 7 · · · · 8 · · · · 9 · · · · 10      1 min
            1              2              3              4              5                               2 min
```

Timing

Set for double spacing. Take two 2-min timings. Circle all errors. Calculate Gross Words Per Minute (GWPM). Record your best timing on your personal progress chart.

SI 1.38

Production 1

Arrange the following material in correct business letter format on Mimico High School letterhead. Not all the letter parts are given below. Input the letter as a full block letter with mixed punctuation. Include all the missing letter parts. Input an appropriate envelope or envelope label.

Remember to include all missing letter parts.

MIMICO HIGH SCHOOL

A Proud Tradition!

1924 -1988

April 10, 19-

Ms. Franca Franceschini
213 Royal York Road
Toronto, Ontario
M8V 2V5

The plans for our FOND FAREWELL to a PROUD TRADITION
are firming up and enthusiasm is growing quickly.
Enclosed is your ticket confirmation. Please retain
it for use when picking up the actual tickets
May 16-21.

We have received letters and calls from many distant
places--Calgary, Vancouver, Florida, Arizona, and
California. Of the 1800 people who have already
registered, about one third are pre-1945, one third
1945-1965 and the remainder from 1965 to the present.

We would like to thank all of the many volunteers
that have helped on various committees. See you at
the FOND FAREWELL!

D. B. Thorburn
Principal

Open Tables with Shorter Column Headings

Format
50-character line
Single spacing

Practise each line twice.
Practise as quickly as you can.

Skill Building

Practise each line once.
Repeat *or* take two
15-s timings on each line.

Practise each line once.
Practise each line again.

Edit each line by correcting
two errors.
Practise each line once with
the corrections.

Production Practice

The symbol ◡ means close
up the space.

One-Hand Words

1 be on egg oil bar lip vest pool save junk bear hop

2 in as pin sad saw milk fast zest look great get on

Common-Word Sentences

3 Address an envelope so that I can mail the letter.

4 We hope you will work hard and learn to ride well.

5 Get the task done and you will be able to go home.

Sentences with Numbers

6 Maria, be sure to be here by 07:30 to take bus 46.

7 Radio 630 plays rock from 08:20 to 11:45 each day.

Editing Practice

8 Summer is a time of freedom,holidays,and travel.

9 Congratulation on your new job; hope you like it!

10 over 500 animals and birds live at at the Valley Zoo.

· · · · 1 · · · · 2 · · · · 3 · · · · 4 · · · · 5 · · · · 6 · · · · 7 · · · · 8 · · · · 9 · · · · 10

Production 1

Using the Backspace Method, attractively arrange the following table on a half sheet of paper.

CANADIAN NATURE TOURS

Date	Tour
July 6◡–◡12	CAPE BRETON Backpacking in the National Park
July 13◡–◡19	KILLARNEY CANOEING Novice canoeing in beautiful Killarney
July 27 – Aug. 2	NORTH SHORE OF SUPERIOR Spectacular islands, travel by boat and van
Aug. 18 – 22	PARRY SOUND RIDING On horseback, Georgian Bay area
Aug. 24 – 30	MONTREAL RIVER CANOEING A delightful week for the experienced novice

Letters

Format

60-character line
Single spacing

Practise each line twice.
Practise as quickly as you can.

Speed Drills

■ Try to practise each timing faster.
Take two 15-s timings on each line. Take one 30-s timing on the set of lines.

Take two 15-s timings on each line. Take one 30-s timing on the set of lines.
■ Did you do each timing faster?

Practise each line once.
Practise each line again.

Read the definition of each word.
Practise each sentence once using the correct word in parentheses.

Common Phrases

1 may write/may wash/may send/may walk/may play/may not/may we/

2 are here/are there/are not/are very/are somewhat/are correct/

Sentences with Double-Letter Words

3 Ginny cannot go shopping tomorrow for the food and supplies.

4 This committee's assignment was to seek effective processes.

5 Keep the callers in the office until the letters are issued.

Common-Word Sentences

6 Due to the cold weather, the cars and truck would not start.

7 I do not want to pass up their offer to visit them in Banff.

8 On the long weekend, he stopped in to visit them five times.
   · · · · 1 · · · · 2 · · · · 3 · · · · 4 · · · · 5 · · · · 6 · · · · 7 · · · · 8 · · · · 9 · · · 10 · · · 11 · · · 12

Number Practice

9 It will take 23 months to finish the 95 doors and 74 frames.

10 The date on the 376 invoices was 1990 05 30, not 1990 04 22.
   · · · · 1 · · · · 2 · · · · 3 · · · · 4 · · · · 5 · · · · 6 · · · · 7 · · · · 8 · · · · 9 · · · 10 · · · 11 · · · 12

Basic English

all together: in one group
altogether: completely

11 The committee made the decision (all together, altogether).

12 Turn to page 57. Repeat lines 3 to 10 (all together, altogether).

13 Anton is an (all together, altogether) different person since the

accident.

Production 2

Attractively centre the following table on a half sheet of paper. Use double spacing.

Title: Calendar of Canadian Events
Column Headings: City / Event / Date

Vancouver	Vancouver Sea Festival	July 2-20
Calgary	Calgary Exhibition and Stampede	July 4-13
Edmonton	Klondike Days	July 16-26
Toronto	Canadian National Exhibition	Aug. 15-Sept. 2
Montreal	Man and His World	July 1-Sept. 1
St. John	Loyalist Days Celebrations	July 15-19
Halifax	Acadian Festivities	July 10-13

(St. circled — spell out)

Two-Minute Timing

		1	CW	2
Money is usually not an answer. Far too much		10	10	5
time is spent hoping for more money. Do not waste		20	20	10
energy in dreams about being rich. The only means		30	30	15
most of us have for getting rich is hard work.		39	39	19
Most people who are given a fortune or win in		10	49	24
a lottery are still not happy all of the time. It		20	59	29
takes more than money to be happy. Happiness does		30	69	34
depend on other factors as well.		36	75	37

· · · · 1 · · · · 2 · · · · 3 · · · · 4 · · · · 5 · · · · 6 · · · · 7 · · · · 8 · · · · 9 · · · · 10   1 min
          1   2   3   4   5   2 min

Composition

Each of the following statements explains a word beginning with the letters "stu". Centre each answer on a separate line.

```
to prepare for a test
pupil
sensational feat
to trip and almost fall
artist's workroom
lacking fresh air
part of a tree after the top is cut
short, used up pencil
to knock senseless
material used inside a pillow
```

Sidebar

Timing

Set for double spacing. Take two 2-min timings. Circle all errors. Calculate Gross Words Per Minute (GWPM). Record your best timing on your personal progress chart.

SI 1.34

Composing Practice

Think and answer as quickly as you can without hesitating.

Production 3

Compose a personal letter to a friend or relative. Input an appropriate envelope or an envelope label.

Three-Minute Timing

Loyal fans were shocked the day Gretzky was traded. It
was one of the biggest trades in hockey history. This trade
involved eight players and millions of dollars. The players
had to move and make changes to play with their new teams.

Gretzky is a small-town boy who worked hard to become a
great hockey player. He began playing on the river near the
farm where he grew up. Later he played on the backyard rink
made by his dad. It was there that he learned many skills.

His name has come to mean success. He has helped teams
win many games. He has played world junior games and broken
numerous records. In fact, it could be said that his talent
has rewritten all of the hockey record books.

1	CW	3
12	12	4
24	24	8
36	36	12
47	47	16
12	59	20
24	71	24
36	83	28
48	95	32
12	107	36
24	119	40
36	131	44
45	140	47

· · · · 1 · · · · 2 · · · · 3 · · · · 4 · · · · 5 · · · 6 · · · · 7 · · · · 8 · · · · 9 · · · 10 · · · · 11 · · · 12   1 min

        1   2   3   4   3 min

Composition

Compose a short descriptive paragraph on one of the following subjects:

hockey   pets   hobbies

Timing

Set for double spacing. Take two 3-min timings. Circle all errors. Calculate Gross Words Per Minute (GWPM). Record your best timing on your personal progress chart.

SI 1.25

Composing Practice

Think and answer as quickly as you can without hesitating.

43

Open Tables with Longer Column Headings

Format
50-character line
Single spacing

Practise each line twice.
Practise as quickly as you can.

Skill Building

Practise each line once.
Repeat *or* take two
15-s timings on each line.

Practise each line once.
Practise each line again.

Edit each line by correcting
two errors.
Practise each line once with
the corrections.

Composing Practice

Think and answer as quickly
as you can without hesitating.

One-Hand Words

1 we no are nil bad joy tea were noun best pill moon

2 on at dad lip was you vat jump date pony ease join

Common-Word Sentences

3 Ask them to show you the red ball before the game.

4 There is a good view of the beach along this road.

5 Call them just in case they sleep in and miss you.

Sentences with Numbers

6 Ken, you save $9.82 if you buy 7 watches by 14:45.

7 The amount of the last bill was $36.90, not $3.90.

Editing Practice

8 We are enjoying much more liesure time these days.

9 May, Jully and Au gust are my very favourite months.

10 Forty per cent of the people vo ted for this mayer.

. . . . . 1 . . . . . 2 . . . . 3 . . . . 4 . . . . 5 . . . . 6 . . . . 7 . . . . 8 . . . . 9 10

Composition

The following short paragraph has 10 words that have been transposed. Revise the paragraph so that the words appear in their proper order.

How Tell to a Frog From Toad a: A frog slender

is, has moist smooth skin and leaps long on hind

legs. A toad stocky is, has dry rough skin hops

and on short legs hind. A frog in lives or water

near. A toad is often far found from water.

Production 2

Input the following personal letter on a plain sheet of paper. Use full block letter style with mixed punctuation. Input an appropriate envelope or an envelope label.

1055 Ducharme Avenue
Winnipeg, Manitoba
R3V 1B3
Current Date

Dear Pat

No luck in the job hunting as yet. I almost took a job on Saturdays in a pet store, but I discovered that it would take me an hour to get there so I decided against that.

I joined the school yearbook staff this year. I work twice a week, inputting material for the printer. I find my inputting speed is improving and the material is interesting too.

I haven't made any specific summer plans yet, but I know my parents will also be taking a vacation during the summer. We might rent a cottage in the Riding Mountain Park area. We did that two summers ago and had a lot of fun.

We're on a semester system this year for the first time so our exams come at different times. We have 70-minute classes, and we take only half our subjects at a time. In January we write final exams for half of our subjects. Then, we begin classes for the remainder of our subjects. At first, I thought I would dislike the system, but it has lots of advantages. Best of all, you only have to worry about half of your courses at one time.

What are you doing for winter break? Will you be visiting your sister? Be sure to let me know if you do. Maybe we can get together.

Your friend

Chris

Open Tables with Column Headings Longer than Columns

```
*French Word            English Translation*

    douze                   twelve
    fin                     end
    manger                  to eat
    soie                    silk
    vert                    green
```

*The key line is: French Word   English Translation
                           | 6 spaces |

Backspace Method

To Input the Column Headings

1. Backspace **once** for every two letters and spaces in the two column headings and the six spaces in between the headings. You have now centred the key line.

2. Input the first column heading at this point. Forward space six times for the spaces between the two columns. Input the second column heading. (It is unnecessary to set a left margin or tab at this point since the columns themselves are shorter than the column headings.)

To Set a Left Margin and a Tab for Column 2

3. • To set a left margin, start at the beginning of the first column heading and forward space **once** for every two letters and spaces in the column heading. This is the centre point of the heading.

```
French Word*
Ↄ Ↄ Ↄ Ↄ Ↄ *
```

Then, backspace **once** for every two letters in the key word of column 1.

```
manger
ↄ ↄ ↄ
```

• Note the character or cursor position.
• Set a left margin at this point.

4. • Clear all tabs.
• To set the tab for the second column, start at the beginning of the second column heading and follow the same procedure. Forward space **once** for every two letters and spaces in the second column heading.

```
English Translation*
Ↄ Ↄ Ↄ Ↄ Ↄ Ↄ Ↄ Ↄ Ↄ *
```

• Then, backspace **once** for every two letters and spaces in the key word(s) of column 2.

```
twelve
ↄ ↄ ↄ
```

• Note the character or cursor position.
• Set a tab at this point.

*Ignore odd letters or spaces.

Note: Master the Backspace Method.

12↓

217 Clinton Place
Swift Current, Saskatchewan
S9H 4K2
Current Date (Line 15)

4↓

Dear Chris:

Have you found a part-time job yet? I am thinking
of giving up my paper route, but I know I would
miss the spending money.

2↓

We played our basketball quarter final game
yesterday. We were up against the best team in
the city. They wiped us out 69 to 18--a humiliating
experience! If we had won our second last game,
which we lost by one point, we might have had a better
chance in the play-offs.

2↓

What are your plans for this summer? My family is
going to spend the month of July canoe tripping
and backpacking. I will probably go to a sports
camp for a couple of weeks in August. A friend of
mine (from our basketball team) may go with me.
The camp is up north.

2↓

How's school? Some of my courses are quite easy,
but others require more effort and lots of
homework.

2↓

Our second set of exams starts tomorrow. We write
at 10:45 each day, which is a welcome change from
having to get up at 6:30 for basketball practice
(there has to be some advantage to having been
knocked out of the play-offs).

2↓

Now that basketball season is over, I thought I
would really enjoy having all this spare time, but
I probably will try out for track and field. The
season starts after exams. I am interested in the
high jump, the 100-metre dash, and relay races.

2↓

Hope to hear from you soon.

2↓

Your friend,

Pat

Personal Letters

50-character line (pica — 10 pitch)

Production 1

Using the Backspace Method, centre the following two-column table on a half sheet of paper. *Note:* One of the column headings is longer than the column items.

```
        LONG DISTANCE AREA CODES

       Area code          Locality

          403             Alberta
          808             Hawaii
          204             Manitoba
          305             Miami
          514             Montreal
          613             Ottawa
          416      | 10 |  Toronto
```

■ Did you centre the key line?

Production 2

Using the Backspace Method, centre the following two-column table on a half sheet of paper.

```
            HOW OLD IS YOUR DOG?

      Age of Dog          Age of Person
       (Years)              (Years)

          1                   7
          2                  14
          3                  21
          4                  28
          8                  56
         12                  84
```

■ Did you centre the key line?

Personal Letters

A letter written from one friend to another is called a personal letter. The inside address and the signature line are omitted. This letter is on a plain sheet of paper with the writer's address (return address) directly above the date line.

Production 1

Input the following personal letter on a plain sheet of paper. Use full block letter style with mixed punctuation. Input an appropriate envelope or an envelope label.

```
12↓
   217 Clinton Place
   Swift Current, Saskatchewan
   S9H 4K2
   Current Date  (Line 15)
 4↓
   Dear Chris:

   Have you found a part-time job yet?  I am thinking of giving
   up my paper route, but I know I would miss the spending money.
 2↓
   We played our basketball quarter final game yesterday.  We
   were up against the best team in the city.  They wiped us
   out 69 to 18--a humiliating experience!  If we had won our
   second last game, which we lost by one point, we might have
   had a better chance in the play-offs.
 2↓
   What are your plans for this summer?  My family is going to
   spend the month of July canoe tripping and backpacking.  I
   will probably go to a sports camp for a couple of weeks in
   August.  A friend of mine (from our basketball team) may go
   with me.  The camp is up north.
 2↓
   How's school?  Some of my courses are quite easy, but others
   require more effort and lots of homework.
 2↓
   Our second set of exams starts tomorrow.  We write at 10:45
   each day, which is a welcome change from having to get up at
   6:30 for basketball practice (there has to be some advantage
   to having been knocked out of the play-offs).
 2↓
   Now that basketball season is over, I thought I would really
   enjoy having all this spare time, but I probably will try out
   for track and field.  The season starts after exams.  I am
   interested in the high jump, the 100-metre dash, and relay
   races.
 2↓
   Hope to hear from you soon.
 2↓
   Your friend,

   Pat
```

Personal Letters
60-character line (elite — 12 pitch)

SI 1.33

Two-Minute Timing

	1	2

There are many fine books to read. No matter
what interests you, you will be able to read about
it. There are books for science fiction fans, the
old classics, and love stories. Perhaps you would
prefer a good mystery story. The local library is
the best spot for you to start. Begin your search
for a good book by finding a section that you feel
would appeal to you. Browse through several books
before you make your choice. Many enjoyable hours
can be spent reading a good book.

10	5
20	10
30	15
40	20
50	25
60	30
70	35
80	40
90	45
96	48

• • • 1 • • • • 2 • • • • 3 • • • • 4 • • • • 5 • • • • 6 • • • • 7 • • • • 8 • • • • 9 • • • • 10   1 min

1   2   3   4   5   2 min

Personal Letters

Format

60-character line
Single spacing

Practise each line twice.
Practise as quickly as you can.

Accuracy Drills

Think **accuracy**. Practise
each line once. Repeat *or* take
two 30-s timings on each line.

Take two 30-s timings on each
line. Take one 1-min timing on
the set of two lines.
■ Did you have two errors or
less with each timing?

Practise each underlined word
four times. Practise each line
once concentrating on the
underlined words.

Edit each line by correcting
two errors. Practise the
paragraph once with the
corrections.

Common Words

1 summary credit money form date last provide following review

2 open quickly before nothing year around painting choice have

Alternate-Hand Words

3 of men bush hair blend keys pair girls rug work chair handle

4 it box dock curl firm sight widow antique fish bus six towns

Common-Word Sentences

5 Has your family received a free sample of their new product?

6 Branches are conveniently located in several downtown areas.

7 If these repairs are very costly, Chris will sell her truck.
· · · · 1 · · · · 2 · · · · 3 · · · · 4 · · · · 5 · · · · 6 · · · · 7 · · · · 8 · · · · 9 · · · ·10· · · ·11· · · ·12

Spelling Practice

8 <u>Disastrous</u> accidents are often caused by <u>changeable</u> weather.

9 His <u>commitment</u> to the <u>campaign</u> was a fine example to others.
· · · · 1 · · · · 2 · · · · 3 · · · · 4 · · · · 5 · · · · 6 · · · · 7 · · · · 8 · · · · 9 · · · ·10· · · ·11· · · ·12

Editing Practice

10   The tiney hummingbord beats its wings 55 to 100 times

a second--the tips move at as much at 30 km an hour--usinh

powerful muscles that account for mre than 25 per cent of i

its mass. unlike the wings of most bird, the humming-

bird's rotate on swivel joints at the showlders. Tomaintai

maintain energy it feesd on nectar/

44

Open Tables with Longer Column Headings

Format
50-character line
Single spacing

Practise each line twice.
Practise as quickly as you can.

Skill Building

Practise each line once.
Repeat or take two
15-s timings on each line.

Practise each line once.
Practise each line again.

Practise each underlined word
four times. Practise each line
once concentrating on the
underlined words.

Read the definition of each
word.
Practise each sentence once
using the correct word in
parentheses.

Alternate-Hand Words

1 go hay cut fog lay wig row tusk firm malt shape so

2 to if but man rub duck fight male fish worm do sit

Common-Word Sentences

3 Is it difficult to back my truck into your garage?

4 The children like to visit the new animal shelter.

5 Three of the eight players had to leave the field.

Sentences with Numbers

6 He owes $5.09 to Ann and $17.62 to Beth for meals.

7 Math 13 meets in Room 76 at 09:35 until August 28.

Spelling Practice

8 We guarantee that he will be offered the job soon.

9 Please do not interrupt me unless it is necessary.

Basic English

fewer: refers to things that can be counted individually
less: refers to quantity or money

10 (Fewer, Less) people attended the games this year.

11 (Fewer, Less) capital is necessary for this project.

12 Our profit this year is (fewer, less) than we had expected.

· · · · 1 · · · · 2 · · · · 3 · · · · 4 · · · · 5 · · · · 6 · · · · 7 · · · · 8 · · · · 9 · · · · 10

Production

Input the following personal business letter on a plain sheet of paper. Use full block letter style with mixed punctuation. Input a small envelope or an envelope label. Fold the letter for insertion.

Wings Point, Newfoundland
A0G 4T0
May 20, 19--

Power Skating School
Brother O'Hehir Arena
St. John's, Newfoundland
A1B 2X5

Gentlemen

Enclosed is a cheque for $25 to cover the cost of two weeks of your power skating and conditioning school. Also enclosed is my registration form.

I am registering in Group B and understand that these classes will be from 10:15 to 11:15, August 18 to 22, and August 25 to 29.

Please send a receipt indicating that I have been accepted for the course.

Sincerely

Ron Bellizia
Enclosure

Production 1

Using the Backspace Method, centre the following table attractively on a half sheet of paper.

Nevada Bob's
Smashing Racquet Sale

Manufacturer	Name of Racquet	Cost (Unstrung)
Prince	Pro 90	$ 50.00
Kennex	Silver Ace	99.95
Head	Graphite Pro	129.95
Wilson	Profile	299.88
Dunlop	McEnroe	59.95
Puma	Becker Super	79.99

Production 2

Centre the following table attractively on a half sheet of paper. Double space the body of the table.

Title: Subcompact Cameras

Column Headings:

Manufacturer / Model No. / Suggested Retail Price / Mass (g)

```
Pentax  / Auto 110 / $239.95 / 172
Rollei  / A110 / 299.95 / 185
Minox   / 35G1 / 354.00 / 190
Rollei  / 35S / 308.50 / 320
Olympus / XA / 328.50 / 225
Minolta / 110 Zoom / 349.95 / 465
```

SI 1.26

Three-Minute Timing

		1	CW	3
We are able to listen to music on compact discs. Discs		12	12	4
do not contain any music. The sounds are stored on discs in		24	24	8
binary code. Each sound is recorded as a series of ones and		36	36	12
zeroes. As the laser reads the code, the player assigns the		48	48	16
proper sounds. On records, sounds are in the grooves of the		60	60	20
vinyl. Most grooves also contain dust and grease which will		72	72	24
affect the sound we hear.		77	77	26
Discs will last much longer than records, but they also		12	89	30
need care. A disc should be handled only by its edges. Put		24	101	34
each disc back in its case after use. To wash a disc, rinse		36	113	38
the side without the label with warm water. This will clean		48	125	42
dirt from the disc before it is wiped from the centre to the		60	137	46
outside with a cloth, chamois, or cotton ball.		69	146	49

· · · 1 · · · · 2 · · · · 3 · · · · 4 · · · · 5 · · · · 6 · · · · 7 · · · · 8 · · · · 9 · · · 10 · · · · 11 · · · · 12   1 min

        1   2   3   4   3 min

Composition

How many addresses of friends, relatives, or companies do you know from memory? Begin with your own address. Remember to include the postal code as the final line.

        Skill Building

Set for double spacing. Take two 2-min timings. Circle all errors. Calculate Gross Words Per Minute (GWPM). Record your best timing on your personal progress chart.

SI 1.21

Two-Minute Timing

		1	2
The rush of a first plane ride is super. The		10	5
feelings cannot be fully told to others. The trip		20	10
to the airport seems to take forever. As you look		30	15
around the terminal, the tension mounts. All work		40	20
for the flight has been done so you can board from		50	25
gate two. At last the engines roar and your plane		60	30
moves down the runway. With great force you leave		70	35
the ground for the sky above.		75	37

· · · · 1 · · · · 2 · · · · 3 · · · · 4 · · · · 5 · · · · 6 · · · · 7 · · · · 8 · · · · 9 · · · · 10   1 min

1   2   3   4   5   2 min

Skill Building

Format

60-character line
Single spacing

Practise each line twice.
Practise as quickly as you can.

Analyze Your Progress

Practise each line once.
Repeat *or* take one 1-min
timing on each line. Circle all
errors. If you have two errors or
less on most of your timings,
go to line 9. If not, practise
lines 3-8.

One-Hand Words

1 only onion loop junk hymn hilly opinion puppy you pupil link

2 tar feed safe ear dart cast eat dress was eraser trace crews

Accuracy Drives

3 egg act beg edge rear fast eager drawer water streets trades

4 mop ill mink pull jolly milk holy pink kill pulp up look ink

5 to jam own tick clay burn shrub profit theme their foam fork

6 ooze funny giddy bubble puppet follow beggar pioneer cutting

7 The office staff agreed not to accept poorly-shipped ribbon.

8 There is little excuse for misspelling common words, Dennis.

Practise each line once.
Repeat *or* take one 1-min
timing on each line. Practise
as quickly as you can.

Speed Drives

9 It is important to accept those who might think differently.

10 Several current popular groups have been together for years.

11 She wrote the songs and did a fantastic job singing as well.

12 The leafless trees outside were covered with the crisp snow.

13 The new bus makes two return trips to the airport each hour.

14 Sometimes friends seem angry when they are actually jealous.
　　　·　·　·　·　1　·　·　·　·　2　·　·　·　·　3　·　·　·　·　4　·　·　·　·　5　·　·　·　·　6　·　·　·　·　7　·　·　·　·　8　·　·　·　·　9　·　·　·　10　·　·　·　11　·　·　·　12

Number Practice

15 Trains to Regina leave at these times: 09:30, 12:40, 16:00.

16 Channels 10 and 17 will be showing this program on the 14th.

17 Your Credit Memo 472, dated 1989 03 21, should be for $9.25.
　　　·　·　·　·　1　·　·　·　·　2　·　·　·　·　3　·　·　·　·　4　·　·　·　·　5　·　·　·　·　6　·　·　·　·　7　·　·　·　·　8　·　·　·　·　9　·　·　·　10　·　·　·　11　·　·　·　12

Practise each line once.
Practise each line again.

Graduated Speed Practice

1. Turn to Lesson 54, page 161.
2. Drill on the appropriate Graduated Speed Practice.

45

Skill Building

Format
50-character line
Single spacing

Practise each line twice.
Practise as quickly as you can.

Skill Building

Practise each line once.
Repeat or take two
15-s timings on each line.

Practise each line once.
Repeat or take two
15-s timings on each line.

Practise each line once.
Practise each line again.

Take two 30-s timings on each line. Practise each phrase as quickly as you can.

Analyze Your Practice

Take two 1-min timings on each sentence.
Each sentence contains the alphabet.
Circle all errors.

One-Hand Words

1 up ear hip red mop age lump only tear yolk bear at

2 be my pump sew bee base honk beef fear seat street

3 at was bad exact ear data wed hum lip case race up

Alternate-Hand Words

4 go toe the fur sir kept hand cubic flake snap worn

5 me end but rug man name lake they bush pay due tow

6 do and she bye cod male tuck dusk them gland right

Alternate-Hand Sentences

7 She made vivid red banners for their new bicycles.

8 Glen cooks ham, turkey, and lamb for the busy men.

9 It is the duty of the girl to pay for both tutors.

Sentences with Numbers

10 The 5 tabs must be set at 35, 50, 65, 80, and 125.

11 The trailor hit a truck at 1490 - 52 St. at 08:25.

12 The 1989 03 25 invoice for $2 524.71 must be paid.

Common Phrases

13 at this/at your/at the/at it/at our/at their/at my/

14 to me/to them/to you/to him/to get/to which/to her/

15 from you/from here/from it/from our own/from which/

Alphabetic Sentences

16 When the Quincy family had their garage sale, Jova

sold her exotic kite but kept the zany clown suit.

17 Mr. Bjorg, our science teacher, asked us to define

twelve terms including quartz, dioxide, and pyran.

· · · · 1 · · · · 2 · · · · 3 · · · · 4 · · · · 5 · · · · 6 · · · · 7 · · · · 8 · · · · 9 · · · · 10

Three-Minute Timing

		1	CW	3

In Canada pronghorns live only in the sagebrush country   12 | 12 | 4

of extreme southern Alberta and Saskatchewan. Sagebrush and   24 | 24 | 8

grass are their main sources of food. They are sociable and   36 | 36 | 12

are usually found in herds. They have one or two fawns late   48 | 48 | 16

in June. The adults are constantly on the alert for danger,   60 | 60 | 20

and if an enemy such as a coyote is sighted, the white hairs   72 | 72 | 24

on the rump become erect. Thus the warning signal is passed   84 | 84 | 28

from group to group. Prior to the arrival of white settlers   96 | 96 | 32

on the prairies, pronghorns were very abundant.   105 | 105 | 35

Although the body is chunky, the legs are long, and the   12 | 117 | 39

neck and head are slender and graceful. The horns have only   24 | 129 | 43

one tine or point. Each year, the sheath covering the horns   36 | 141 | 47

is shed by the bucks and does--a unique characteristic found   48 | 153 | 51

only in pronghorns.   51 | 156 | 52

```
· · · · 1 · · · · 2 · · · 3 · · · · 4 · · · · 5 · · · 6 · · · · 7 · · · · 8 · · · 9 · · · ·10· · · ·11· · · ·12    1 min
              1                    2                    3                    4              3 min
```

SI 1.39

Composition

The following expressions contain redundant words; that is they contain unnecessary words. In each case, one word can replace the expression. Develop a list of words to replace these expressions:

absolutely complete, exactly identical, first and foremost,

if and when, personal opinion, right and proper, true facts,

very unique

Composition

Input as many words as you can that begin with the following prefixes. Follow the instructions below for the set-up of each column. An example has been given for each column.

20 (margin)	35 (tab)	50 (tab)	65 (tab)
be	de	re	in
before	decide	receive	into

Graduated Speed Practice

1. Turn to Lesson 30, page 84.
2. Drill on the appropriate Graduated Speed Practice.

Timing

Set for double spacing. Take two 2-min timings. Circle all errors. Calculate Gross Words Per Minute (GWPM). Record your best timing on your personal progress chart.

SI 1.25

Two-Minute Timing

	1	CW	2

The view of the city and river was great. It   10 | 10 | 5

was the best park in the south area. It was never   20 | 20 | 10

crowded or noisy. Cars or trucks were not allowed   30 | 30 | 15

to drive through this park.   35 | 35 | 17

They went to the park many nights. There was   10 | 45 | 22

always a flock of birds to feed. They enjoyed the   20 | 55 | 27

walk on the trail along the river bed. It was the   30 | 65 | 32

perfect way to relax after a busy day.   37 | 72 | 36

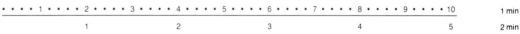

· · · · 1 · · · · 2 · · · · 3 · · · · 4 · · · · 5 · · · · 6 · · · · 7 · · · · 8 · · · · 9 · · · · 10   1 min

1   2   3   4   5   2 min

Production 2

Input the following business letter on Cooper Canada letterhead. Use full block letter style with mixed punctuation. Input a Number 10 envelope or an envelope label. Fold the letter for insertion. Remember to include all missing letter parts.

To: Ms. Lisa Ng / 1519 Henderson House / Howe Hall / Dalhousie University / Halifax, Nova Scotia / B3H 4J5 /

Many thanks for your letter telling us of your interest in hockey helmets and your need for assistance with your project.

In terms of developing your own homemade helmet, the only material you would use is fibreglass, and the technical skills necessary for you to accomplish this are very substantial and complex. Also, a fibreglass helmet would be sufficiently heavy that you would not be able to wear it.

I am sorry that we are not able to be of more assistance to you. We appreciate your interest in Cooper equipment and wish you well with your physical education studies.

John H. Cooper

■ Did you listen for the right margin signal? OR Did you use word wrap?

46

Open Tables with Centred Column Headings

Format
50-character line
Single spacing

Practise each line twice.
Practise as quickly as you can.

Skill Building

Practise each line once.
Repeat *or* take two
15-s timings on each line.

Practise each line once.
Practise each line again.

Edit each line by correcting
two errors.
Practise each line once with
the corrections.

Production Practice

■ Did you centre the key
line?

One-Hand Words

1 no as race limp you tar him weeds link beat art up

2 my be no gas grab deed loop treat nun ink star lip

Common-Word Sentences

3 He applied for a credit card sometime last spring.

4 The firm pays them when they load crates of fruit.

5 Snow fell all night and it was deep on the street.

Sentences with Numbers

6 The 538 albums were $12.97 and she had 36 of them.

7 Oma bought 36 pens, 175 pencils, and 2 856 papers.

Editing Practice

8 I am selling tickets. Would you like to buy some

9 he is now the manger of the Regina district area.

10 I recieved the bill on May 1. I paid it on May8.

· · · · 1 · · · · 2 · · · · 3 · · · · 4 · · · · 5 · · · · 6 · · · · 7 · · · · 8 · · · · 9 · · · · 10

Production 1

Using the Backspace Method, centre the following table on a half sheet of paper. Use centred column headings.

CANADIAN PROVINCIAL AND NATIONAL PARKS

Province	No. of Parks	Name of Largest Park
British Columbia	73	Tweedsmuir
Alberta	36	Wood Buffalo
Saskatchewan	23	Prince Albert
Manitoba	18	Riding Mountain
Ontario	80	Algonquin
Quebec	21	Mistassini
New Brunswick	16	Kouchibouguac
Prince Edward Island	17	Prince Edward Island
Nova Scotia	15	Cape Breton Highlands
Newfoundland	34	Gros Morne

Production 1

Input the following personal business letter on a plain sheet of paper. Use full block style with mixed punctuation. Input a small envelope or an envelope label. Fold the letter for insertion. Remember to include all missing letter parts.

To: Cooper Canada Ltd. / 501 Alliance Avenue / Toronto, Ontario / M6N 2J3 /

From: 1519 Henderson House / Howe Hall / Dalhousie University / Halifax, Nova Scotia / B3H 4J5 /

I am a second year physical education student at Dalhousie University. I am taking a course entitled History of Sport where we must do a practical assigned project. It was suggested that we examine a sport, or even the history of a particular piece of sporting material.

I have always been interested in all facets of ice hockey. For my project, I have decided to construct a homemade helmet, much like those used before helmets were mass produced.

I would greatly appreciate your assistance in providing me with any suggestions on how I may go about developing a homemade helmet.

Lisa Ng

■ Did you use your judgment for spacing?

■ Did you remember to omit your initials?

Production 2

Centre the following table attractively on a half sheet of paper. Use centred column headings. Double space the body of the table.

Canadian Products, Inc.
DEPARTMENTAL MANAGERS

Name of Manager	Department	Extension
DeWitt, John	Sales	2957
Fainstein, Jay	Accounting	3908
Garbor, Lisa	Office Services	3867
Ho, Raymond	Manufacturing	3897
Oboyowana, Joy	Purchasing	8927
Mancini, Mary	Accounts Receivable	1289
Parshan, Dov	Personnel	2175
Walker, Lina	Payroll	6137

■ Did you centre the key line?

Two-Minute Timing

Timing

Set for double spacing. Take two 2-min timings. Circle all errors. Calculate Gross Words Per Minute (GWPM). Record your best timing on your personal progress chart.

SI 1.16

	1	CW	2

The big house on the top of the high hill had — 10 10 5

been empty for years. The last family moved after — 20 20 10

the fatal fire in the guest house. Not one person — 30 30 15

had set foot in the yard since. — 36 36 18

On dark nights, the house moaned in the wind. — 10 46 23

The sad sound was heard in the distance. When the — 20 56 28

moon was out, it never shone on the house. It was — 30 66 33

the type of setting for a good mystery thriller. — 39 75 37

`. . . . 1 . . . . 2 . . . . 3 . . . . 4 . . . . 5 . . . 6 . . . 7 . . . 8 . . . 9 . . . 10`

`1        2        3        4        5`

1 min
2 min

Composition

Composing Practice

Think and answer as quickly as you can without hesitating.

The following is a list of items usually found in a supermarket. What brand name would you buy for each of these items? Set up your list in two columns (margin 25 and tab of 50) with the items in one column and the brands in the second column. Supply a suitable title for each column (blocked).

cookies, pickles, pineapple, oranges, razors,

cereal, soft drinks, peanuts, milk, ice cream

Personal Business Letters

Format
60-character line
Single spacing

Practise each line twice.
Practise as quickly as you can.

Speed Drills

■ Try to practise each timing faster.
Take two 15-s timings on each line. Take one 30-s timing on the set of lines.

Take two 15-s timings on each line. Take one 30-s timing on the set of lines.
■ Did you do each timing faster?
■ *colourful* or *colorful*
Know the preference in your area of Canada.

Practise each line once.
Practise each line again.

Read the definition of each word.
Practise each sentence once using the correct word in parentheses.

Double-Letter Words

1 mill greed class tipped offer grammar spelling written needs

2 reel added middle comma hurry thrilled bottle kettle support

Sentences with Double-Letter Words

3 Elliott and his three buddies took the little car to school.

4 The small bellboy still cannot attach all the muddy luggage.

5 Tammy was happy to be called upon to assist with the kitten.

Common-Word Sentences

6 There are several unique problems facing the general public.

7 We should work together to keep our country united and free.

8 The colourful flag stirred gently in the warm spring breeze.
· · · · 1 · · · · 2 · · · · 3 · · · · 4 · · · · 5 · · · · 6 · · · · 7 · · · · 8 · · · · 9 · · · 10 · · · 11 · · · 12

Number Practice

9 He has 29 or 30, she has 74 or 75, and I have only 10 or 11.

10 On April 30, 1989 there were 45 houses and 273 barns burned.
· · · · 1 · · · · 2 · · · · 3 · · · · 4 · · · · 5 · · · · 6 · · · · 7 · · · · 8 · · · · 9 · · · 10 · · · 11 · · · 12

Basic English

advice: recommendation or information (noun)
advise: to give advice (verb)

11 It seemed logical to follow his (advice, advise).

12 The guide (adviced, advised) us to take the short route home.

13 It is a difficult decison——I really need some (advice, advise).

Folding Letters for Personal-Size Envelopes

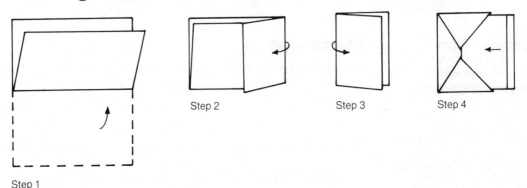

Step 1   Step 2   Step 3   Step 4

Open Tables with Centred Column Headings

Format
50-character line
Single spacing

Practise each line twice.
Practise as quickly as you can.

Alternate-Hand Words

1 go he ham pan visit them city snap torn gown forms

2 pan us blend dig ivy bye pale bush lake the quench

Skill Building

Practise each line once.
Repeat or take two
15-s timings on each line.

Common-Word Sentences

3 He cleaned his brushes and rollers after painting.

4 I want to enroll in more than one term of physics.

5 The spiders are killing the apple trees this year.

Practise each underlined word
four times. Practise each line
once concentrating on the
underlined words.

Spelling Practice

6 Occasionally, we receive requests for these books.

7 The description of the accident was very thorough.

Basic English

all ready: entirely ready
already: previously, by this time

Read the definition of each
word.
Practise each sentence once
using the correct word in
parentheses.

8 Alice had (all ready, already) arrived when Jack appeared.

9 We were (all ready, already) to leave at a moment's notice.

10 Can you believe it is (all ready, already) the end of term

one?

· · · · 1 · · · · 2 · · · · 3 · · · · 4 · · · · 5 · · · · 6 · · · · 7 · · · · 8 · · · · 9 · · · · 10

Production 1

Centre the following table on a half sheet of paper.

Bilingual keyboards have
accent keys. If you do not have
a bilingual keyboard, insert
accents by hand **after** the
production exercise is
completed.

SI UNITS NAMED AFTER SCIENTISTS

Unit	Scientist	Country of Birth	Dates
ampere	Ampère, André-Marie	France	1775–1836
degree Celsius	Celsius, Anders	Sweden	1701–1744
newton	Newton, Sir Isaac	England	1642–1727
ohm	Ohm, Georg Simon	Germany	1787–1854
pascal	Pascal, Blaise	France	1623–1662
volt	Volta, Count Alessandro	Italy	1745–1827
watt	Watt, James	Scotland	1736–1819

Three-Minute Timing

Note the accent marks in the word mâché. Insert the accent marks after you have finished the timed writing.

		1	CW	3
Of the various types of puppets the two most common are		12	12	4
glove puppets and marionettes. A glove puppet has a head, a		24	24	8
hole through the neck, and a glove with three fingers. This		36	36	12
allows the thumb and second finger to work both arms and the		48	48	16
first finger to work the head. Some puppets have legs which		60	60	20
are visible to the audience, but are not used for walking.		72	72	24
Marionettes are complete figures with jointed limbs. A		12	84	28
string is attached to each limb. These puppets are moved by		24	96	32
pulling the various strings. The better ones are carved out		36	108	36
of prime wood. Others are made on a wire base; papier mâché		48	120	40
is used for the head, hands, and feet. The limbs are padded		60	132	44
with cloth. Marionettes are sometimes made to be life-size.		72	144	48

· · · ·1· · · ·2· · · ·3· · · ·4· · · ·5· · · ·6· · · ·7· · · ·8· · · ·9· · ·10· · · ·11· · · ·12   1 min

       1   2   3   4   3 min

Composition

Do you know in which provinces the following cities are located? Input a rough copy of the cities and the provinces. If you are using a computer, print a copy. Edit your work and make any necessary corrections in pen or pencil on the rough copy. Then, input a good copy in two-column format. Supply a suitable main title and column headings.

Winnipeg	Saskatoon	Edmonton	Sault Ste. Marie
Vancouver	Montreal	Guelph	Calgary
Ottawa	Yarmouth	Moncton	Trail
Gander	Red Deer	Hull	Charlottetown

Production 2

Centre the following table attractively on a half sheet of paper.

Title: Canine Crossbreeds

Column Headings: 1st Breed / 2nd Breed / Name of Crossbreed

basset / beagle / bagel
poodle / chow chow / pooch
Pekingese / bouvier / peekaboo
cocker spaniel / poodle / cockapoo
boxer / schnauzer / bowzer
pug / yorkie / porky

Timing

Set for double spacing. Take two 2-min timings. Circle all errors. Calculate Gross Words Per Minute (GWPM). Record your best timing on your personal progress chart.

SI 1.15

Two-Minute Timing

		1	CW	2
The cabin at the lake was finally empty. The		10	10	5
last car had just turned on to the main road. Now		20	20	10
one could hear the wind in the trees and the songs		30	30	15
of the birds. It had been a busy four days.		39	39	19
Next week there were many things to do. Most		10	49	24
of the summer was over, and the cabin must be made		20	59	29
ready for winter. The wood pile should be a metre		30	69	34
high, and the winter doors must be put back on.		39	78	39

· · · · 1 · · · · 2 · · · · 3 · · · · 4 · · · · 5 · · · 6 · · · · 7 · · · · 8 · · · · 9 · · · · 10   1 min

1   2   3   4   5   2 min

Production 2

Input the following business letter on Laura Secord letterhead. Use full block letter style with mixed punctuation. Input a Number 10 envelope or an envelope label. Remember to include all missing letter parts.

```
Current date

To:  Ms. Lilian Beckstrom / 34211 Redwood Avenue /

     Abbotsford, British Columbia / V2X 2T6

From:  Denise Laporte / Director, Public Relations

Thank you for your letter requesting material for the
family studies project you are researching.  ¶  We would be
happy to help you with your project.  Enclosed are
several pamphlets which describe the Laura Secord story,
as well as literature on the historical background of
Laura Secord Candy Shops.  ¶  Good luck with your research!
When you have completed your project, we would be very
pleased to receive a copy of your work.
```

■ Did you read the body of the letter?

Unit Review

Format
50-character line
Single spacing

Practise each line twice.
Practise as quickly as you can.

Skill Building

Practise each line once.
Repeat *or* take two
15-s timings on each line.

Practise each line twice.

One-Hand Words

1 be hum mop fade hymn ward upon drag nylon extra we

2 up cab lip as monk refer phony freeze milk were in

Common-Word Sentences

3 She took a dozen comic books to the exchange shop.

4 The amounts on the bill were not for that account.

5 When you receive the marks, you should check them.

· · · · 1 · · · · 2 · · · · 3 · · · · 4 · · · · 5 · · · · 6 · · · · 7 · · · · 8 · · · · 9 · · · · 10

Drill and Practice

6 Gary and Liz like to listen to 1050 CHUM and Q107.

7 Her address is 692 – 84 Street, Edmonton, Alberta.

8 Pick 6 tomatoes, 3 onions, 8 carrots, and 7 beets.

9 Frank's speed went from 35 to 48 in only 6 months.

10 Account 5127-A shows a balance owing of $1 490.46.

11 Mystery, romance, humour--the book has everything.

12 Evan would enjoy Klondike Mike by Merrill Denison.

13 Add these prices: $7.92, $9.54, $21.95 and $3.68.

14 Answer questions 9 to 24 (see page 83, section 2).

· · · · 1 · · · · 2 · · · · 3 · · · · 4 · · · · 5 · · · · 6 · · · · 7 · · · · 8 · · · · 9 · · · · 10

Timing

Set for double spacing. Take
two 2-min timings. Circle all
errors. Calculate Gross Words
Per Minute (GWPM). Record
your best timing on your
personal progress chart.

SI 1.48

Two-Minute Timing

	1	CW	2
The kayak was first built and used for Inuit.	10	10	5
It is a low, sleek vessel with covered decks. The	20	20	10
kayak is very light and is faster than a canoe.	29	29	15
The kayak was first built for hunting. Today	10	39	20
it is mainly used for recreation or racing. Inuit	20	49	25
kayaks are still covered with sealskin, but modern	30	59	30
ones are usually made of fibreglass.	37	66	33

· · · · 1 · · · · 2 · · · · 3 · · · · 4 · · · · 5 · · · · 6 · · · · 7 · · · · 8 · · · · 9 · · · · 10   1 min

1   2   3   4   5   2 min

Return Address

Date Line

Use your judgment for spacing.

Line Length
50 characters (pica — 10 pitch)

Note: Do not include your initials.

12

34211 Redwood Avenue
Abbotsford, British Columbia
V2X 2T6
May 7, 19-- (Line 15)

6

Ms. Denise Laporte
Director, Public Relations
Laura Secord
Laura Secord Walk
P.O. Box 1812, Station D
Scarborough, Ontario
M1R 4Z2

2

Dear Ms. Laporte:

2

I have been asked to research a Canadian food
product for the family studies course I am taking
this year. I have chosen Laura Secord candies as
my topic.

2

Would it be possible for you to send me any
pamphlets or literature on the candy industry, or
specifically, on the historical background of
Laura Secord candies.

2

I would very much appreciate receiving any material
you feel might be useful for my project.

2

Sincerely,

4-6

Lilian Beckstrom

Personal Business Letter

50-character line (pica — 10 pitch)

Composition

The following is a list of abbreviations that are often used. Input each abbreviation and what it stands for. Compose your list in the following manner:

Example: doz. stands for dozen
  amt.   amount

```
acct., approx., assn., bldg., e.g., i.e., mdse., encl.,
Esq., etc., govt., no., pkg., rpm, wpm, Dr., Blvd., vs.
dept., mfg., bros., a.k.a.
```

Review of Hyphenation Rules

Rule 1: Hyphenate words between speech syllables (pic-ture).
Rule 2: Hyphenate words between double letters of speech syllables (gram-mar).
Rule 3: Divide only after the hyphen in a compound word (twenty-one).
Rule 4: Do not hyphenate words of one syllable (washed).

Instructions:

Input a copy of the following words, dividing each with a hyphen (or hyphens) according to the above rules. Set the words up in four columns and supply a suitable main title.

style	subsidy	padding	give–away
frankness	handbook	grotesque	mid–eastern
stairs	warrant	vouched	whipping
sluggish	contests	chamber	break–even
shipped	bluffing	loafing	solving
growth	displays	dumped	dumping
past–due	torture	toastmaster	trend
spotlight	south–bound	bookstore	censorship
spinning	staffing	staging	mystery
mustache	furnished	gossip	calling

Personal Business Letters

A letter from an individual to a business organization is called a personal business letter. This letter is on a plain sheet of paper with the individual's address (return address) directly above the date line.

Production 1

Input the following personal business letter on a plain sheet of paper. Input a small envelope or an envelope label.

Production Practice

Return Address

Date Line

Use your judgment for spacing.

Line Length
60 characters (elite — 12 pitch)

Note: Do not include your initials.

```
12↓

   34211 Redwood Avenue
   Abbotsford, British Columbia
   V2X 2T6
   May 7, 19--  (Line 15)

6↓


   Ms. Denise Laporte
   Director, Public Relations
   Laura Secord
   Laura Secord Walk
   P.O. Box 1812, Station D
   Scarborough, Ontario
   M1R 4Z2
2↓
   Dear Ms. Laporte:
2↓
   I have been asked to research a Canadian food product for the
   family studies course I am taking this year.  I have chosen
   Laura Secord candies as my topic.
2↓
   Would it be possible for you to send me any pamphlets or
   literature on the candy industry, or specifically, on the
   historical background of Laura Secord candies.
2↓
   I would very much appreciate receiving any material you feel
   might be useful for my project.
2↓
   Sincerely,

4-6↓


   Lilian Beckstrom
```

Personal Business Letter
60-character line (elite — 12 pitch)

Production

Centre the following announcement attractively on a full sheet of paper.

THE TENTH ANNUAL ATHLETIC BANQUET

will be held

at the

B O U L E V A R D   C L U B — spread centre

on

Thursday, May 28

featuring

buffet dinner
guest speakers
awards presentations

TICKETS AVAILABLE FROM STUDENT COUNCIL MEMBERS

% / **Personal Business Letters**

Common Words

1 large special offer product with after natural there nothing

2 north initials written shown when lines taken request orders

Sentences with Double-Letter Words

3 The office down the corridor will be too small for meetings.

4 Three small deer leaped out of the woods and into the creek.

5 Tae Goo served coffee and cookies at the end of the meeting.

Common-Word Sentences

6 It may be difficult for you to understand what is happening.

7 Do not think that you know everything; one can always learn.

8 She caught his eye on the bus and they met in the cafeteria.
• • • • 1 • • • • 2 • • • • 3 • • • • 4 • • • • 5 • • • 6 • • • 7 • • • • 8 • • • • 9 • • • 10 • • • 11 • • • 12

Number Practice

9 He asked us to insert a sheet of P5 paper (14 cm x 21.5 cm).

10 Please phone Area Code 416–576–9921 and ask for Extension 2.
• • • • 1 • • • • 2 • • • • 3 • • • • 4 • • • • 5 • • • 6 • • • 7 • • • • 8 • • • • 9 • • • 10 • • • 11 • • • 12

Reach to % Key

11 fff f5f f%f f%f %%% f% f% %%% f%f f%f %%f %%f f% f% %%f %%ff

12 10% and 20% and 30% and 40% and 50% and 60% and 70% and 100%

13 The statistical groups range from 13% to 19% and 20% to 50%.
• • • • 1 • • • • 2 • • • • 3 • • • • 4 • • • • 5 • • • 6 • • • 7 • • • • 8 • • • • 9 • • • 10 • • • 11 • • • 12

Basic English

accept: take what is offered
except: exclude

14 The union is prepared to (accept, except) the wage offer.

15 (Accept, Except) for our lost luggage, our trip was very enjoyable.

16 Please (accept, except) my apologies for not writing sooner.

Unit Review

Format
50-character line
Single spacing

Practise each line twice.
Practise as quickly as you can.

Skill Building

Practise each line once.
Repeat or take two
15-s timings on each line.

Metric Practice

Practise each line twice.

Timing

Set for double spacing. Take
two 2-min timings. Circle all
errors. Calculate Gross Words
Per Minute (GWPM). Record
your best timing on your
personal progress chart.

SI 1.39

Common Words

1 have store much luck pass if not idea does gift at

2 list that often type each your used can may mostly

Common-Word Sentences

3 Send the card and your money to the above address.

4 She needs new equipment for the game on Wednesday.

5 We were unable to get tickets for the school play.

Metric Practice

6 Jay's race time was 2.7 min, while Hugh's was 3.5.

7 This rope is 28 m long. We need one that is 40 m.

8 Many prefer the numeric form of date: 1995 07 02.

9 That steel ball-bearing is about 3 mm in diameter.

10 Christopher's temperature rose to a feverish 39°C.

· · · · 1 · · · · 2 · · · · 3 · · · · 4 · · · · 5 · · · · 6 · · · · 7 · · · · 8 · · · · 9 · · · · 10

Two-Minute Timing

	1	CW	2

Visitors who hurry through our provincial and | 10 | 10 | 5

national parks looking for wildlife are sure to be | 20 | 20 | 10

disappointed. The best way to see park life is to | 30 | 30 | 15

head for a side road early or late in the day. | 39 | 39 | 19

Look for moose, deer, rabbits, and chipmunks. | 10 | 49 | 24

Turtles and other reptiles can be seen near lakes, | 20 | 59 | 29

ponds, and marshy valleys. | 25 | 64 | 32

Loud noises or sudden movements will frighten | 10 | 74 | 37

away most animals. Quiet patience will reward you | 20 | 84 | 42

with a good view of park wildlife. | 26 | 90 | 45

· · · · 1 · · · · 2 · · · · 3 · · · · 4 · · · · 5 · · · · 6 · · · · 7 · · · · 8 · · · · 9 · · · · 10   1 min

         1   2   3   4   5   2 min

Production

Input the following addresses on small envelopes or envelope labels using correct format. Use provincial or territorial symbols for the last four envelope addresses.

Kodak Canada Inc. 3500 Eglinton Avenue West TORONTO, Ontario M6M 1V3	Ms. Mary Nurse 1005 - 10101 Saskatchewan Drive Edmonton, Alberta T6E 4R6
Mrs. Mary Cobierski 67 Country Road CORNER BROOK, Newfoundland A2A 1X5	Mr. Howard Mah 3624 Hillgrass Place Port Alberni, British Columbia V9Y 7P2
Chrysler Corporation 12000 Chrysler Drive HIGHLAND PARK, MI 48288-1919 U.S.A.	Mr. Henry Ghostkeeper 101 Tweedsmuir Street Flin Flon, Manitoba R8A 0R7
Mlle Marie Beauchamp 1420, rue Marchesseault ST. HYACINTHE, Quebec J2T 2Y9	Beaver Lumber Company Limited P.O. Box 2700 Whitehorse, Yukon Territory Y1A 3V5
Mr. Gregory Mathus 1608 Nogales Street, #108 ROWLAND HEIGHTS, CA 91748-2257 U.S.A.	Ms. Dianne C. Warnick, Press Officer Beaver Lumber Company Limited 245 Fairview Mall Drive Willowdale, Ontario M2J 4T1

Three-Minute Timing

Timing

Set for double spacing. Take two 3-min timings. Circle all errors. Calculate Gross Words Per Minute (GWPM). Record your best timing on your personal progress chart.

SI 1.47

	1	3
The rubber tree grows wild in the forests of Brazil. A	12	4
milky substance oozes out of the tree when a slanting groove	24	8
is made in the bark. This liquid contains particles of what	36	12
becomes tires, gloves, boots, etc. The liquid has been used	48	16
for over 400 years. By the 19th century people realized how	60	20
important rubber really was. In 1839 Charles Goodyear found	72	24
a method of treating rubber with sulfur and heat. This made	84	28
it possible to manufacture rubber products that retain their	96	32
shape at hot or cold temperatures.	103	34

```
• • • • 1 • • • • 2 • • • • 3 • • • • 4 • • • • 5 • • • • 6 • • • • 7 • • • • 8 • • • • 9 • • • • 10 • • • • 11 • • • 12     1 min
              1                    2                    3                    4          3 min
```

Review of Hyphenation Rules

Rule 5: Do not leave a one-letter syllable at the beginning or end of a line (agree).

Rule 6: Avoid leaving a two-letter syllable at the beginning or end of a line (reply).

Rule 7: A one-letter syllable in the middle of a word should not be carried over to the new line. When two separately sounded vowels come together in a word, divide between them (dedi-cate).

Rule 8: Do not hyphenate proper names (Canada).

Rule 9: Do not hyphenate abbreviations, numbers, or contractions (couldn't).

Instructions:

Input a rough copy of the following words, dividing each word with a hyphen (or hyphens) according to the above rules. Set the words up in four columns and supply a suitable main title.

unwrap	science	oblige	abandon
acid	accident	cunningly	Cosell
isolation	825–R68	questionnaire	river
Winnipeg	sacred	noisy	onions
N.S.F.	employment	entertainment	firstly
$184.26	final	hasn't	impress
laminate	resign	wagon	sharply
saturate	sunny	Charlottetown	uneven
it's	venison	upholding	M9B 3B6
china	closely	battery	baritone

Production 1

Centre the following table on a half sheet of paper.

OFFICE SUPPLIES AND EQUIPMENT

letterhead	envelopes	staplers	scratch pads
desks	notebooks	typewriters	writing supplies
file cabinets	collators	dicta-machines	calculators
credenzas	room dividers	computers	word processors
diskettes	modems	fax machines	laser printers

Small Envelope (92 mm × 165 mm)

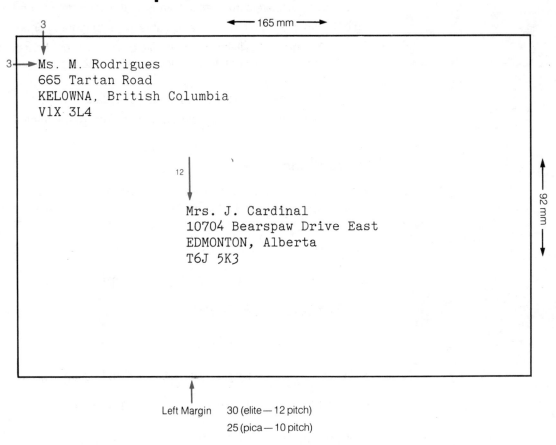

Formatting Guide for Personal-Size Envelopes

(Small) (92 mm × 165 mm)

General Principle

The address is blocked ten characters to the left of the vertical centre of the small envelope and two lines below its horizontal centre. If an address line is very long, adjust the left margin.

Mailing Address	• Starts on line 12 • 30 spaces from the left edge (elite — 12 pitch) 25 spaces (pica — 10 pitch)
Return Address	• Starts on line 3 • 3 spaces from the left edge
Special Instructions	• Start on line 8 • 3 spaces from the left edge

Production 2

Centre the following table attractively on a full sheet of paper.

Title: *Synonyms and Antonyms*

Column Headings: *Word / Synonym / Antonym*

Column Items:
```
grasp / seize / surrender
kind / thoughtful / cruel
near / close / distant
often / frequently / seldom
prohibit / prevent / permit
remember / recall / forget
spacious / roomy / cramped
triumph / victory / defeat
```

Production 3

Centre the following table attractively on a full sheet of paper. Provide a suitable title.

Country	Capital	Currency
Vietnam	Hanoi	Dong
Thailand	Bangkok	Baht
Singapore	Singapore	Singapore Dollar
Philippines	Manila	Philippine Peso
Malaysia	Kuala Lumpur	Ringgit
South Korea	Seoul	Won
Japan	Tokyo	Yen
Indonesia	Jakarta	Rupiah
China	Beijing	Yuan

vb

Place countries in alphabetical order

Small Envelopes

Format
60-character line
Single spacing

Practise each line twice.
Practise as quickly as you can.

Accuracy Drills

Think **accuracy**. Practise
each line once. Repeat *or* take
two 30-s timings on each line.

Take two 30-s timings on each
line. Take one 1-min timing on
the set of two lines.
■ Did you have two errors or
less with each timing?

Practise each underlined word
four times. Practise each line
once concentrating on the
underlined words.

Edit each line by correcting
two errors. Practise the
paragraph once with the
corrections.

Alternate-Hand Words

1 of eye fox lake clan wish shelf ant turkey penalty half held

2 am hen pant duck melt world elbow bushel visitor problem own

Double-Letter Words

3 book issues follow happen smooth supply current called spell

4 pass keep sorry common succeed manner arrange correspondence

Sentences with Double-Letter Words

5 Try to control your errors by stressing accuracy, not speed.

6 Millions of dollars are lost if unnecessary errors are made.

7 Pierre took the toboggan to the village during the blizzard.
    · · · ·1· · · ·2· · · ·3· · · ·4· · · ·5· · · ·6· · · ·7· · · ·8· · · ·9· · · ·10· · · ·11· · · ·12

Spelling Practice

8 Is this the most efficient method of calculating the answer?

9 We were referred to the authority in charge of ticket sales.
    · · · ·1· · · ·2· · · ·3· · · ·4· · · ·5· · · ·6· · · ·7· · · ·8· · · ·9· · · ·10· · · ·11· · · ·12

Editing Practice

10   Life jakkets are a must for water sports.   A life

jacket is for saveing a life, so use only the best..

Acceptable jackets are Approved by the federal MiNistry

of Transport. To test a jacket, wade into chest--deep

water and bend your nees; the jacket should support you

in a back ward position with your mouoth and nose clear of

the water.

Evaluate Your Progress

Format
50-character line
Single spacing

Practise each line twice.
Practise as quickly as you can.

Skill Building

Practise each line once.
Repeat *or* take two
15-s timings on each line.

Timing

Set for double spacing. Take
two 2-min timings. Circle all
errors. Calculate Gross Words
Per Minute (GWPM). Record
your best timing on your
personal progress chart.

SI 1.24

Common Words

1 will tray into your dirt hurry ever must jog first

2 time enter break like her foot ask went give cross

Common-Word Sentences

3 By this time next week, I shall be on my holidays.

4 They are looking for a house in the north section.

5 We are planning to spend the weekend at a cottage.

· · · · 1 · · · · 2 · · · · 3 · · · · 4 · · · · 5 · · · · 6 · · · · 7 · · · · 8 · · · · 9 · · · · 10

Two-Minute Timing

	1	CW	2
Cooking with clay is an ancient practice, one	10	10	5
which the Indians used for centuries. Vegetables,	20	20	10
birds and small animals can be cooked in this way.	30	30	15
It is also a good method of baking fish.	38	38	19
A layer of clay or mud is packed on the items	10	48	24
to be cooked. Coals are then heaped over the clay	20	58	29
and left to cook overnight.	25	63	31
In the morning the coals are removed from the	10	73	36
clay shell which will be baked hard. The clay can	20	83	41
then be broken by giving it a sharp rap.	28	91	45

· · · · 1 · · · · 2 · · · · 3 · · · · 4 · · · · 5 · · · · 6 · · · · 7 · · · · 8 · · · · 9 · · · · 10   1 min

      1   2   3   4   5   2 min

Production 2

Input the following on Olympia Sports Camp letterhead. Use full block letter style with mixed punctuation. Input a Number 10 envelope or an envelope label. Remember to include all missing letter parts.

Current date

To: Mr. Jeff Aman, 425 Norwood Avenue, North Bay, Ontario, P1B 5E5

From: David Grace, Camp Director

We are most pleased that you will be with us at OLYMPIA SPORTS CAMP this summer.

We look forward to having you with us for the following sessions:

Basketball – July 13-19
Basketball – July 20-26

horizontally centre

Please have your family physician complete the enclosed health certificate and return it to us as soon as possible.

In May, I will send you more details regarding departure and arrival times, clothing suggestions, etc. In the meantime, if I can be of any further help, please do not hesitate to write or call.

■ Did you include the four missing letter parts?

Three-Minute Timing

	1	3
A major food for most of the population of the world is	12	4
some form of grain. Wheat, rice, and corn are the important	24	8
members of the grain family. Grains are plants whose single	36	12
seeds contain small amounts of what is required for good and	48	16
stable nutrition. Grains contain sugar, vitamins, proteins,	60	20
and minerals. Wheat is the oldest grain used by humans. We	72	24
know of about 14 types of wheat. Scientists experiment with	84	28
new types of wheat, hoping to develop new types that will do	96	32
well with little water or sunlight.	103	34

· · · 1 · · · · 2 · · · · 3 · · · · 4 · · · · 5 · · · · 6 · · · · 7 · · · · 8 · · · · 9 · · · ·10· · · ·11· · · ·12   1 min

1   2   3   4   3 min

Timing

Set for double spacing. Take two 3-min timings. Circle all errors. Calculate Gross Words Per Minute (GWPM). Record your best timing on your personal progress chart.

SI 1.43

Production 1

Centre the following three-column table on a half sheet of paper. Double space the body.

CANADIAN WILDLIFE

wolf	musk-ox	Rocky Mountain bighorn
caribou	wapiti	white-tailed deer
badger	moose	mountain goat
bison	raccoon	cougar
polar bear	lynx	beaver
sea mink	river otter	grizzly bear
prairie dog	arctic hare	coyote

Production 2

Centre the following two-column table on a half sheet of paper.

(WORDS) spread

from

A Dictionary of Canadianisms

on

Historical Principles

Word	Meaning
Bluenose	a Nova Scotian
Canuck	a native or citizen of Canada
castor	a beaver pelt
dasher	hockey rink fence (the boards)
kayak	a light sealskin boat
mush	move ahead!
muskeg	an organic bog
musquash	another name for muskrat
sault	a waterfall or rapids

Cooper Canada Limited

July 7, 19—

National Gym Clothing Ltd.
10, rue Deslauriers
Rivière du Loup, Québec
G5R 3E2

Gentlemen:

Enclosed is a revised hockey price list effective
August 1. The increases have been kept as moderate
as possible. Hockey sticks, sweaters and socks
have not been increased.

As of the same date, we shall revise the prices
for some sport bags illustrated on the separate
brochure mailed previously. Here are the new
prices:

DS ↓

BG11 — $18.75
BG12 — 11.00   Horizontally centre
BG13 — 13.00
BG15 — 10.75

DS ↓

Thank you for your co-operation and support. We
hope you enjoy record fall and winter business.

Yours truly,

Cliff Gabel
Executive Vice President
Sporting Goods Division

cr
Enclosure

Full Block Letter with a Display

50-character line (pica — 10 pitch)

Production 3

Centre the following program attractively on a full sheet of paper.

The Theatre Arts Club

presents

"YOU'RE A GOOD MAN CHARLIE BROWN"

by

Charles M. Schulz and Clark Gesner

Cast

```
Charlie Brown ............... Carl Maolo
Linus ..................... Domenic Sala
Schroeder ................... Ken Roche
Lucy ................ Roxanne Ingeborg
Patty ..................... Ruth Dartis
Snoopy ................... Michele Cole
Sally ................... Maria Argento
```

Production 1

Input the following letter on Cooper Canada letterhead. Input a Number 10 envelope or an envelope label.

Cooper Canada Limited

July 7, 19--

National Gym Clothing Ltd.
10, rue Deslauriers
Rivière du Loup, Québec
G5R 3E2

Gentlemen:

Enclosed is a revised hockey price list effective August 1.
The increases have been kept as moderate as possible. Hockey
sticks, sweaters and socks have not been increased.

As of the same date, we shall revise the prices for some sport
bags illustrated on the separate brochure mailed previously.
Here are the new prices:

DS

BG11 - $18.75
BG12 - 11.00   *Horizontally centre*
BG13 - 13.00
BG15 - 10.75

DS

Thank you for your co-operation and support. We hope you
enjoy record fall and winter business.

Yours truly,

Cliff Gabel
Executive Vice President
Sporting Goods Division

cr
Enclosure

Full Block Letter with a Display

60-character line (elite — 12 pitch)

Unit III

Objectives

By completing this unit *you* will:

1 Improve keyboard control.

2 Learn and apply the rules of capitalization.

3 Learn to format full block letters with mixed punctuation.

4 Learn to format letters with enumerations and displays.

5 Learn to format envelopes.

6 Learn to format enumerated copy.

7 Learn to input on lines and on printed forms.

8 Learn to correct errors in your copy.

9 Learn to spread and squeeze letters in a word.

10 Work toward developing a minimum speed of 30 words per minute with six or fewer errors on a three-minute timing.

Note: Additional production practice for this unit may be found on page 338.

This includes three production exercises for letters and three production exercises for enumerated material.

Letters with Displays

Format
60-character line
Single spacing

Practise each line twice.
Practise as quickly as you can.

Accuracy Drills

Think **accuracy**. Practise
each line once. Repeat or take
two 30-s timings on each line.

Take two 30-s timings on each
line. Take one 1-min timing on
the set of two lines.
■ Did you have two errors or
less with each timing?

Practise each underlined word
four times. Practise each line
once concentrating on the
underlined words.

Edit each line by correcting
two errors. Practise the
paragraph once with the
corrections.

Common Words

1 western nation travel aware simple metric language post word

2 clever perhaps order plants help lucky change owner like sea

Alternate-Hand Words

3 by cod rib disk lane coal blame eight sleuth bicycle torment

4 me pay tub girl duty rush flake formal firm pan body but own

Common-Word Sentences

5 Our company is interested in receiving a copy of the letter.

6 It really is not necessary for May to meet us at the office.

7 It will be a long time before I am able to visit them again.
      · · · ·1· · · ·2· · · ·3· · · ·4· · · ·5· · · ·6· · · ·7· · · ·8· · · ·9· · ·10· · · ·11· · · ·12

Spelling Practice

8 The inspector was definite; the building would be condemned.

9 I find it difficult to develop a resistance to winter colds.
      · · · ·1· · · ·2· · · ·3· · · ·4· · · ·5· · · ·6· · · ·7· · · ·8· · · ·9· · ·10· · · ·11· · · ·12

Editing Practice

10   Birds with eyes on the sides of th head can seee

almost 360°. Owls have front-facing eye, which giv them

a narowwer field of vision but a greater arae of binocular

sight (The ability to see an object w ith both eyes and get

one image). An owl is capable of turninging it head through

most of a circle andeven upside down for all-round visiion.

Format
60-character line
Single spacing

Practise each line twice.
Practise as quickly as you can.

Accuracy Drills

Think **accuracy**. Practise each line once. Repeat *or* take two 30-s timings on each line.

Take two 30-s timings on each line. Take one 1-min timing on the set of two lines.
■ Did you have two errors or less with each timing?

Use the left shift key and ; finger.

Practise each line twice.

Practise each underlined word four times. Practise each line once concentrating on the underlined words.

Edit each line by correcting two errors. Practise the paragraph once with the corrections.

Alternate-Hand Words

1 if end pen they dial clay right their height antique soap do

2 it and tight them foam bowls surname both turn make sign aid

Double-Letter Words

3 add see egg tell inn dull sorry guess fuzzy commit doll room

4 zoo off all lass call happy allow buddy agree ribbon baggage

Sentences with Double-Letter Words

5 The current tariffs on coffee and tobacco will be cancelled.

6 All meetings will be held in the upper staff room this week.
• • • •1• • • •2• • • •3• • • •4• • • •5• • • •6• • • •7• • • •8• • • •9• • • •10• • • •11• • • •12

Reach to the ” Key

7 ;;; ;"; ;"; ;"; """" ;" ;" ;;; ;"; ;"; ""; ""; ;" ;" ""; "";;

8 "Where is the ball," asked Andrea, "that broke the windows?"

9 Dale said, "Over here." She asked, "Shall I throw it back?"

Spelling Practice

10 The <u>secretary</u> notified the <u>committee</u> members of the meeting.

11 I read an interesting <u>pamphlet</u> on personal <u>financial</u> advice.
• • • •1• • • •2• • • •3• • • •4• • • •5• • • •6• • • •7• • • •8• • • •9• • • •10• • • •11• • • •12

Editing Practice

12   Do you know the diference between a loon and a duck.

Loons have largerand longer bodies than ducks. loons'

bills are shraply pointed, andthe ducks' bills are round-

tipped and flat. There sounds are very different:ducks

quack; the loons cry is   long, haunting, and lonely.
• • • •1• • • •2• • • •3• • • •4• • • •5• • • •6• • • •7• • • •8• • • •9• • • •10• • • •11• • • •12

Graduated Speed Practice

1. Turn to Lesson 54, page 161.
2. Drill on the appropriate Graduated Speed Practice.

1. Turn to Lesson 54, page 161.

Timing

Set for double spacing. Take two 3-min timings. Circle all errors. Calculate Gross Words Per Minute (GWPM). Record your best timing on your personal progress chart.

SI 1.19

Three-Minute Timing

	1	CW	3

When you reach into the glove box of a car or truck for — 12 / 12 / 4

a folded road map, you might take out a cassette tape. This — 24 / 24 / 8

tape is an electronic map which shows up as green lines on a — 36 / 36 / 12

screen mounted on the dash. The map moves as the car moves; — 48 / 48 / 16

streets that go past outside also go past on the screen. An — 60 / 60 / 20

arrow lets you know where you are and a flashing star lights — 72 / 72 / 24

where you are going. The map also shows you what streets to — 84 / 84 / 28

take to get there. — 87 / 87 / 29

You can zoom in for a close look at passing streets and — 12 / 99 / 33

city freeways. It takes no longer for a driver to glance at — 24 / 111 / 37

a screen than to look at any other gauge on the dash. It is — 36 / 123 / 41

faster to glance at a screen than to fumble with a paper map — 48 / 135 / 45

or squint at street signs. An electronic map is the perfect — 60 / 147 / 49

gift for drivers who tend to get lost going places. — 70 / 157 / 52

```
· · · · 1 · · · · 2 · · · · 3 · · · · 4 · · · · 5 · · · · 6 · · · · 7 · · · · 8 · · · · 9 · · · · 10 · · · · 11 · · · · 12     1 min
           1              2              3              4      3 min
```

Composition

As a bystander at an accident, answer the following questions. Use a separate sentence for each answer.
1. Who was driving the car at the time of the accident?
2. How did the accident happen?
3. How much damage was done to the car?
4. With what was the driver charged?
5. When will the case be heard in court?

Capitalization

Rule 1: Capitalize the first word in:
- sentences
- direct quotations
- complimentary closings

Are you ready?
Mary said, "We are late."
Yours very truly,

Capitalization Practice

13 we look forward to meeting with you soon. very truly yours,

14 the salesman replied, "the car is available in four shades."

15 thank you for your assistance with our survey. yours truly,

16 "no," he insisted, "the information is not for publication."

17 would you like us to return the entire shipment? sincerely,

• • • •1• • • •2• • • •3• • • •4• • • •5• • • •6• • • •7• • • •8• • • •9• • • •10• • • •11• • • •12

Alignment

How is this typed line sitting on your alignment scale?

OR

1. Locate the alignment scale on your typewriter.

2. Input: How is this typed line sitting on your alignment scale?

3. Know your typewriter:
   - Is the bottom of each letter sitting on the horizontal line, below the horizontal line, or above the horizontal line of the alignment scale?
   - Are the letters "i" and "l" aligned with a vertical line or between two vertical lines of the alignment scale?

1. Input: How is this typed line

2. Take the paper out of your typewriter.

3. Reinsert the paper.

4. Align the letter "i" with the alignment scale.
   - To move the line up or down, use the variable line spacer.
   - To move the line to the right or left, use the paper release.

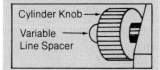

Cylinder Knob
Variable Line Spacer

5. Test the first letter to be input: s
   - Backspace with the correcting key. Make the necessary adjustments to correctly align the letter "s".

6. After the letter is aligned correctly, finish the sentence by adding:

   sitting on your alignment scale.

Production

Input the following letter on Cooper Canada letterhead. Use full block letter style with mixed punctuation. Input a Number 10 envelope or an envelope label. Remember to include all missing letter parts.

Kule's Sporting Goods Ltd.
1843 Hamilton Street
Regina, Saskatchewan
S4P 2B9

Gentlemen

We are pleased to enclose our new hockey catalogue. Many new and exciting products are shown throughout the catalogue.

Our new line of sweaters and stockings is shown on pages 10 to 15. New elbow pads, shinguards and a new European-style of hockey pants are but a few of the items awaiting your inspection. A new Cooper helmet is illustrated on pages 28 and 29.

Your Cooper representative has the details on all our new products, and will be in touch with you shortly.

Thanks for your support during the past year. We look forward to working with you again. Please use our newly expanded WATS lines to place your orders.

Yours truly

Cliff Gabel
Executive Vice-President
Sporting Goods Division

■ Did you listen for the right margin signal? OR Did you use word wrap?

■ Did you read the body of the letter?

Reinsertion Practice

Input each sentence leaving the number of spaces indicated in the parentheses. Remove your paper from the typewriter. Reinsert your paper, realign the line, and insert the word(s) indicated in the parentheses at the end of the sentence. If you are using a computer, move your cursor to the blank spaces and insert the word(s) indicated in parentheses at the end of the sentence. Follow this procedure for each of the practice lines.

19 Word processing can be (11) as a communication system. (described)

20 It is a (8) method of processing office communication. (speedy)

21 Letters and (11) are keyed--typed--on a machine. (documents)

22 The (6) is corrected--edited--before (4) is printed. (copy)   (it)

23 Usually, the copy can be (8) on a video screen. (viewed)

24 The revision may be (9) and stored for future use. (printed)

Production Practice

■ If you are using a computer, did you ask your teacher for another exercise?

Production

You wish to apply for a Social Insurance Number (SIN). Complete the SIN application form provided by your teacher.

Skill Building

Format
60-character line
Single spacing

Practise each line twice.
Practise as quickly as you can.

Analyze Your Progress

Practise each line once.
Repeat *or* take one 1-min
timing on each line. Circle all
errors. If you have two errors or
less on most of your timings,
go to line 9. If not, practise
lines 3-8.

Practise each line once.
Repeat or take one 1-min
timing on each line. Practise
as quickly as you can.

Practise each line once.
Practise each line again.

Read the definition of each
word.
Practise each sentence once
using the correct word in
parentheses.

One-Hand Words

1 far rat tea east fed add faster attract verb grave trade sea

2 joy pill link you hulk loop hum hymn minimum nylon lump lily

Accuracy Drives

3 raw tag ewe wave race test brass weave excess savage retread

4 hop oil inn junk only poppy kimono milk noon moon ill in nun

5 small floor supper getting yellow roof green callers meeting

6 feel happy sudden supply illness offer staff letters follows

7 Millie is willing to keep the office accounts in the summer.

8 Lee cooked some goose gizzard and broccoli in smooth batter.

Speed Drives

9 The members should pay their annual dues before the meeting.

10 They made more noise when coming back into the quiet garden.

11 Much less solar energy is received during the winter months.

12 The older folks had problems getting out and buying records.

13 Fishing vessels remained in the harbour while being checked.

14 The cold steady rain kept the children inside for nine days.
· · · ·1· · · ·2· · · ·3· · · ·4· · · ·5· · · ·6· · · ·7· · · ·8· · · ·9· · · ·10· · · ·11· · · ·12

Number Practice

15 There were 27 cousins, 16 aunts and 9 uncles at the reunion.

16 Bring 527 samples of blue candies and 308 samples of toffee.
· · · ·1· · · ·2· · · ·3· · · ·4· · · ·5· · · ·6· · · ·7· · · ·8· · · ·9· · · ·10· · · ·11· · · ·12

Basic English

principal: a head of a school or a sum of money (noun)
main or chief (adjective)
principle: a rule or law (noun)

17 Mr. Stock, our (principal, principle), is retiring this year.

18 The (principal, principle) of gravity was discovered by Newton.

19 How much interest does the bank pay on a (principal, principle) of

$15 000?

SI 1.26

Two-Minute Timing

		1	CW	2
They have caring eyes and sad faces. They roam through		12	12	6
the cold and lonely tundra of the north, grazing on moss and		24	24	12
lichen. Natives call them the bearded ones and we call them		36	36	18
musk oxen. Although they are neither oxen nor smell of musk		48	48	24
this name has stayed with them.		54	54	27
The musk oxen is very friendly and easy to train. They		12	66	33
are not pretty but are charming, playful, and clever. Since		24	78	39
they have been kept in zoos they have lost their yoke-shaped		36	90	45
horns. They come when called by name and love exploring new		48	102	51
places. Their wool is very warm and light. One kilogram of		60	114	57
their wool can be spun into over sixty kilometres of wool.		71	125	63

· · · · 1 · · · · 2 · · · · 3 · · · · 4 · · · · 5 · · · · 6 · · · · 7 · · · · 8 · · · · 9 · · · · 10 · · · · 11 · · · · 12   1 min

  1   2   3   4   5   6   2 min

Set for double spacing. Take
two 3-min timings. Circle all
errors. Calculate Gross Words
Per Minute (GWPM). Record
your best timing on your
personal progress chart.

SI 1.47

Three-Minute Timing

	1	3
It is possible for everyone to swim. The body contains	12	4
enough air to enable one to remain on the surface, if proper	24	8
breathing can be sustained. Sea water has a greater density	36	12
than fresh water, and is more buoyant. Some bodies of water	48	16
are so dense that it is difficult to keep the body immersed.	60	20
Many people enjoy swimming. It is a healthy sport; all	72	24
muscles of the body are exercised. Doctors prescribe it for	84	28
patients to help regain strength and the use of limbs. Some	96	32
towns and cities have indoor pools, which usually have a set	108	36
temperature. In outdoor pools the temperature always varies	120	40
with the weather. Many places now have both types of pools.	132	44

```
• • • • 1 • • • • 2 • • • • 3 • • • • 4 • • • • 5 • • • • 6 • • • • 7 • • • • 8 • • • • 9 • • • • 10 • • • • 11 • • • • 12      1 min
          1                        2                    3                    4          3 min
```

Composition

How many of the following abbreviations do you recognize? Input the words for which each abbreviation stands. Use a separate line for each one.

Example: MP -- Member of Parliament

CFL, CPR, CNR, UFO, PC, NDP, CIA, IBM, TV, NHL, LED, LCD,
UNICEF, SCUBA, BASIC, UPC, MICR, ROM, RAM

52

Format
60-character line
Single spacing

Practise each line twice.
Practise as quickly as you can.

Accuracy Drills

Think **accuracy**. Practise each line once. Repeat *or* take two 30-s timings on each line.

Take two 30-s timings on each line. Take one 1-min timing on the set of two lines.
■ Did you have two errors or less with each timing?

Use right shift key and **D** finger.
Keep other fingers in home position.
Practise each line twice.

Spelling

Practise each underlined word four times. Practise each line once concentrating on the underlined words.

Editing Practice

Edit each line by correcting two errors. Practise the paragraphs once with the corrections.

/ Inputting on Lines / Forms

One-Hand Words

1 we bad was acre best date aware barge beaver secrets average

2 nip you mop him pill plump hook limp loop jump hop lip plunk

Alternate-Hand Words

3 ham aid may pair sit maid vogue handle problem bicycle handy

4 so cob ape slap goal dusk fight chair eighty naughty element

Sentences with Alternate-Hand Words

5 Nancy works for both of them on the island half of the time.

6 That signal by the big firm is the key to the civic problem.
· · · · 1 · · · · 2 · · · · 3 · · · · 4 · · · · 5 · · · · 6 · · · · 7 · · · · 8 · · · · 9 · · · 10 · · · 11 · · · 12

Reach to the # Key

7 ddd d3d d#d d#d ### d# d# ### d#d d#d ##d ##d d# d# ##d ##dd

8 #28 and #59 or #72 and #40 or #56 and #27 or #48 and #91 and

9 We will pay these invoices now: #36, #598, #270, and #3376.

Spelling Practice

10 Expenses for this contract will exceed the budget estimates.

11 My cousin has a permanent position with a government agency.
· · · · 1 · · · · 2 · · · · 3 · · · · 4 · · · · 5 · · · · 6 · · · · 7 · · · · 8 · · · · 9 · · · 10 · · · 11 · · · 12

Editing Practice

12   The mos practical way to determine direction inthe

wilderness is bye means of a compass. ^Compasses--for the

most part-are foolproof and realiabe. They rarely require

maintenance, and they are usually simple operate to. By

the best modal for hiking that your budget will allow.

Production 2

Input the following letter on Bell Canada letterhead. Use full block letter style with mixed punctuation. Use the current numeric date. Input a Number 10 envelope or an envelope label. Remember to include all missing letter parts.

Bell Canada

Bell

Current date

To: Mr. Carl Weylman, 4110 Sherbrooke Street West Westmount, Quebec, H3Z 1K9

Thank you for your letter inquiring about Bell payphone policies. The following information will answer the questions you were asking:

1. Bell Canada has over 90 000 payphones in Ontario and Quebec.

2. Coin change is not required to make a local or long distance call from most payphones.

3. You can charge local and long distance calls to your Bell Calling Card at any payphone, or to a credit card when using one of Bell's new Card-Phones, located in Toronto and Montreal.

4. There is no charge to call the operator, emergency services, directory assistance, or repair service from a payphone.

Please do not hesitate to contact us again if you have any further questions about Bell services.

From: Leslie Solway, Public Relations Department

■ Did you listen for the right margin signal? OR Did you use word wrap?

■ Did you include the four missing letter parts?

■ Did you use your judgment for spacing?

Capitalization

Rule 2: Capitalize proper nouns:

• names of people	Mr. William Goer
• places and geographic locations	Montreal, Quebec Lake Simcoe
• days of the week and months of the year	Sunday August 20
• holidays	Good Friday
• animals	our pet, Simon
• trade names	Big Mac

Capitalization Practice

Read the Capitalization Rule. Edit each line by using the Capitalization Rules. Practise each line once with the correct capitalization.

13 roy and ann plan to visit the cottage on labour day weekend.

14 how many days does sue get for christmas holidays this year?

15 nobu's pet dog, toby, likes to go for a walk after his meal.

16 the vending machine in the cafeteria sells pepsi and sprite.

17 steffi and christopher plan to canoe down the nahanni river.

    · · · ·1· · · ·2· · · ·3· · · ·4· · · ·5· · · ·6· · · ·7· · · ·8· · · ·9· · · ·10· · · ·11· · · ·12

Reinsertion Practice

Input each sentence leaving the number of spaces indicated in the parentheses. Remove your paper from the typewriter. Reinsert your paper, realign the line, and insert the word(s) indicated in the parentheses at the end of the sentence. If you are using a computer, move your cursor to the blank spaces and insert the word(s) indicated in the parentheses at the end of the sentence. Follow this procedure for each of the practice lines.

18 Word processing operators (6) possess many basic skills. (must)

19 As well as basic skills, (9) and spelling are important. (grammar)

20 Proofreading (9) is another necessary skill. (ability)

21 Also, an operator (9) trained to use a computer. (must be)

 **BEAVER**

Beaver Lumber Company Limited
Executive Offices
245 Fairview Mall Drive, Willowdale, Ontario M2J 4T1
Telephone (416) 494-2161

August 12, 19—

Mr. A. S. Rapada
National Leasing Limited
441 North Market Street
Summerside, Prince Edward Island
C1N 1M2

Dear Mr. Rapada:

Would you please have your computer updated with
the following information:

DS↓

1. Unit #41169 (A. Crosby) Code 0100 instead of
    1430

DS↓

2. Unit #41167 (E. Bradley) Code 0034 instead of
    0125

DS↓

3. Unit #61150 (H. Baxter) Code 0140 instead of
    1356

DS↓

Also, would you please clarify the attached invoice.
According to our calculations, the amount should
be $338.67.

Yours very truly,

R. G. Richter, Manager
Operating Services

cr

Enclosure

Full Block Letter with Enumerations

50-character line (pica — 10 pitch)

Inputting on Lines

Move your cylinder forwards or backwards by depressing the left cylinder knob or the variable line spacer. Input slightly above the line. Use your alignment scale as a guide.

This is too high.

This is too low.

This is just right.

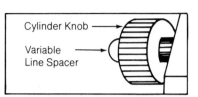

Production 1

Input the following with appropriate underscores. Remove the paper from your typewriter. Reinsert to input on the lines.

Surname: ————————————————

Date of Birth: ————————————

DS

Home Address: ————————————

————————————————————

TS | Postal Code: ————————————

Telephone Number: area code ————————

SS number ————————————————

TS

You are the winner of a new *car* ——————————

The records were on sale for *$9.98* and *$10.50* ——————

DS The last school I attended was ————————————

I will graduate ————————————————————

Two of my classmates are ———————— and ————————

TS

Air Canada and *Canadian Airlines* are two major commercial

DS airlines in Canada. They both have flights to *Europe* .

Production 2

You wish to attend two sessions at Olympia Sports Camp this summer. Complete the application form.

Basketball	or	Aqua-Sport	session 1	June 29-July 5
Competitive Swim	or	Basketball	session 2	July 6-July 12
Soccer	or	Basketball	session 3	July 13-July 19
Tennis	or	Soccer	session 4	July 20-July 26
Cheerleading	or	Wrestling	session 5	July 27-August 2
Football	or	Baseball	session 6	August 3-August 9
Cross Country	or	Dance	session 7	August 10-August 16

Production 1

Input the following letter on Beaver Lumber letterhead. Input a Number 10 envelope or an envelope label. Fold the letter for insertion.

 **BEAVER**

Beaver Lumber Company Limited
Executive Offices
245 Fairview Mall Drive, Willowdale, Ontario M2J 4T1
Telephone (416) 494-2161

August 12, 19--

Mr. A. S. Rapada
National Leasing Limited
441 North Market Street
Summerside, Prince Edward Island
C1N 1M2

Dear Mr. Rapada:

Would you please have your computer updated with the following information:
DS↓
1.   Unit #41169 (A. Crosby) Code <u>0100</u> instead of 1430
DS↓
2.   Unit #41167 (E. Bradley) Code <u>0034</u> instead of 0125
DS↓
3.   Unit #61150 (H. Baxter) Code <u>0140</u> instead of 1356
DS↓
Also, would you please clarify the attached invoice. According to our calculations, the amount should be $338.67.

Yours very truly,

R. G. Richter, Manager
Operating Services

cr

Enclosure

Full Block Letter with Enumerations

60-character line (elite — 12 pitch)

OLYMPIA
Sports Camp

OLYMPIA SPORTS CAMP — SUMMER SESSIONS
OLYMPIA SPORTS CAMP — A DIVISION OF OLYMPIA ATHLETIC CAMPS LTD.

APPLICATION FORM
62 Ridgevale Drive — Toronto, Ontario, M6A 1L1 — (416) 783-0589

Please state the SPECIFIC SPORT, DATES FOR EACH SESSION that you wish your son/daughter to attend:
e.g. OLYMPIA _Basketball_ CAMP   SESSION NO. _1_ _June 28 – July 4_

I would like my son/daughter to attend:

SPORT		SESSION	DATES
_____		NO. _____	_____
_____		NO. _____	_____
_____		NO. _____	_____

Name _____ Male _____ Female _____
         Surname   First   Middle

Address _____
         Number   Street   Apartment No.

City _____ Province _____ Postal Code _____ Tel: _____
                                                              Area Code   No.

Present Age _____ Date of Birth _____ Height _____ Mass _____
                        Day   Month   Year

Grade completed as of June _____ School _____

Name of Parent or Guardian _____

Business No. _____ Telephone No. to call while
                        son or daughter at Camp _____

Summer Address while
son or daughter at camp _____

Two-Minute Timing

	1	2
They left Victoria at 06:30 on Monday for a 26-day trip	12	6
of 3 755 km. On Friday, they decided to add 9 days to their	24	12
holiday. Most of the motels cost $73.00 a night. The meals	36	18
cost about $8.75 each, unless they had a picnic. Total food	48	24
expenses were $495.36 for the first 14 days. Every gasoline	60	30
station had different prices, from $0.47/L to $0.68/L.	70	35

• • • • 1 • • • • 2 • • • • 3 • • • • 4 • • • • 5 • • • • 6 • • • • 7 • • • • 8 • • • • 9 • • • •10 • • • •11 • • • •12   1 min

   1   2   3   4   5   6   2 min

Letters with Enumerations

Format
60-character line
Single spacing

Practise each line twice.
Practise as quickly as you can.

Speed Drills

■ Try to practise each timing faster.
Take two 15-s timings on each line. Take one 30-s timing on the set of lines.

Take two 15-s timings on each line. Take one 30-s timing on the set of lines.
■ Did you do each timing faster?

Practise each line once.
Practise each line again.

Read the definition of each word.
Practise each sentence once using the correct word in parentheses.

Double-Letter Words

1 bee pool skill sweet seeks error class puppet begged cabbage

2 all toss added dress comma green goods effect goose colleges

Common-Word Sentences

3 Being able to speak a second language may help in some jobs.

4 Each morning, the blinds and curtains were opened for light.

5 They lit the first fire in their new fireplace last evening.

Sentences with Alternate-Hand Words

6 Ruby may have to give half of the turkey to the eight girls.

7 She may go to the big island to visit with them and to fish.

8 The city paid the busy auditor to fight their civic problem.
• • • • 1 • • • • 2 • • • • 3 • • • • 4 • • • • 5 • • • • 6 • • • • 7 • • • • 8 • • • • 9 • • • •10 • • • •11 • • • •12

Number Practice

9 Our committee needed 25 people to register 10 000 delegates.

10 We will meet every 15 days for 18 months to plan 3 seminars.

Basic English

leave: to depart or abandon
let: allow

11 I must (leave, let) now, or I will be late for the opening.

12 Will the company (leave, let) you take your holidays in March?

13 (Leave, Let) me help you with those heavy boxes.

Full Block Letter with Enumerations

A common style for enumerations in the body of a letter is to align (block) the enumerated material with the left and right margins.

Example:

The following precedures should be followed in the event of
an accident:

1.   Telephone the nearest police station and report the
     location of the accident.

Forms

Format
60-character line
Single spacing

Practise each line twice.
Practise as quickly as you can.

Speed Drills

■ Try to practise each timing faster.
Take two 15-s timings on each line. Take one 30-s timing on the set of lines.

Take two 15-s timings on each line. Take one 30-s timing on the set of lines.
■ Did you do each timing faster?

Practise each line once.
Practise each line again.

Capitalization Rule

Read the Capitalization Rule. Edit each line by using the Capitalization Rules. Practise each line once with the correct capitalization.

Double-Letter Words

1 egg too bee well keep staff spoon hilly apple accuse pioneer

2 drill zoo see error pass teeth funny gloom suggest off queen

Common-Word Sentences

3 It was the last day of classes for the first semester group.

4 The girls and boys washed their hands and feet in the water.

5 When the weather turned cold, they had to move their plants.

Sentences with Alternate-Hand Words

6 The doctor with the giant, hairy dogs laughs at their shape.

7 The two men blame the sick dog for the fight over the rifle.

8 Their recent guest may go to the chapels in the city by bus.

· · · ·1· · · ·2· · · ·3· · · ·4· · · ·5· · · ·6· · · ·7· · · ·8· · · ·9· · · 10· · · ·11· · · ·12

Number Practice

9 The speed limit is 60 km/h here; on highways it is 100 km/h.

10 Invoice #93, dated 1989 04 10, was received by us yesterday.

Capitalization

Rule 3: Capitalize the following names:

• departments	Personnel Department
• companies	Lawson & Jones, Inc.
• organizations	Red Cross
• historical events or documents	the Middle Ages
• specific courses in schools or colleges	Computronics 201

11 katy's new job involves working in the marketing department.

12 the bank of canada interest rates dropped to 10.95 per cent.

13 the history classes discussed the british north america act.

14 cynthia chose french 101, art 141, and music 151 as options.

15 koo's junior achievement group meets every monday at school.

· · · ·1· · · ·2· · · ·3· · · ·4· · · ·5· · · ·6· · · ·7· · · ·8· · · ·9· · · 10· · · ·11· · · ·12

Timing

Set for double spacing. Take two 3-min timings. Circle all errors. Calculate Gross Words Per Minute (GWPM). Record your best timing on your personal progress chart.

SI 1.46

Three-Minute Timing

People have been greatly interested in their dreams for	12	4
many years. In earlier days, it was sometimes believed that	24	8
the soul left the body during sleep and actually visited the	36	12
sites of the dreams. To some, dreams are a simple form of a	48	16
natural thought. Dreams occur only when the activity of the	60	20
brain is slowed down. When one awakes, the actual events of	72	24
dreams might be forgotten. Most dreams are the result of an	84	28
external influence on a person. Many people dream about one	96	32
particular thought or experience that might have happened to	108	36
them during the preceding day.	114	39

```
• • • •1• • • •2• • • •3• • • •4• • • •5• • • •6• • • •7• • • •8• • • •9• • • •10• • • •11• • • •12        1 min
        1                2                3                4        3 min
```

Composing Practice

Think and answer as quickly as you can without hesitating.

Composition

An employee of any organization is an important public-relations representative. He or she reflects the attitude of a firm in many ways. Often, people judge the quality and efficiency of a company by the employees that they come in contact with.

Assume that you have a specific part-time job with a company. In your role as an employee of the company, what personal qualities would you consider as essential for that job? Use sentence form to describe the qualities. List as many qualities as you can in enumerated format.

Basic English

effect: result (noun)
to bring about (verb)
affect: to change (verb)

Read the definition of each word.
Practise each sentence once using the correct word in parentheses.

16 How does the hot weather (effect, affect) you?

17 What you say will never (effect, affect) our decision.

18 The speaker had a tremendous (effect, affect) on the audience.

Production 1

Production Practice

■ If you are using a computer, you may be asked to create a master form.

Complete the Consumer Questionnaire provided by your teacher.

■ Did you use your alignment scale as a guide?
■ Did you use the variable line spacer?

CONSUMER QUESTIONNAIRE

1. What items have you purchased in the last month? (Do not include food purchases.)

_____ _____ _____

_____ _____ _____

2. Select the most expensive purchase from the above list and answer the following:

   a)   Was this purchase a planned or an impulse decision?

   _____

   b)   Did you price competitive brands before buying?

   _____

   c)   Who was with you at the time of the purchase?

   _____

   d)   How did you feel about the purchase afterwards?

   _____

   e)   Did you see this product advertised before you purchased it?

   _____

   f)   If so, where was it advertised?

   _____

   g)   Where did you buy it?

   _____

   h)   Would you judge this product to be a need or a want?

   _____

Production

Set a 60-character line and input a rough draft in order to determine the number of lines. Vertically centre and prepare a second copy on a full sheet of paper. Use correct format for enumerated material.

Title: CARE OF YOUR RECORDS

Enumerations: 1. Records attract dust. Even a new album can

carry minuscule particles. To keep your records dust-free,

wipe them frequently with a lint-free cloth or chamois.

2. If your records are very dirty, wash them with warm

water and a mild detergent. Then dry them immediately with

a clean, lint-free cloth.

3. The natural oils present on your fingertips will soil

your records. Handle an album by tipping it out of its

jacket and holding it with the edges between your palms, or

with your thumb on the edge and your middle fingers

balancing on the label.

4. As soon as you have finished playing a record, return it to its jacket. To help prevent dust accumulation, place the open end of the paper sleeve at the closed end of the jacket.

5. Don't pile up records on your turntable -- this makes them susceptible to warping. Also, store records upright.

6. Keep albums away from damp areas and from exposure to extreme heat or cold. Never leave a record in the car on a hot summer day or in the dead of winter.

7. Don't listen to a stereo album on a mono record player. It may damage the record because the needles on mono players are too thick. On the other hand, it is acceptable to play mono disks on a stereo system.

Production 2

Complete the registration form provided by your teacher and apply for one of the programs offered by Parks and Recreation Services.

PARKS & RECREATION SERVICES
Fall Programs

BADMINTON	Monday	20:00-21:30	$12/9 wks.
GUITAR II (teen)	Monday	19:00-20:00	15/9
GOLF	Wednesday	18:30-20:00	14/9
DANCERCISE	Thursday	19:00-20:00	17/9
BRIDGE	Friday	19:00-20:00	16/9
DRESSMAKING	Friday	19:00-21:00	22/9

REGISTRATION FORM

NAME

DATE OF BIRTH   Year   Month   Day

ADDRESS

TELEPHONE NUMBER

PROGRAM   Day

TIME   Fee

Signature   Date

Amount enclosed. (Do not send cash in the mail.)

¢ / Enumerations

Format
60-character line
Single spacing

Practise each line twice.
Practise as quickly as you can.

Speed Drills

■ Try to practise each timing faster.
Take two 15-s timings on each line. Take one 30-s timing on the set of lines.

Take two 15-s timings on each line. Take one 30-s timing on the set of lines.
■ Did you do each timing faster?

Practise each line once.
Practise each line again.

Use left shift key and **J** finger. Keep other fingers in home position.

Practise each line twice.

Know your keyboard.

Read the definition of each word.
Practise each sentence once using the correct word in parentheses.

Common Words

1 small rate high freight summer when dream another part print

2 growth autumn climate number arrive hand friend together dig

Common-Word Sentences

3 He felt he had a right to know which number had been chosen.

4 The children were told a different bedtime story each night.

5 They looked at the map, but it was very difficult to follow.

Sentences with Double-Letter Words

6 Anna should allow three weeks for all the new mitten orders.

7 The committee feels that caffeine and tobacco cause illness.

8 The cook rang the dinner bell to call the loggers to supper.
····1····2····3····4····5····6····7····8····9····10····11····12

Number Practice

9 They will deposit $2 500, which leaves a balance of $37 000.

10 Turn to page 375 and do questions 9 to 27, part B, by 10:30.

Reach to the ¢ Key

11 jjj j6j j¢j j¢j ¢¢¢ j¢ j¢ ¢¢¢ j¢j j¢j ¢¢j ¢¢j j¢ j¢ ¢¢j ¢¢jj

12 These are the prices for the candies: 9¢, 35¢, 45¢ and 99¢.

13 3 sheets @ 15¢; 25 boxes @ 99¢; 12 typewriter ribbons @ 86¢;
····1····2····3····4····5····6····7····8····9····10····11····12

Basic English

sight: vision
cite: to quote or refer to
site: location

14 He (sighted, cited, sited) many sources for his statistics.

15 The Board has chosen the (sight, cite, site) for the new library.

16 Following the accident, he had (sight, cite, site) in only one eye.

Set for double spacing. Take
two 3-min timings. Circle all
errors. Calculate Gross Words
Per Minute (GWPM). Record
your best timing on your
personal progress chart.

SI 1.46

Three-Minute Timing

	1	3
Many cities have ripped the tracks from the streets but	12	4
they have left the streetcar rights of way in large suburban	24	8
areas. With increased subway costs, the surface routes will	36	12
likely be revived. Several cities are planning and building	48	16
new streetcar systems. The intent is to promote rail travel	60	20
service and to raise it from an age of steam and soot to the	72	24
era of silent speed. Bombardier Inc. is a leader in various	84	28
aspects of rail and subway vehicle development in the world.	96	32

```
• • • •1• • • •2• • • •3• • • •4• • • •5• • •6• • • •7• • • •8• • • •9• • • •10• • • •11• • • •12      1 min
         1                  2                  3                  4           3 min
```

Composing Practice

Think and answer as quickly
as you can without hesitating.

Composition

Input as many names of Canadian cities as you can in the next five minutes. Each succeeding name must begin with the last letter of the preceding name. Begin with the city in which you live or the name of the city closest to your home. Use commas to separate the names.

Example:

Montreal, Lethbridge, Edmonton, etc.

Production 2

Set a 60-character line and input a rough draft in order to determine the number of lines. Vertically centre and input a second copy on a half sheet of paper. Use correct format for enumerated material.

Choosing a Camera

1. Learn the basics. A few simple principles govern all cameras. Pick up pointers from a good photography book or talk to a pro.
2. Know your needs. The camera market offers a wide variety of choices: cartridge-loaded cameras, cameras with self-developing film, 35 mm cameras with automatic exposure control, single-lens reflex or twin-lens reflex cameras.
3. Try before you buy. Ask to see the cameras at a photo dealer, and take your time to determine which one feels most comfortable for you.
4. Comparison shop. Prices vary widely. Check newspapers, discount catalogues, etc.

■ Did you set a tab? OR Did you use the indent option?

■ Did you listen for the right margin signal? OR Did you use word wrap?

Timing

Set for double spacing. Take two 2-min timings. Circle all errors. Calculate Gross Words Per Minute (GWPM). Record your best timing on your personal progress chart.

SI 1.22

Two-Minute Timing

		1	2
Sue's room is 6.95 m long and 3.75 m wide. The ceiling		12	6
is 2.53 m high. The windows are 1.83 m long and 1.5 m high.		24	12
She has 27 blouses, 9 dresses, 8 pairs of jeans, 6 sweaters,		36	18
and 17 pairs of shoes in her closet. The new rug was 0.75 m		48	24
too short for the family room so she got it. She had to ask		60	30
her brother for $35.10 and her friend for $10.50 to buy it.		71	35

```
· · · · 1 · · · · 2 · · · · 3 · · · 4 · · · · 5 · · · 6 · · · 7 · · · · 8 · · · · 9 · · · ·10· · · ·11· · · ·12      1 min
              1                    2                    3                    4               2 min
```

Skill Building

Format
60-character line
Single spacing

Practise each line twice.
Practise as quickly as you can.

One-Hand Words

1 him union yolk plum noon onion pupil opinion pumpkin you pin

2 bar draw greet tear scar cafe address face crease waste fast

Accuracy Drives

Analyze Your Progress

Practise each line once.
Repeat *or* take one 1-min
timing on each line. Circle all
errors. If you have two errors or
less on most of your timings,
go to line 9. If not, practise
lines 3-8.

3 art web fat weed feat grab swear badge streets breeze trades

4 you pink pop him lull plunk monk lion imply mummy junk union

5 pass arrest staff occur smooth commit bottle connect depress

6 full flood dizzy dinner assist arrive cocoon village quitter

7 The jogger will accept the odds and run in the annual event.

8 A restless class left a mess of books by the classroom door.

Speed Drives

Practise each line once.
Repeat *or* take one 1-min
timing on each line. Practise
as quickly as you can.

9 There are many time zones in our gracious extending country.

10 Solar energy is most efficient when receiving southern rays.

11 It is sometimes a problem to determine who has called again.

12 Many customers are not ready when the taxi arrives for them.

13 It is an individual decision if a day will have many smiles.

14 Her sleek fingers passed gracefully over the piano keyboard.
· · · · 1 · · · · 2 · · · · 3 · · · · 4 · · · · 5 · · · · 6 · · · · 7 · · · · 8 · · · · 9 · · · · 10 · · · · 11 · · · · 12

Number Practice

Practise each line once.
Practise each line again.

15 The 24 quotes for 96 brushes and 78 cards were 15 days late.

16 She sold 215 in May, 1 074 in June, and 896 or more in July.

17 They bought 98 chairs, 41 tables, 35 lamps, and 60 blankets.

Spelling Practice

Practise each underlined word
four times. Practise each line
once concentrating on the
underlined words.

18 A separate schedule was included for each of the applicants.

19 Chaos resulted as the mischievous tots tore around the room.

20 One should have personal pride in the achievement of a goal.
· · · · 1 · · · · 2 · · · · 3 · · · · 4 · · · · 5 · · · · 6 · · · · 7 · · · · 8 · · · · 9 · · · · 10 · · · · 11 · · · · 12

Formatting Guide for Enumerations

Line Length	• Set a 60-character line (elite — 12 pitch) or a 50-character line (pica — 10 pitch) unless a different line length is required. Enumerations in a report use the same line length as the body of the report.
Tab	• Set a tab to leave two characters between the numbers and the sentences.
Top and Bottom Margins	• Centre vertically.
Spacing	• Single space each enumeration. • Double space between enumerations.
Continuation Line	• Input the second line (and following lines) of each enumeration aligned with the beginning of the sentence: not with the number.
Title	• Capitalize and centre the title. Then, triple space to the enumerations.

Production 1

Set a 60-character line. Vertically centre the following enumerated material on a half sheet of paper.

TAB OR INDENT

HOMEWORK TIPS

TS

1. ∧∧Be organized. Keep a list of homework items which must
   be done. A small notebook just for that purpose is a
   good idea—notes can be entered during each class.

   DS

2. Be efficient. Schedule your homework time for the hours
   you feel best. You'll be able to concentrate, and
   you'll finish faster.

   DS

3. Have a special work area. A large desk or table is best
   so that there is enough space available for all the
   texts and supplies you need.

   DS

4. Divide a long task. Instead of trying to complete a
   very long assignment in one sitting, plan your schedule
   so that you are able to tackle it in several sessions.

Your teacher will select one of the time intervals indicated at the right of the drill lines. Select the line that you think you can complete in that interval.

If you complete the line, try the next line which is longer. If not, try again or adjust your goal to a shorter line.

If your objective is speed, concentrate on speed by **pushing** to complete the line in the time limit. Errors should not be a concern.

If your objective is accuracy, concentrate on accuracy by attempting to complete the line with one error or less in the time limit.

Graduated Speed Practice

20 s 15 s 12 s

#	Line	12	16	20
21	Send the list to me.	12	16	20
22	She wants to go home.	13	17	21
23	They went to the city.	13	18	22
24	Make some tea for them.	14	18	23
25	Hang that picture there.	14	19	24
26	We know you want to come.	15	20	25
27	Bring me a glass of water.	16	21	26
28	The bus and train are here.	16	22	27
29	The jars fell to the ground.	17	22	28
30	Classes are over in one week.	17	23	29
31	Go to the school without them.	18	24	30
32	Carry the books to the library.	19	25	31
33	Trees have many shades of green.	19	26	32
34	Her baby is growing very quickly.	20	26	33
35	Brown curtains hung in the window.	20	27	34
36	They will be going later this week.	21	28	35
37	Take the deposits to the bank later.	22	29	36
38	It will make a great name for itself.	22	30	37
39	She was the link between the two ages.	23	30	38
40	The tots caused much chaos in his room.	23	31	39
41	The lights went out while you were away.	24	32	40
42	Both sides of the old story must be told.	25	33	41
43	The next five years were very long for us.	25	34	42
44	Those cheques must be sent to their office.	26	34	42
45	He does not need those wheels for his truck.	26	35	44
46	They peeked in the window and saw him inside.	27	36	45
47	Radio stations are playing more popular music.	28	37	46
48	We expect a detailed report from you next week.	28	38	47
49	More people are listening to country-rock songs.	29	38	48
50	Many hope peace can be restored there next month.	29	39	49

· · · · 1 · · · · 2 · · · · 3 · · · · 4 · · · · 5 · · · · 6 · · · · 7 · · · · 8 · ·

@ / Enumerations

Format
60-character line
Single spacing

Practise each line twice.
Practise as quickly as you can.

Alternate-Hand Words

1 tie cow pans clam whale cycle duty keys work burnt lake worn

2 air snap down lamb tight firm bus handle right box men towns

Accuracy Drills
Think **accuracy**. Practise
each line once. Repeat *or* take
two 30-s timings on each line.

Double-Letter Words

3 off need still abbey upper added goods bigger dollar illness

4 zoo toss petty drill shall flood occur middle happen vaccine

Sentences with Double-Letter Words

Take two 30-s timings on each
line. Take one 1-min timing on
the set of two lines.
■ Did you have two errors or
less with each timing?

5 Suzannah called Jimmy to suggest that he attend the meeting.

6 All the volleyball supporters cheered for the happy winners.
····1····2····3····4····5····6····7····8····9····10····11····12

Spelling Practice

Practise each underlined word
four times. Practise each line
once concentrating on the
underlined words.

7 A current trend of our <u>society</u> is towards more <u>leisure</u> time.

8 On the <u>fourth</u> attempt, Sue did the manuscript without error.

Reach to the @ Key

Use right shift key and **S**
finger.

9 sss s2s s@s s@s @@@ s@ s@ @@@ s@s s@s @@s @@s s@ s@ @@s @@ss

10 Buy the 60 @ $0.29 each; 600 @ $1.75 each; 230 @ $1.44 each.

Practise each line twice.

11 They quoted us 780 @ $1.50; 36 @ $2.99; and 15 @ $9.95 each.
····1····2····3····4····5····6····7····8····9····10····11····12

Editing Practice

Edit each line by correcting
two errors. Practise the
paragraph once with the
corrections.

12   The first makers of chewinggum in america were the

Indians who used the resin from spruce bark., It did't

be come a comercial success until an inventor, Thomas

Adams, processed teh sapodilla plant, known today as.

chicle. He called it Admas New York Gum. It had no

flavour or sugar, but kids loved it-in spit of the oppo-

sition of ministers, teachers parents, and the press

Timing

Set for double spacing. Take two 3-min timings. Circle all errors. Calculate Gross Words Per Minute (GWPM). Record your best timing on your personal progress chart.

SI 1.26

Composing Practice

Think and answer as quickly as you can without hesitating.

Three-Minute Timing

She walked across the hall and opened the door. As she	12	4
went upstairs she opened the bag and thought about what they	24	8
had done. She came down again, wearing her new green dress.	36	12
The towels and newspapers she was carrying were neatly under	48	16
her arm. One or two little touches and things would be back	60	20
in order. She glanced at the clock beside the window as she	72	24
hurried toward the basement door. It was almost noon and if	84	28
they were on time they would be home in five minutes. Later	96	32
she could relax and tell them what had happened to the desk.	108	36

`· · · ·1· · · ·2· · · ·3· · · ·4· · · ·5· · · ·6· · · ·7· · · ·8· · · ·9· · · ·10· · · ·11· · · ·12`   1 min

1   2   3   4   3 min

Composition

A paragraph is a group of sentences that deals with a single topic. The main theme of the paragraph should be clear to the reader. This theme may or may not be at the beginning of the paragraph. Each sentence in a paragraph must be connected in some way to the preceding sentence.

Input a rough draft of a short story using one of the following sentence beginnings:

> The explosion...
> No one was...
> A creepy feeling...
> I discovered...

If you are using a computer, print a copy of your story. Edit your rough draft and make any necessary corrections in pen or pencil. Then, input a good copy.

Folding Letters for Business-Size Envelopes

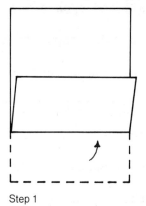

Step 1

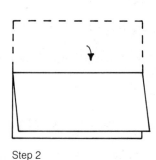

Step 2

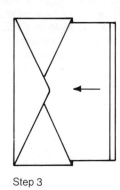

Step 3

Timing

Set for double spacing. Take two 2-min timings. Circle all errors. Calculate Gross Words Per Minute (GWPM). Record your best timing on your personal progress chart.

SI 1.46

Two-Minute Timing

	1	2
Many rivers and lakes now cover almost one sixth of the	12	6
province and help make it a popular vacation spot. Tourists	24	12
enjoy boating and swimming in the clear and sparkling water.	36	18
Fishermen catch bass, pike, and trout. In the thick forests	48	24
hunters can track caribou, elk, moose, and smaller game. In	60	30
the marshes and on the prairie, they can shoot ducks, geese,	72	36
and partridge. Manitoba does have something for everyone.	83	41

• • • 1 • • • • 2 • • • • 3 • • • • 4 • • • • 5 • • • • 6 • • • • 7 • • • • 8 • • • • 9 • • • • 10 • • • • 11 • • • • 12   1 min
     1   2   3   4   5   6   2 min

& / Envelope Addresses

Format
60-character line
Single spacing

Practise each line twice.
Practise as quickly as you can.

Accuracy Drills

Take two 30-s timings on each line. Practise each phrase as quickly as you can.

Take two 30-s timings on each line. Take one 1-min timing on the set of two lines.
■ Did you have two errors or less with each timing?

Use left shift key and **J** finger. Keep other fingers in home position.
Practise each line twice.

Practise each underlined word four times. Practise each line once concentrating on the underlined words.

Edit each line by correcting two errors.
Practise the paragraph once with the corrections.

Common Words

1 has done make trade willing that road group these must every

2 strong heavy glass meat acquire receive luck bread does hope

Common Phrases

3 we are/we will/we know/we cannot/we must/we might/we suggest/

4 to go/to stay/to read/to write/to know/to play/to be/to come/

Common-Word Sentences

5 She said she does not wish to be disturbed until break time.

6 They promised to pay for the damages to the trucks and cars.
••••1••••2••••3••••4••••5••••6••••7••••8••••9••••10••••11••••12

Reach to the & Key

7 jjj j7j j&j j&j &&& j& j& &&& j&j j&j &&j &&j j& j& &&j &&jj

8 1 & 2 and 3 & 4 and 5 & 6 and 7 & 8 and 9 & 10 and 11 & 12 &

9 The company in question is James R. Robertson & Company Ltd.

10 Mr. & Mrs. A. T. Kells attended the annual business meeting.

Spelling Practice

11 Can you recommend a dependable shop that can repair our car?

12 Pat's dessert course was irresistible--we all had a portion.
••••1••••2••••3••••4••••5••••6••••7••••8••••9••••10••••11••••12

Editing Practice

13   The beaver---along with mice, squirrels, muskrat and

porcupine--blongs to a group of animal known as rodents.

These animals all have two two upper teeth and two lower te teeth

in the front of the jaw;these teeth are calledincisors

are are used primarily for gnawing. The beaver's in cisors

are long large and very shrap.

Production 2

Input the following in full block style with mixed punctuation on the 3M letterhead. Use the current numeric date. Read the letter to determine if there should be an enclosure notation. Remember to include all missing letter parts. Input a Number 10 envelope or an envelope label. Fold the letter for insertion.

3M Canada Inc.

Post Office Box 5757
London, Ontario N6A 4T1

3M

Current date
To: Mr. Richard Guthrie
    6625 Arlington Street, Vancouver,
    British Columbia V5S 3P1

Thank you for your letter requesting information about Thinsulate thermal insulation.

Made by 3M, Thinsulate provides nearly twice the warmth of equal thicknesses of down, polyester, fibrefill, or wool. Yet it adds little bulk or volume, so garments can be sleek and trim. This insulation does not lose its loft under damp conditions because the fibres absorb less than 1 per cent of their mass in water.

The enclosed list gives the names of manufacturers that are currently featuring Thinsulate in their activewear garments (for hunting, cross-country skiing, backpacking, mountain climbing, and snowmobiling) as well as in their dress and casual outerwear.

We hope this summary will answer your questions. We appreciate your interest in our product.

From: D.J. Ferguson, Public Relations

Where ideas come to life.

■ Did you listen for the right margin signal OR Did you use word wrap?

■ Did you include the complimentary closing?

■ Did you include your initials?

Capitalization

Rule 4: Capitalize the first word of a title (book, magazine, article, etc.,) and all other words, except joining words such as *of*, *to*, *the*, etc.

Note: Underscore titles of complete works published as separate items e.g. books, magazines, newspapers, titles of movies, plays, etc. Enclose in quotation marks titles that represent part of a complete published work e.g. chapters, lessons, and sections in a book; articles for newspapers and magazines, etc.

- book   The Lord of the Rings
- newspaper   The Sudbury Star
- article   "Beating a Player at the Net"
- chapter   "Road Tests and Off-Road Tests"
- play   The Elephant Man
- movie   The Empire Strikes Back
- magazine   Sports Illustrated

Read the Capitalization Rule. Edit each line by using the Capitalization Rules. Practise each line once with the correct capitalization.

14 we have subscribed to runner's world for the past six years.

15 did you read the article about skiing in the globe and mail?

16 be sure to read "shoes and feet", an article by Dr. D. Brit.

17 alfred hitchcock's movie, north-by-northwest, starts friday.

18 the servant of two masters played for stratford this summer.

· · · ·1· · · ·2· · · ·3· · · ·4· · · ·5· · · ·6· · · ·7· · · ·8· · · ·9· · · ·10· · · ·11· · · ·12

Formatting Guide for Envelope Addresses

City	• The city is preferred in upper case.
Province and Territory	• Businesses and individuals usually use complete addresses without abbreviations and symbols. Two-letter address symbols of provinces and territories may be used by large volume mailers.
Postal Code	• The postal code is preferred as the last line of the address. If it has to be on the same line as the province, it must be separated by at least two spaces.
Foreign Addresses	• The country of destination, in capital letters, is the last line of the address.

Canadian Provinces and Territories

Provinces and Territories	Symbols	Provinces and Territories	Symbols
Alberta	AB	Nova Scotia	NS
British Columbia	BC	Ontario	ON
Labrador	LB	Prince Edward Island	PE
Manitoba	MB	Quebec	~~PQ~~ QC
Newfoundland	NF	Saskatchewan	SK
New Brunswick	NB	Yukon	YK
Northwest Territories	NT	NUNAVUT	NT

BEAVER LUMBER COMPANY LIMITED

245 Fairview Mall Drive, Willowdale, Ontario M2J 4T1 Telephone (416) 494-2161

August 27, 19--

Ms. Renata Jacot
5703 Dalton Drive N.W.
Calgary, Alberta
T3A 1C4

Dear Ms. Jacot:

In response to your recent request, we are pleased
to send you a copy of our article entitled "Exterior
Painting, The Quick Home Remedy".

Our Group Merchandising Department prepared this
article for consumers. It contains many helpful
suggestions on choosing the right paint and tools
for the job, preparing the surface to be painted,
etc.

Please do not hesitate to call your local Beaver
store, or to write our Group Merchandising Department
at the above address if you require additional
information.

Yours very truly,

Dianne C. Warnick
Press Officer
2↓
cr
2↓
Enclosure

Full Block Letter with Enclosure Notation

50-character line (pica — 10 pitch)

Postal Code Reminders

1. The postal code is a permanent part of the address.
2. Always enter the code using numbers and upper case letters.
3. Do not use periods or other punctuation marks in the code.
4. Never underscore the postal code.
5. Leave one space between the two parts of the code. Do not join the code in any way.
6. No part of the address should appear below the code. The word CANADA should be above the code or the word before the code.

Production Practice

Production 1

Input the following envelope addresses. Both styles for the provinces and territories are given.

The American Postal Code (Zip Code) is at least a five-digit number. It is placed on the same line as the city and state.

The state is a two-letter abbreviation in capital letters.

There is one space between the state and the Zip Code.

Mr. John H. Cooper
Executive Vice President
Cooper Canada Limited
501 Alliance Avenue
TORONTO, Ontario
M6N 2J3

Mr. D. J. Ferguson
Public Relations
3M Canada Inc.
P.O. Box 5757
LONDON, ON
N6A 4T1

Mrs. J. Sakamoto
209 Lavigne Street
BATHURST, New Brunswick
E2A 1J3

British Columbia Railway Company
221 West Esplanade
NORTH VANCOUVER, BC
V7M 3J1

Canadian Pacific Limited
910, rue Peel
MONTREAL, Quebec
H3C 3E4

Hudson's Bay Company
77 Main Street
WINNIPEG, MB
R3C 2R1

Mr. Joseph Falke
1221 Avenue of the Americas
NEW YORK, NY 10124-0027
U.S.A.

Brookfield Ice Cream Limited
312 Lemarchant Road
ST. JOHN'S, NF
A1C 5J4

Ms. R. D. Recchi
86 Whelan Avenue
CHIPPING NORTON
2170 N.S.W.
AUSTRALIA

Mr. Lin Song
Director, Foreign Affairs Office
Xinghua University
Haidian District
BEIJING
PEOPLE'S REPUBLIC OF CHINA

Full Block Letter with Enclosure Notation

When an item is included with the letter, the word *Enclosure* is below your initials. This is called an Enclosure Notation.

Production 1

Input the following letter on Beaver Lumber letterhead. Input a Number 10 envelope or an envelope label. Fold the letter for insertion.

 BEAVER LUMBER COMPANY LIMITED

245 Fairview Mall Drive, Willowdale, Ontario M2J 4T1 Telephone (416) 494-2161

August 27, 19--

Ms. Renata Jacot
5703 Dalton Drive N.W.
Calgary, Alberta
T3A 1C4

Dear Ms. Jacot:

In response to your recent request, we are pleased to send you a copy of our article entitled "Exterior Painting, The Quick Home Remedy".

Our Group Merchandising Department prepared this article for consumers. It contains many helpful suggestions on choosing the right paint and tools for the job, preparing the surface to be painted, etc.

Please do not hesitate to call your local Beaver store, or to write our Group Merchandising Department at the above address if you require additional information.

Yours very truly,

Dianne C. Warnick
Press Officer
2
   cr
2

Enclosure

Full Block Letter with Enclosure Notation
60-character line (elite — 12 pitch)

■ Did you use your judgment for the signature space?

Production 2

Input the following using the correct format for envelope addresses. Remember the cities are in upper case. In the last three envelope addresses, use the provincial or territorial symbols.

The Gazette, Dept. 11521, P.O. Box 6036, Station A, Montreal, Quebec H3C 3E2

Ms. Mora Guthrie, 13 Erncliffe Street, Amherst, Nova Scotia B4H 1A7

Mr. David Dale, GWG Limited, 5240 Calgary Trail, Edmonton, Alberta T6H 5G8

Mr. Clifford Guest, 66 Victory Avenue, Charlottetown, Prince Edward Island C1A 5G1

Mr. Joseph Victor, 41 - 12 Avenue East, Whitehorse, Yukon Territory Y1A 4J7

Dome Petroleum Limited, P.O. Box 200, Calgary, Alberta T2P 2H8

Timing

Set for double spacing. Take two 2-min timings. Circle all errors. Calculate Gross Words Per Minute (GWPM). Record your best timing on your personal progress chart.

SI 1.19

Two-Minute Timing

	1	2
There are many ways to say hello when meeting a friend.	12	6
Most of the time we extend our right hand when we say hello.	24	12
In one country people greet a friend by jumping up and down.	36	18
Some people fall on the ground when they meet. Other people	48	24
put one foot up in the air when they meet someone they know.	60	30
In some countries people kiss the hand of a friend. Another	72	36
way of greeting is to take the foot of a friend and place it	84	42
on one's face. No one knows the best way to greet a friend,	106	53
but it is usually more fun to say hello than farewell.	117	58

```
• • • • 1 • • • • 2 • • • • 3 • • • • 4 • • • • 5 • • • • 6 • • • • 7 • • • • 8 • • • • 9 • • • •10• • • •11• • • •12    1 min
         1              2              3              4              5              6               2 min
```

Spacing Reminder: Period .

* One space follows a period at the end of an abbreviation.
  Example: Mr. A. T. Kells

Letters with Enclosure Notations

Format
60-character line
Single spacing

Practise each line twice.
Practise as quickly as you can.

Accuracy Drills

Think **accuracy**. Practise each line once. Repeat *or* take two 30-s timings on each line.

Take two 30-s timings on each line. Take one 1-min timing on the set of two lines.
■ Did you have two errors or less with each timing?

Practise each underlined word four times. Practise each line once concentrating on the underlined words.

Edit each line by correcting two errors. Practise the paragraph once with the corrections.

Common Words

1 answer name person place sure get right down habit cares for

2 letter method week above been service stood possible friends

Alternate-Hand Words

3 is the half chairman handle usual sleigh theory visit turkey

4 or she got city sight laugh bible signal bowl this when soak

Sentences with Alternate-Hand Words

5 The problem odour of fish may torment or sicken the visitor.

6 Both the dog and the boy rush by the man with the big rifle.
• • • • 1 • • • • 2 • • • • 3 • • • • 4 • • • • 5 • • • • 6 • • • • 7 • • • • 8 • • • • 9 • • • •10 • • • •11 • • • •12

Spelling Practice

7 Our accommodation was adjacent to the hotel recreation area.

8 A sound knowledge of good grammar is a must for secretaries.

Editing Practice

9   Cave exploring--^{a}lso called spelunking or caving--iss

an exciting and intrigu ing sport. Experenced spelunkers

      carry a compass and a relaible source of light, such as

a carbide lamp. $_M$ost caves are damp and cool, so warm/

clothing is a must, as is a helmut. Leather gloves prevnt

cuts from sharp roocks;hiking boots are good protection

against snakes.

56

Number 10 Envelopes

Format
60-character line
Single spacing

Practise each line twice.
Practise as quickly as you can.

Accuracy Drills

Think **accuracy**. Practise
each line once. Repeat *or* take
two 30-s timings on each line.

Take two 30-s timings on each
line. Take one 1-min timing on
the set of two lines.
■ Did you have two errors or
less with each timing?

Practise each underlined word
four times. Practise each line
once concentrating on the
underlined words.

Edit each line by correcting
two errors.
Practise the paragraph once
with the corrections.

Capitalization Rule

Use periods without spacing
when abbreviating academic
degrees.
Read the Capitalization Rule.
Edit each line by using the
Capitalization Rules. Practise
each line once with the correct
capitalization.

Alternate-Hand Words

1 to for pale both fork gown when eight wish fox and field due

2 he but turn shame quake ambush goal lane dish kept soak town

Double-Letter Words

3 off add all feel dull tooth week muddy guess wheel seek fuss

4 see will cliff green lobby occur free smooth office need ill

Sentences with Double-Letter Words

5 Business essays must fully discuss annual asset commitments.

6 The groom suddenly happened to see the pretty wedding dress.
•　•　•　•1•　•　•　•2•　•　•　•3•　•　•　•4•　•　•　•5•　•　•　•6•　•　•　•7•　•　•　•8•　•　•　•9•　•　•　•10•　•　•　•11•　•　•　•12

Spelling Practice

7 Sometimes it is difficult to <u>listen</u> to one's own <u>conscience</u>.

8 <u>Vice versa</u> is a Latin term meaning "with the order changed."

Editing Practice

9　　A bat is not blind,as the saying goes, but its eyes

are weak. To detect obsta les or insects, it emits high-

frequency sounds And picks up the echoes. It varies the

the frequency and rate of the sounds to determin the position,

distance, size, & movement of objectx.

Capitalization

Rule 5:　Capitalize titles or degrees that come before or after proper nouns.
　　　　　Will Inspector Renouf handle the case?
　　　　　Mora Guthrie received her M.B.A. from Western.

10 alice mae thinks that mayor deluca is planning to run again.

11 the lectures given by professor gauvin are most interesting.

12 rolf parsons jr. is the head of their purchasing department.

13 lawrence hopes to pursue a college program leading to a b.a.

14 according to dean yates, the course must be taken this year.
•　•　•　•1•　•　•　•2•　•　•　•3•　•　•　•4•　•　•　•5•　•　•　•6•　•　•　•7•　•　•　•8•　•　•　•9•　•　•　•10•　•　•　•11•　•　•　•12

Production 2

Arrange the following material in correct letter format on Cooper Canada letterhead. Not all the letter parts are given below. Input the letter as a full block letter with mixed punctuation. Include all the missing parts. Use the current alphabetic date.

The symbol / means end of the line.

To: Mr. Ralph Winters / 6 Skaling Court / Saint John, New Brunswick / E2K 4G8

From: Lynne Pheeney / Customer Service
Thank you for your recent letter bringing to our attention the problem you have experienced with our 4R41-CD Golf Bag (Model 754-520).

The problem ~~you have~~ *that you* described--the strap tearing from the bag--can easily be repaired by stitching. If you return the bag to us, we shall gladly ~~make~~ *effect* the necessary repairs; or if more convenient, we would refer you to a local repair shop.

As we do not deal directly with the public, we cannot offer refunds. We will inspect any of our merchandise to see if it is defective, and if it cannot be repaired, we will replace it.

We thank you for your support of the Cooper line of equipment.

■ Did you include the salutation?

■ Did you listen for the right margin signal OR Did you use word wrap?

■ Did you include the complimentary closing?

Number 10 Envelopes (105 mm x 242 mm)

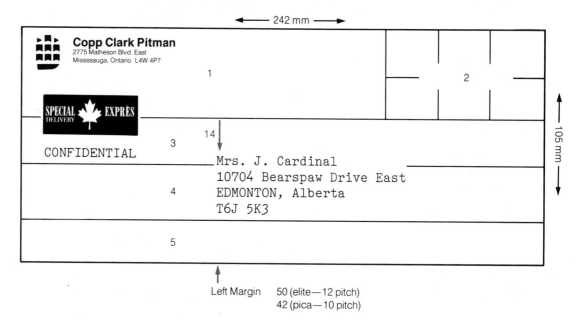

Sections of an Envelope
1. This space is for the return address.
2. This space is reserved for the stamp.
3. This space is used for special instructions.
4. This space is for the mailing address. The Postal Code must appear in section 4.
5. This space is reserved for the bar-coding at the post office. The Postal Code **must not** appear in this section.

Formatting Guide for Business-Size Number 10 Envelopes (105 mm × 242 mm)

General Principle

This address is blocked five characters to the left of the vertical centre of the Number 10 envelope and two lines below its horizontal centre. If an address line is very long, adjust the left margin.

Mailing Address	• Starts on line 14
	• 50 spaces (elite—12 pitch) from the left edge or 42 spaces (pica—10 pitch) from the left edge
Return Address	• Starts on line 3
	• 3 spaces from the left edge
Special Instructions	• Start on line 10
	• 5 spaces from left edge

Alphabetic dating consists of
month   day year

December 6, 19– –

Numeric dating consists of
year   month   day

19– – 12 06

Both are acceptable.

■ Did you listen for the right
margin signal? OR Did you
use word wrap?

Production 1

Input the following as a full block letter with mixed punctuation. Use the correct numeric date. Use the Cooper Canada letterhead. Listen for the right margin signal if you are using a typewriter.

Current date:

Mr. Peter H. Holten
Holten Dart Supplies
R.R. 2
Hampton, New Brunswick
EOG 1ZO
Dear Mr. Holten:

¶ We recently received your letter requesting information on darts, which was forwarded to us by General Sportcraft in New Jersey. We do carry the Unicorn line of darts. However, we sell directly only to dealers who have an account with us.

¶ New accounts are opened on the recommendation of Louis Boudreau, our representative for the area. Mr. Boudreau is familiar with the territory and how many accounts we have covering the locality at the present time.

¶ We will ask Mr. Boudreau, P.O. Box 1150, Shediac, to contact you to discuss the Cooper line of merchandise, our policies, and other relevant details.

Yours truly,

Lynne Pheeney
Customer Service

yi

Production

Input the following addresses on Number 10 envelopes. Use correct format. On the last four envelope addresses, use the provincial or territorial symbols.

General Motors of Canada Limited
215 William Street East
OSHAWA, Ontario
L1G 1K7

Belarus Equipment of Canada Limited
1200, rue Nobel
Boucherville, Quebec
J4B 5L2

Mrs. Alice Beddoe
34211 Redwood Avenue
ABBOTSFORD, British Columbia
V2S 2T6

Sklar Manufacturing Limited
617 Victoria Street East
Whitby, Ontario
L1N 5S7

McDonald's Corporation
One McDonald's Plaza
OAKBROOK, IL 60521-1250
U.S.A.

Dr. William Garvock
81 Wishingwell Road
St. John's, Newfoundland
A1B 1G9

Mr. G. T. Bakker
Vice-President, Personnel
Laura Secord
P. O. Box 1812, Stn. D
SCARBOROUGH, Ontario
M1R 4Z2

Mrs. Teresa Oman
1081 - 109 Street
North Battleford, Saskatchewan
S9A 2E3

CONFIDENTIAL
Mr. John Barsczewski
P. O. Box 2700
DAUPHIN, Manitoba
R7N 2V5

Mr. Robert Reisen
Tuktoyaktuk,
Northwest Territories
X0E 1C0

Two-Minute Timing

	1	2
The latest inventory figures show 1 726 pairs of 185 cm	12	6
skis. Prices range from $69.25 to $374.00. The 39 cm poles	24	12
were ordered 67 days ago. Send the size 11 gloves to the 24	36	18
clubs in Vernon. They will need 350 jackets: 95 small, 100	48	24
medium, and 155 large. Deliver them before 09:30 on Friday.	60	30

· · · 1 · · · 2 · · · 3 · · · 4 · · · 5 · · · 6 · · · 7 · · · 8 · · · 9 · · · 10 · · · 11 · · · 12   1 min

   1   2   3   4   5   6   2 min

Sentences with Numbers

57 An exhibition soccer tournament will be held on August 16 at
19:00 at Centennial Park, 1875 Redgrave Street. The line-up
will be as follows: Cougars (Team 1) vs. Lions (Team 3) and
Tigers (Team 2) vs. Jaguars (Team 4).
· · · ·1· · · ·2· · · ·3· · · ·4· · · ·5· · · ·6· · · ·7· · · ·8· · · ·9· · · ·10· · · ·11· · · ·12

Take two 1-min timings on each sentence. Circle all errors.

Selected Number Practice

1. Circle all errors in the Sentences with Numbers.
2. From your errors, choose the number or numbers which gave you difficulty.
3. Select the appropriate drill lines in the Selected Number Practice.
4. Practise each line twice concentrating on accuracy.
5. If you had no errors in the Sentences with Numbers, or if you complete the accuracy lines before your teacher calls **time**, start at line 0 and **push** for speed. Practise each line once.

After Selected Number Practice, take two 1-min timings on the Sentences with Numbers and determine if you have improved.

1 58 type 1 and 1 or 11 and 111 for 12 or 13 but not 151 or 1 112

2 59 2 or 22 by 12 nor 212 by 2 maybe 21 or 12 not 2 122 or 1 211

3 60 try 3 and 13 but not 131 or 232 then 333 not 123 but 3 or 33

4 61 4 or 41 or 444 not 144 maybe 424 but 234 and 441 or 444 44 4

5 62 send 55 to 15 not 45 to 515 maybe 555 not 532 or 151 or 5355

6 63 the 6 or 16 then 616 or 61 or 16 666 or 66 by 16 and 26 or 6

7 64 a 7 and a 77 or 71 or 73 but 72 not 73 among 7 734 and 1 771

8 65 the 8 and 18 and 88 by 82 yet 8 248 not 81 nor 18 and 8 or 8

9 66 or 9 and a 99 but not 29 or 39 since 89 are 9 999 not 9 or 9

0 67 0 and 040 and 050 not 900 or 290 but 200 and 7 000 not 8 000
· · · ·1· · · ·2· · · ·3· · · ·4· · · ·5· · · ·6· · · ·7· · · ·8· · · ·9· · · ·10· · · ·11· · · ·12

57

Full Block Letters

Format
60-character line
Single spacing

Practise each line twice.
Practise as quickly as you can.

Speed Drills

■ Try to practise each timing faster.
Take two 15-s timings on each line. Take one 30-s timing on the set of lines.

Take two 15-s timings on each line. Take one 30-s timing on the set of lines.
■ Did you do each timing faster?

Practise each line once.
Practise each line again.

Capitalization Rule

Read the Capitalization Rule. Edit each line by using the Capitalization Rules. Practise each line once with the correct capitalization.

Common Words

1 rock bring before stop boys might car spent work without big

2 this himself just some trip time few white able looking from

Common-Word Sentences

3 The search helicopter found the downed airplane in the bush.

4 He donated the used clothing to the charitable organization.

5 The solid gold pin looked very nice on her new pink sweater.

Sentences with Double-Letter Words

6 The current committees will canvass the village for support.

7 Will you need more staff for the committee meeting tomorrow?

8 The pioneers agree on that matter but cannot assure success.

· · · · 1 · · · · 2 · · · · 3 · · · · 4 · · · · 5 · · · · 6 · · · · 7 · · · · 8 · · · · 9 · · · ·10· · · ·11· · · ·12

Number Practice

9 Please send $85.29 to Box 8770B, Edmonton, Alberta, T5K 0M1.

10 I sent surveys to 63 of the 80 schools during 1989 and 1990.

Capitalization

Rule 6: Capitalize nouns when they are followed by figures or letters indicating sequence.

• number	Licence No. 13823		• exhibit	Exhibit A
• chapter	Chapter IV		• room	Room 119
• section	Section 11		• volume	Volume II
• model	Model No. 2901		• policy	Policy No. 88567
• clause	Clause 3		• lesson	Lesson 27

Note: Do not capitalize the following nouns indicating minor divisions:

page	line	paragraph	note	size	verse

11 answers to the homework questions may be found in chapter 3.

12 the lawyer referred to clause 13 of their mortgage document.

13 we purchased our humidifier, model no. 3836-27, in february.

14 you will find that quotation on page 6, line 27 of the book.

15 the driver education course meets in room 230 on wednesdays.

· · · · 1 · · · · 2 · · · · 3 · · · · 4 · · · · 5 · · · · 6 · · · · 7 · · · · 8 · · · · 9 · · · ·10· · · ·11· · · ·12

R 39 or regular regard relax restore rarely remember pride replay
40 Ralph repaired the arrow and rapidly ran to target practice.

S 41 savings senses sky status space house west street list store
42 Susan and Simon play squash on Saturdays at the sports club.

T 43 table tourist tomato trust twist title tender trip interests
44 Twelve students talked to teachers about the trivial matter.

U 45 usual upset urge unity useful under crust umbrella us unions
46 The four individuals uttered unusual but useful union views.

V 47 vulture vogue convent vicar valid prevent veto voyage virtue
48 Vicky values vitamins if they give her added vim and vigour.

W 49 werewolf weak weather straw wheel who cow forward water view
50 Gwen wants to wear her white winter coat on Wednesday night.

X 51 mixture lynx express extras exaggerate oxen axe examinations
52 Rex examined the sixty examples of latex paint in the annex.

Y 53 young yield lazy youth yearly yours beyond yard sorry mainly
54 May I ask the young lady why all the youngsters are yelling?

Z 55 zodiac zebra zoo lizard zone sneeze amaze freeze ooze zipper
56 Zelda liked to puzzle over the zodiac signs on the zoo gate.

• • • •1• • • •2• • • •3• • • •4• • • •5• • • •6• • • •7• • • •8• • • •9• • • •10• • • •11• • • •12

Basic English

council: an advisory body
counsel: advice, or to give advice (verb)
a lawyer (noun)

Read the definition of each word.
Practise each sentence once using the correct word in parentheses.

16 The (council, counsel) was composed of fifteen representatives.

17 She asked for his (council, counsel), but he refused to give it.

18 The Student (Council, Counsel) meets once a week on Wednesdays.

• • • • 1 • • • • 2 • • • • 3 • • • • 4 • • • • 5 • • • • 6 • • • • 7 • • • • 8 • • • • 9 • • • •10• • • •11• • • •12

Full Block Letters

A full block letter is one in which all letter parts are at the left margin. Mixed punctuation uses a colon after the salutation and a comma after the complimentary closing.

Formatting Guide for Full Block Letters

If you are using a computer, read the manuals to determine if there is a software or printer default for top/ bottom margins.

Line Length	• Set a 60-character line (elite — 12 pitch) or a 50-character line (pica — 10 pitch).
Date Line	• Start on line 15 or 2-3 lines below the letterhead.
Inside Address (envelope address)	• Space down 6 lines or use your judgment.
Salutation	• Double space before and after salutation.
Body	• Single space the body but double space between paragraphs. *Note:* There are no paragraph indentations.
Complimentary Closing	• Double space before the complimentary closing.
Signature Space	• Space down 4-6 lines. Use your judgment.
Signature Lines	• Input sender's name and sender's official title.
Your Initials	• Input in lower case double spaced below the signature lines or use your judgment.
Notations	• Input below your initials e.g. Enclosure. Use your judgment for spacing.

Production Practice

Production 1

Input the letter to Mr. George Campbell illustrated on the next pages on the Laura Secord letterhead provided by your teacher. Use full block letter style with mixed punctuation.

G 17 gift flag guilty huge right great gold pig gloomy eggs rigid
18 It is great to get a gift of luggage before going to Greece.

H 19 house fish high dash horizon hike holiday hole help heal hot
20 Hugh thought Helen should chat with the other hurt children.

I 21 insist inquiry ironing alias indoors dirt impossible invites
22 I wish to invite Ivor and Iris to visit our office in April.

J 23 janitor jazz juice journal jewel jam just rejoice jump judge
24 Judith rejoiced when the jewel was found just near the lake.

K 25 kit knock kennel kitchen kick keep rink sunk bunk monk kites
26 Karl knocked the kettle off his backpack into a rocky creek.

L 27 land lazy label lawful logical loyal lilac little limp light
28 Lend Lou your clipboard for the lecture in literature class.

M 29 memory medium must many bomb meant impossible master million
30 Remember that some of our members may make this mistake too.

N 31 nation nylon none napkin ankle night invite never know enter
32 Norman went to the ninth annual national dinner in November.

O 33 over outlook often opinion oven older wrong only some wonder
34 The four monopoly opponents lost their hotels in two rounds.

P 35 perhaps pepper popcorn prompt puzzle price appear proper dip
36 Paul helped Pat prepare purple posters for the parish party.

Q 37 request acquire quality quit require queen quite requisition
38 He was required to quote from two Quebec authors to qualify.
• • • • 1 • • • • 2 • • • • 3 • • • • 4 • • • • 5 • • • • 6 • • • • 7 • • • • 8 • • • • 9 • • • • 10 • • • • 11 • • • • 12

Date Line

Inside Address
(envelope address)

Salutation

Body

Complimentary Closing

Signature Lines

Your Initials

Laura Secord LAURA SECORD WALK. P.O. BOX 1812, STN. 'D'
SCARBOROUGH, ONT. M1R 4Z2. (416)751-0500

15 or | 2-3 below letterhead

September 5, 19--

6

Mr. George Luong
70 St. Ninians Street
Antigonish, Nova Scotia
B2G 1Y8
2
Dear Mr. Luong :
2
Thank you for your letter of August 28, addressed to Mr. W. H.
Wardle, in which you inquire about employment possibilities
with us.
2
Unfortunately, at the present time, we do not have an opening
that would suit a person with your particular interests and
background. However, we will retain your letter in our active
file and contact you should an appropriate position become
available.
2
Your interest is appreciated. We wish you every success in
your future endeavours.
2
Yours truly,

4-6

G. T. Bakker
Vice-President, Personnel
2
cr

DIVISION AULT FOODS (1975) LTD. - LES ALIMENTS AULT (1975) LTÉE.
LAURA SECORD CANDY SHOPS — SMILES 'N CHUCKLES

Full Block Letter with Mixed Punctuation

60-character line (elite — 12 pitch)

Analytical Practice

Format
60-character line
Single spacing

Practise each line twice.
Practise as quickly as you can.

Analyze Your Practice

Take two 1-min timings on
each sentence. Each
sentence contains the
alphabet. Circle all errors.

Alternate-Hand Words

1 sit tie pair fur burnt panel island their rock turn quantity

2 fit an own shape usual goal visitor handle pen lane sick men

• • • • 1 • • • • 2 • • • • 3 • • • • 4 • • • • 5 • • • • 6 • • • • 7 • • • • 8 • • • • 9 • • • 10 • • • 11 • • • 12

Alphabetic Sentences

3 Frank's hurried request for an extra copy of the Global Wars

bulletin puzzled Marjorie very much.

4 The frightened monkey was quite sure his life was in danger,

but the very lazy lynx just yawned and went back to sleep.

Selected Letter Practice

1. Circle all errors in the Alphabetic Sentences.
2. From your errors, choose the letter or letters which gave you difficulty.
3. Select the appropriate drill lines in the Selected Letter Practice.
4. Practise each line twice concentrating on accuracy.
5. If you had no errors in the Alphabetic Sentences, or if you complete the accuracy lines before your teacher calls **time**, start at line A and **push** for speed. Practise each line once.

After Selected Letter Practice,
take two 1-min timings on each
Alphabetic Sentence and
determine if you have
improved.

A 5 able affair shape lap area another after apple was rather at

6 Alan also asked Anna if Havana was the capital city of Cuba.

B 7 bin boil babble baton probe absorb fibre bay beast tub bonus

8 Barby bought Bobby and Burt black rubber boots and blankets.

C 9 candy sick crayons castle pack muscle couch· occur dock chews

10 The coach accepted courteous criticism of the clumsy centre.

D 11 dried drama addict dynamic depend detail dead digging drapes

12 David and Dorothy's dad told a dull riddle about an old dog.

E 13 entire even eye exit every wave beat jet everybody erase ear

14 Everyone arrived on time for the art exhibits at the Centre.

F 15 find fifth firm fry frozen fun friend refund defend if after

16 Fifteen efficient foresters found four flaming forest fires.

• • • • 1 • • • • 2 • • • • 3 • • • • 4 • • • • 5 • • • • 6 • • • • 7 • • • • 8 • • • • 9 • • • 10 • • • 11 • • • 12

Date Line

Inside Address
(envelope address)

Salutation

Body

Complimentary Closing

Signature Lines

Your Initials

Laura Secord LAURA SECORD WALK. P.O. BOX 1812, STN. 'D'
SCARBOROUGH, ONT. M1R 4Z2. (416)751-0500

15 or | 2-3 below letterhead

September 5, 19—

6

Mr. George Luong
70 St. Ninians Street
Antigonish, Nova Scotia
2 B2G 1Y8

2 Dear Mr. Luong:

Thank you for your letter of August 28, addressed
to Mr. W. H. Wardle, in which you inquire about
2 employment possibilities with us.

Unfortunately, at the present time, we do not have
an opening that would suit a person with your
particular interests and background. However, we
will retain your letter in our active file and
contact you should an appropriate position become
2 available.

Your interest is appreciated. We wish you every
2 success in your future endeavours.

Yours truly,

4-6

G. T. Bakker
Vice-President, Personnel
2
cr

DIVISION AULT FOODS (1975) LTD. - LES ALIMENTS AULT (1975) LTÉE.
LAURA SECORD CANDY SHOPS — SMILES 'N CHUCKLES

Full Block Letter with Mixed Punctuation

50-character line (pica — 10 pitch)

SI 1.37

Composing Practice

Think and answer as quickly as you can without hesitating.

Three-Minute Timing

	1	3
Fires destroy millions of hectares of useful forests in	12	4
one year. Most fires are caused by humans. A lit cigarette	24	8
or match carelessly thrown from a vehicle can start a deadly	36	12
blaze. It is necessary to put a campfire out with water and	48	16
to cover the coals with dirt or sand. To prevent fires from	60	20
completely destroying our forests, a network of huge lookout	72	24
towers are used to check for signs of smoke. Please be sure	84	28
you are not responsible for starting a forest fire.	94	31

· · · · 1 · · · · 2 · · · · 3 · · · · 4 · · · · 5 · · · · 6 · · · · 7 · · · · 8 · · · · 9 · · · ·10· · · ·11· · · ·12   1 min

1　　　　　　2　　　　　　3　　　　　　4   3 min

Composition

A title of courtesy should be used before a person's name when addressing a letter. For example, the title of courtesy for a man is Mr. What would the title of courtesy be for each of the following? Answers should be in sentence form.

1. A married woman
2. An unmarried woman
3. A young boy (under 12 years of age)
4. A woman (marital status unknown)
5. Two or more men

Production 2

Input the following letter in full block letter style with mixed punctuation. Use the Laura Secord letterhead.

Current date

Ms. Edna Manygreyhorses, Director
Staff Development
Cariboo College
P.O. Box 3010
Kamloops, British Columbia
V2C 6B7

Dear Ms. Manygreyhorses:

Please accept my apologies in taking so long to respond to your letter of July 9, which somehow did not get here until August 13.

I have discussed your program with our management group and regretfully was unable to arrange something for this year.

We hope you will contact us again next year to see if we can contribute to this worthwhile project.

We appreciate your interest in our company.

Yours truly,

G. T. Bakker
Vice-President, Personnel

yi

■ If you are using a computer,
• Did you use word wrap for the body of the letter?
• Did you check the manuals to determine if there is a software or printer default for top/bottom margins?

■ yi means your initials. These are in lower case characters.

60-character line (elite-12 pitch)

Sentence Practice for Squeezing Letters

Production 1

Practise the following sentences using the Steps for Squeezing. If you are using a computer, input the sentence and revise it using the insert/delete mode.

Input:	The car raced around the track.
Correct by squeezing:	The cars raced around the track.
Input:	Ron had a adverse reaction to th cough medicine.
Correct by squeezing:	Ron had an adverse reaction to the cough medicine.
Input:	Our sudden outburst of anger was very upsetting.
Correct by squeezing:	Your sudden outburst of anger was quite upsetting.
Input:	Its best to check the phone number before dialing.
Correct by squeezing:	It's best to check the phone numbers before dialing.

Steps for Spreading or Removing an Extra Letter from a Word Using a Typewriter

1. Remove the word.
2. Move each letter one-half space to the right.
3. The corrected word will have one and one-half spaces between it and the next word.

We arre happy.

We are happy.

One and one-half spaces

Sentence Practice for Spreading Letters

Production 2

Practise the following sentences using the Steps for Spreading. If you are using a computer, input the sentence and revise using the insert/delete mode.

Input:	I am sure the manager willl be at the next meeting.
Correct by spreading:	I am sure the manager will be at the next meeting.
Input:	When will you be ready to visit your three cousins?
Correct by spreading:	When will you be able to visit your four cousins?
Input:	Cheque the library bullettin board for your notices.
Correct by spreading:	Check the library bulletin board for your notices.
Input:	The childrens liked to visit the new animal shelter.
Correct by spreading:	The children like to visit the new animal shelter.

■ Does your software have a spell check?
■ Did you use the scroll option?
■ Did you ask your teacher or read your software manual in order to know how to set the insert/delete mode?

■ Does your software have a spell check?

Timing

Set for double spacing. Take two 3-min timings. Circle all errors. Calculate Gross Words Per Minute (GWPM). Record your best timing on your personal progress chart.

SI 1.37

Three-Minute Timing

		1	3
In 1986 there were 1 079 motorcycles stolen in Alberta.		12	4
Only 458 of these were recovered. As you can see the chance		24	8
of getting a bike back is not good. Many of these bikes are		36	12
reduced to basket jobs. The parts are stripped and sold. A		48	16
few parts can be traced and returned to the owner. Programs		60	20
have been started to reduce bike theft by placing the serial		72	24
number on whatever items can be removed and sold. The looks		84	28
of the machine will not be affected. The local police force		96	32
will supply the tools for marking and this is free of charge		108	36
to the owner. This program is called Do Your Parts.		118	39

· · · · 1 · · · · 2 · · · · 3 · · · · 4 · · · · 5 · · · 6 · · · · 7 · · · · 8 · · · · 9 · · · ·10 · · · ·11 · · · ·12   1 min
           1   2   3   4   3 min

Composition

People learning English as a second language have difficulty with expressions that don't mean exactly what they say. Such expressions are called idioms.

Explain the meaning of each of the following sentences by composing a new sentence for each one.

1. I'm tied up.
2. Give me a ring.
3. I'll pick you up.
4. What a rip off!
5. He has a chip on his shoulder.
6. They creamed us!
7. I ran out of ink.
8. You drive me bananas.
9. I got burned on the deal.
10. It's a steal.
11. I bombed the test.
12. I'm going nuts.
13. Right on!
14. That's cool.
15. She lucked out at the sale.

Ask your teacher or read the software manual in order to know how to set the delete/insert mode. Your word processing software may have a spell-check feature.

To correct an error after the material has been input:

1. Read your monitor using the scrolling option.
2. Move the cursor to the error.
3. Correct the error using the backspace key, or the insert/delete option.
4. Know your software and use the most efficient method for correcting errors.

Correction Drill

Input the following sentences. Make the necessary corrections.

Here it es.   2.   My neice is seven.   3.   Mamy were away today.

Practice

■ Did you correct the errors so that the original errors cannot be seen?

Squeezing or Spreading Letters in a Word Using a Typewriter

To squeeze or add an extra letter in a word:
1. Determine if your typewriter has a half space key or bar. Know your typewriter.
2. With some typewriters, you can press gently with your hand against the ribbon pack mechanism and watch the print indicator on the alignment scale.

Steps for Squeezing an Extra Letter into a Word

1. Remove the word.
2. Move each letter one-half space to the left.
3. The corrected word will have one-half space between it and the next word.

We ar happy.

We are happy.
↑ ↑
One-half space

Squeezing and Spreading Letters in a Word Using a Computer

On a computer, words are usually corrected using the insert/delete option. Therefore, it is not necessary to squeeze or spread letters in a word. The lines will adjust to the line length which has been set.

If the right margin has been set for right justification, extra spaces may be automatically inserted between some of the words in each line so the right margin will align. Know your software. Is justification a system default? Is justification *on* or *off*?

58

Correcting Errors/ Squeezing and Spreading

Format
60-character line
Single spacing

Practise each line twice.
Practise as quickly as you can.

Speed Drills

■ Try to practise each timing faster.
Take two 15-s timings on each line. Take one 30-s timing on the set of lines.

Take two 15-s timings on each line. Take one 30-s timing on the set of lines.
■ Did you do each timing faster?

Practise each line once.
Practise each line again.

Capitalization Rule

Read the Capitalization Rule. Edit each line by using the Capitalization Rules. Practise each line once with the correct capitalization.

Double-Letter Words

1 breed class written shipped ribbon willing necessary guessed

2 add good sleep shall floor saddle bottle success drill brass

Common-Word Sentences

3 Choices and decisions made now may affect mankind for years.

4 The fresh snow made the streets and highways quite slippery.

5 At this point in time, it may be much too late to turn back.

Sentences with Double-Letter Words

6 Correct your errors while the sheet is still in the machine.

7 It is possible to withhold the full amount of the two bills.

8 Their favourite colours are yellow, maroon, and apple-green.
· · · · 1 · · · · 2 · · · · 3 · · · · 4 · · · · 5 · · · · 6 · · · · 7 · · · · 8 · · · · 9 · · · ·10· · · ·11· · · ·12

Number Practice

9 At 5 years of age, Fay is 98 cm tall, and her mass is 22 kg.

10 Call me at 893-2568 before 18:00 today or by 10:30 tomorrow.
· · · · 1 · · · · 2 · · · · 3 · · · · 4 · · · · 5 · · · · 6 · · · · 7 · · · · 8 · · · · 9 · · · ·10· · · ·11· · · ·12

Capitalization

Rule 7: Capitalize nouns showing family relationship when they are used as specific names or when there is no possessive pronoun in front of mother, father, etc.

Uncle Joe will visit in August.
Did Dad fix the table yet?
My brother works at McDonald's on Saturdays.

11 uncle joe and aunt henrietta are planning a trip to florida.

12 my brother, louis, says the group can use his fender guitar.

13 my sister, teresa, lives in north bay at 425 norwood avenue.

14 my father agrees, but my mother doesn't want me to work yet.

15 do mother and father know about this special surprise party?
· · · · 1 · · · · 2 · · · · 3 · · · · 4 · · · · 5 · · · · 6 · · · · 7 · · · · 8 · · · · 9 · · · ·10· · · ·11· · · ·12

Basic English

stationary: motionless
stationery: materials used for writing or typing

Read the definition of each word. Practise each sentence once using the correct word in parentheses.

16 I usually buy my (stationary, stationery) supplies at The Bay.

17 How many (stationary, stationery) objects do you see in this room?

18 You will find a (stationary, stationery) store in the nearby plaza.

Correcting Errors Using a Typewriter

Errors may be corrected by using an eraser, correction fluid, correction paper, correction tape, or a correction key. Many typewriters now include a correction key and correction tape as part of the standard keyboard.

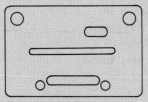

Correction Shield

Erasers

A hard eraser should be used on original copies and a soft eraser should be used on carbon copies.
1. Eraser particles should not fall into the typewriter.
2. Advance the paper until the word(s) to be corrected is/are well above the cylinder or roller.
3. Use an eraser shield, if possible, to protect the other words and lines from smudging.
4. Erase gently using a circular motion following the outline of each letter.
5. Blow or brush the eraser particles away from the typewriter mechanisms.
6. Return the copy to the original position and make the correction.

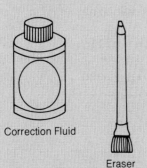

Correction Fluid

Eraser

Correction Tape or Correction Paper

1. Insert the correction tape or paper in front of the word to be corrected.
2. For each incorrect letter, backspace using the backspace key and insert the incorrect letter. This lifts the incorrect letter off the original copy or covers the error.
3. Make the correction.

Correction Key

1. For each incorrect letter, backspace using the correction key and insert the incorrect letter.
2. Make the correction.

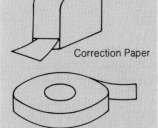

Correction Paper

Correction Tape

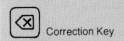

Correction Key

Correcting Errors on Your Computer Monitor

To correct an error when inputting the material, you should know the function of the backspace key, the delete key, and the insert key. This will allow you to insert and delete characters, words, lines, paragraphs, and larger blocks of text. The insert and delete modes are the two most commonly used text-editing features of any word processing program. Know your software.

The backspace key moves the cursor one space to the left removing the character it passes.

The delete key removes the character directly above the cursor.

The insert key adds characters to the left of the cursor.